Import and Customs
Law Handbook

Import and Customs Law Handbook

MICHAEL J. HORTON

Q

Quorum Books
New York • Westport, Connecticut • London

Library of Congress Cataloging-in-Publication Data

Horton, Michael J.
    Import and customs law handbook / Michael J. Horton.
      p. cm.
    Includes bibliographical references and index.
    ISBN 0-89930-665-9
    1. Customs administration—Law and legislation—United States.
2. Tariff—Law and legislation—United States. 3. Foreign trade
regulation—United States. 4. U.S. Customs Service.   I. Title.
KF6694.H67   1992
343.7305'6—dc20
[347.30356]   91-23045

British Library Cataloguing in Publication Data is available.

Library of Congress Catalog Card Number: 91-23045
ISBN: 0-89930-665-9

First published in 1992

Quorum Books, One Madison Avenue, New York, NY 10010
An imprint of Greenwood Publishing Group, Inc.

Printed in the United States of America

The paper used in this book complies with the
Permanent Paper Standard issued by the National
Information Standards Organization (Z39.48-1984).

10 9 8 7 6 5 4 3 2 1

Copyright Acknowledgment

The author and publisher gratefully acknowledge permission to reprint the
following item:

"Explanatory Notes," reprinted from *Explanatory Notes to the Harmonized
Commodity Description and Coding System*, copyright © 1986 by Customs
Cooperation Council.

Contents

Preface

How to become an importer is not the subject of this book. The materials herein are intended to provide guidance to those whose jobs make them responsible for handling U.S. Customs matters, including legal compliance and direct communications with customs officials. The intended audience, thus, includes company owners, company officials, or company employees—depending upon the size of the company and the extensiveness of its import operations. Typically, one employee or department within a company will be responsible for Customs clearances and related matters, while other departments are responsible for product design (engineering), foreign sourcing (purchasing), international payments (finance), and distribution (sales). It is to the former and not the latter that this handbook is addressed.

Import laws and procedures are technical and complex. The purpose of this book is to explain the important legal aspects of importing in a way that is concise and readily understandable. Organization is as important to this purpose as the writing itself. Every subject cannot be included, and those included cannot be completely explored. Deciding what to include and what to leave out has been as difficult certainly as the actual exposition.

No single approach has been applied to all the subjects covered. Each topic has suggested its own manner of presentation. Some of the materials rely heavily on the laws, some on the Customs Regulations, and some on both. Other materials are based on neither, but rather on personal experience. How successful this endeavor has been can be judged by the reader.

Acknowledgments

I wish to express my appreciation to the following people whose assistance, patience, and support were instrumental in completing this volume: Scott Whiteley, Don Fischer, Jim Easterday, Debbie Richmond, and Julie Horton.

RULES, PROCEDURES, AND LAWS EVERY IMPORTER MUST KNOW

The essential items that importers must know in order to prevent costly mistakes from occurring are discussed in this section. The structure of the U.S. Customs Service, the procedures it uses, the customs officers who process the imported goods, and important ground rules and laws the importer should know are explained. Also explored are those legal obligations that Customs most expects the importer to fulfill.

Part I also contains troubleshooting techniques the importer can use to determine if all reportable costs are being properly declared to Customs and methods for reporting such costs. An understanding of the matters discussed in Part I is considered necessary to avoid the most frequently imposed penalties, liquidated damages, and seizures.

Chapter 1

The U.S. Customs Service

Before discussing formal Customs procedures and the important laws that importers should know, it will prove helpful to give some background on the Customs Service itself and the customs officers the importer is most likely to meet. Importing merchandise is, after all, a human enterprise in all respects. Therefore, it is important to understand why Customs employees think the way they do and how the nature of each officer's particular job gives rise to different concerns.

AN HISTORICAL PERSPECTIVE

The Customs Service is one of the oldest federal agencies in existence today. Founded by the First Congress in 1789, Customs was perceived in its infancy as an important source of revenue. Indeed, all important public activity at the federal level was paid for by Customs collections. These funds built railroads, dredged harbors and canals, and paid for territories such as the Louisiana Purchase, Oregon, and Alaska. The construction of the capital in Washington, D.C., was also funded from tariff revenues.

U.S. Customs held its place as the primary source of federal income until the institution of personal income taxes in 1913. Today, Customs revenues are small compared to the collections of the Internal Revenue Service (IRS). Nevertheless, Customs duties are still a meaningful source of federal income. For example, duties collected by Customs in fiscal year 1990 totaled $17.2 billion. Moreover, as enterprises go, Customs is operated very efficiently. For every dollar spent, Customs returns about $18 to the U.S. Treasury.

The important thing to be learned from this history, however, is the overriding concern that all customs officers have for the production of revenue and the protection of its sources. "Revenue" considerations pervade the thinking of customs officers and their decision making. To know this helps the importer understand why customs officers sometimes scrutinize import transactions so closely.

THE AGENCY AND ITS OFFICERS

Size of the Agency

The U.S. Customs Service consists of about 16,000 employees nationwide. As government agencies go, this is not a large organization. Consider, for example, that the Veterans Administration (VA) has approximately 240,000 employees and the IRS has approximately 123,000. Because Customs has so few employees to do the job that Congress has entrusted it to do, the agency has made certain assumptions about how it expects importers to conduct themselves in fulfilling their legal obligations while engaged in importing activities. The assumptions that Customs has made will be considered more fully below when the important rules the importer should know are discussed.

Structure of the Agency

The formal organization of the Customs Service and its place in the federal government may be set forth briefly as follows:

TREASURY DEPARTMENT
Secretary of the Treasury
Washington, D.C.

U.S. CUSTOMS SERVICE
Commissioner of Customs
Washington, D.C.

CUSTOMS REGIONS
Regional Commissioners
(Seven in Number)

CUSTOMS DISTRICTS
District Directors
(Forty-Four in Number)

As can be seen above, the Customs Service, like the IRS, is a unit of the Treasury Department. The Washington, D.C., offices of Customs are referred to as headquarters, while the regional and district offices are referred to as field offices. Each district office has one or more ports of entry for imported goods.

For importers, the most important customs officer is the District Director of Customs for the port where the imported goods are cleared through Customs. The district director's office makes all the final decisions regarding the legal status of the merchandise and its release into the commerce of the United States. Under the Customs Regulations as currently written, the district director is given broad, discretionary authority in interpreting and enforcing the Customs laws and regulations.

What Customs Enforces

The Customs laws are set forth in Title 19 of the United States Code and consist of approximately 500 pages of text. Customs laws are also referred to as statutes, and both terms are used interchangeably throughout this book. The Customs Regulations are found in Title 19 of the Code of Federal Regulations and comprise about 850 pages of text. These two sources of laws and regulations, if printed together, would be about the size of the white pages telephone book for any major U.S. city. In short, these legal materials are extensive. The significance of this fact will become apparent later in this text.

Customs statutes are normally only a half-page to two pages in length. Many of the important statutes will be quoted in this book, either in whole or in part. The various Customs Regulations are written to carry out the letter and the intent of the Customs laws. For this reason, the regulations corresponding to any given law tend to be significantly greater in length than the law itself. Anyone whose job involves Customs compliance should obtain a current copy of the Customs Regulations as set forth in Title 19 of the Code of Federal Regulations, Volume 1. (This volume is published by the Government Printing Office and is available in government bookstores nationwide.)

In addition to enforcing its own laws and regulations, the Customs Service performs compliance services on imported merchandise for approximately 40 other federal agencies. These include the Federal Trade Commission; the Federal Communications Commission; the Food and Drug Administration; the Bureau of Alcohol, Tobacco, and Firearms; the International Trade Commission; the Bureau of Census; the Department of Commerce; and the Department of Agriculture, to name a few. The reason Customs is asked to enforce requirements for other agencies is fairly simple: Customs has complete physical control of imported merchandise and can deny those goods entry into the commerce of the country if they do not comply with applicable laws.

Customs Officers

The most important customs officers are the inspector, the import specialist, the regulatory auditor, and the special agent. These are the customs officers with whom an importer is most likely to come into contact, and some understanding of how their jobs differ is useful.

The Inspector. The Customs inspector works in the Inspection and Control Branch, a unit directly under the district director in each Customs district. The inspector is one of the few customs officers who wears a uniform and a displayed badge. Well known to international travelers, the inspector is the person who processes incoming passengers from foreign locations.

In addition to passenger control, the inspector has important responsibilities for the processing of all incoming and outgoing commercial cargo. As the term "inspection and control" implies, the inspector both examines commercial merchandise and maintains physical control of it until its release into the United States is authorized. At least 95% of all cargo examinations are conducted by inspectors. The importance of cargo examination and the purposes it serves will be explained later. From necessity, Customs inspectors are called to duty at all hours of the day and night. Their tireless efforts largely account for the smooth flow of cargo across U.S. international borders.

The Import Specialist. The import specialist works in the Classification and Value Branch, a unit directly under the district director. The import specialist is responsible for determining where, in the Tariff Schedule, each imported item is classified and, consequently, the rate of duty that applies. Since duties on most imported goods are a percentage of their value, the import specialist also appraises the merchandise. Customs appraisement or valuation is done according to a complex set of rules contained in the valuation law. The acts of classification and appraisement, taken together, determine exactly how much duty is owing on any given importation. Because of this, the import specialist holds a special place in the esteem of importers and customs brokers.

It is important for the importer to know that, while performing classification and appraisement duties, the import specialist has access to a large body of transactional information regarding U.S. importers and foreign manufacturers and shippers. The records available include his or her own records, as well as those of other import specialists throughout the United States.

In most Customs districts, the Tariff Schedule is divided among the available import specialists so that each is assigned a relatively small section of the schedule. All the entries and commercial invoices for a narrow group of industrial products are seen by the same import specialist, who thus becomes very experienced and knowledgeable regarding these goods. Consequently, it becomes extremely difficult for an importer to undervalue merchandise without detection.

In addition, every import specialist is required to report a certain number of Customs transactions to the Customs Information Exchange, a unit of Customs located in New York City. This information, which includes the names of the importer, manufacturer, and shipper; the commodity description; and the price and terms of sale, can be distributed to all import specialists around the United States. As a result, the import specialist is aware of importations of identical or similar merchandise at other ports and the price at which those goods were purchased.

Another tool available to the import specialist is the Treasury Enforcement Communications System, a nationwide computer system with a centralized data base. This system contains the identity of importers, manufacturers, and shippers who have violated Customs laws and regulations or who are suspected of doing so.

In addition to classification and appraisement, the import specialist is also responsible for ensuring that imported goods meet all other requirements of the laws and regulations—both of Customs and of other federal agencies.

Import specialists, as a group, tend to have closer day-to-day contacts and communications with importers and customs brokers than other Customs officers, because providing adequate information to this industry group facilitates the correct filing of Customs entries and makes the import specialist's job easier.

The Regulatory Auditor. The regulatory auditor works in the Regulatory Audit Branch, a unit directly under the Regional Commissioner of Customs in each Customs region. As the term "audit" implies, the auditor conducts examinations of a company's business records and Customs documents to determine whether laws and regulations are being complied with and whether the proper amount of duty has been paid. Because most auditors have extensive training in accounting, they tend to conduct in-depth audits involving every aspect of a company's accounting system, from general ledger to actual supporting documents.

Auditors examine the books of importers, customs brokers, bonded warehouse proprietors, and foreign trade zone operators, among others. Customs audits, however, are not conducted by surprise. Usually, the party to be audited receives a letter from the Director of Regulatory Audit setting forth (1) a proposed date and time for the audit, (2) the length of time the audit is estimated to take, (3) the documents the auditors would like to examine, and (4) the time period to be covered by the audit.

From a practical standpoint, a visit by a Customs auditor is the functional equivalent of a visit by an IRS auditor. Auditors frequently discover that importers owe the Customs Service additional duties.

The Special Agent. The Customs special agent works for a branch of Customs that has its own chain of command outside the formal organization that covers other customs officers. This unit, known as the Office of Enforcement, is headquartered in Washington, D.C., and reports directly to the Commissioner of Customs. Under the Washington office are the regional offices and, below them, the offices of the Special Agent in Charge. The Special Agent in Charge (SAC), is roughly the equivalent of the district director in the formal structure discussed previously. The Office of Enforcement has a separate and independent organizational chain of command in order to protect the integrity of its investigations and to prevent intermeddling by other Customs field officers.

Each special agent carries a badge and has the power to make arrests for serious violations of federal law. Because of this, Customs special agents have been known to carry handguns from time to time.

Although the average special agent spends a considerable amount of time in the interdiction of drugs and narcotics, he or she also has important duties involving the investigation of commercial fraud. A special agent may begin a formal investigation of an importing company or individual based upon a tip from the public (often a disgruntled former employee) or based upon a request by another customs officer, usually an import specialist.

The special agent's investigation is conducted through interviews of company officers or employees and the examination of company records. Unlike the auditor, the agent may not give the importer much prior notice of his or her visit. Often, the company will receive a phone call from the agent requesting an appointment to see someone that day or the next. By using surprise and putting themselves on the scene quickly, special agents feel they can prevent the destruction or alteration of incriminating records and deter efforts by company officials to get their stories straight. Also, special agents are usually disinclined to reveal before they arrive exactly what records they want to examine.

IMPORTANT RULES THE IMPORTER SHOULD KNOW

Certain fundamental rules that the importer should know will now be discussed. Some of these rules have the flavor of legal maxims and should guide the importer's thinking habits. Others are important because they strongly affect the attitudes of customs officers. The rules discussed below are not necessarily related to one another.

Importing Is Not a Right

The U.S. Congress, under the U.S. Constitution's grant of power to control interstate commerce, may completely deny anyone the opportunity to import merchandise into the United States. Congress can deny importing privileges to any individual or company, or it can exclude from entry an entire class of goods. Congress could, if it chose, seal off U.S. borders to all foreign goods. The power that Congress has to control imported merchandise is administered through U.S. Customs and other federal agencies.

By way of example, the U.S. International Tariff Commission issues exclusion orders that prohibit the importation of foreign-made goods that impermissibly utilize the patents of another party. An importer may not even be aware that goods being purchased abroad use these patents and are therefore excluded from entry. Nevertheless, if Customs discovers such goods at the time of entry, the goods will not be released.

In a different case, a number of companies imported wearing apparel manufactured in the People's Republic of China and filed with the entries counterfeit visas which had been forged in Hong Kong. The visa is a required document for most textiles. In almost every case, the importer had absolutely no way of knowing the visa was counterfeit. Nevertheless, the goods were seized by Customs. Since the government of the People's Republic of China would not issue valid visas for these shipments, the goods were forfeited to the U.S. government. These shipments were valued up to $150,000 each. The innocent parties who imported these goods had no recourse whatever.

These examples serve to illustrate that the U.S. government exercises absolute authority and control over imported merchandise.

Rules Used by Revenue Officers

As noted in the discussion of the early history of the Customs Service, revenue collection was an important part of the early Customs mission, and it still is. Customs officers are at heart revenue officers. Therefore, it should come as no surprise that the primary tenet of the customs officer is: *protect the revenue.* This rule pervades the thinking of customs officers. Anyone puzzled by a decision made by a customs officer should reflect back upon this rule to see how often the questioned decision actually makes sense.

The second Customs rule is an offshoot of the first: *resolve all doubts in the government's favor.* For example, if two different duty rates, one higher than the other, might apply to certain goods, the customs officer will always choose the higher and make the importer prove it wrong. If goods might legitimately be appraised at two different values, the higher value will always be chosen by Customs.

The Rule of Voluntary Compliance

As mentioned previously, Customs is a very small federal agency. It lacks the manpower to police every transaction to ensure that the importer has complied with the law. To circumvent this problem, Customs has chosen to make the legal assumption that all importers are in *voluntary compliance* with the law.

What is voluntary compliance? The answer is simple. An importer is in voluntary compliance when he or she has done the following two things:

1. Read all the Customs laws and regulations thoroughly to determine which of them apply to his or her merchandise and Customs transactions
2. Done everything necessary to ensure that all the laws and regulations that apply to his or her merchandise and Customs transactions have been complied with to the letter

It is obvious that the burden rests with the importer to know and comply with the law. As noted earlier, the laws and regulations that the importer is required to know, if printed together, would fill the white pages of a major city telephone book. Therefore, adhering to the rule of voluntary compliance is an onerous, but necessary, task.

All of this comes as a surprise to most importers. Many even think the rule unreasonable. Yet voluntary compliance is the rule. As a result, the old legal maxim applies: ignorance of the law is no excuse. Thus, if an importer is found to have violated the law or regulations, either by something not done (an omission) or something done wrongly (a commission), Customs will not permit the importer to complain that he did not know.

In actual practice, ignorance of the law is not permitted as a defense in a Customs civil penalty action. One may plead inexperience in importing as a mitigating factor. If the facts support a plea of inexperience (usually importing less than two years), the penalty may be reduced, for example, from $50,000 to $35,000. This is small consolation to the one who pays the penalty—particularly since it is true that penalties are not tax deductible business expenses. The subject of civil penalties is covered at more length in Part II.

Duty Due on All Imports, Unless Exempt

Every item is dutiable each time it enters the United States, unless there is a specific exemption. This is a very straightforward rule and it says, in effect, that an importer should expect to pay duty on everything he or she imports, unless a specific provision that permits that exact item to enter duty free is found.

It is necessary to state this rule because there are numerous circumstances that, for one reason or another, lead people to assume that various items are not dutiable. For example, many people believe that if a foreign-made item has been imported once and duty paid, then that item may be reimported without a second payment of duty on it. This is usually not the case. There are some limited circumstances in which duty will not have to be paid a second time. For the most part, however, every item of foreign manufacture is dutiable every time it enters the United States.

Note that the rule, as stated, does not refer to foreign items. The rule refers to every item, whether foreign or domestic. One should not fall into the habit of assuming that goods manufactured in the United States can be imported duty free. Many people assume that if they import a U.S.-made item, either by itself or incorporated into another product, it is duty free. It may be, but in many cases it is not. Therefore, the importer should take steps to determine the dutiable status of all U.S.-made goods before they are imported.

Duty Exemptions—Burden of Proof

There are many circumstances in which an exception to the normal rules of duty apply. Some exemptions permit goods to enter completely duty free. Others permit the payment of reduced duties. In every case, however, there are usually conditions that must be met, either factual conditions or documentary conditions. This rule simply puts the importer on notice that, to qualify for an exemption, he or she must prove, beyond doubt, that the necessary conditions are met. As usual, doubts are resolved in favor of the government. Some of the most common duty exemptions are discussed in Part II.

Items Purchased in the United States
May Be Foreign Made

Some duty exemptions are permitted for goods manufactured in the United States. For example, U.S.-made goods assembled abroad into another article may be subject to reduced duties if all requisite conditions are met. Unfortunately, many people assume that an item was made in the United States simply because they purchased it from a company located in the United States. Obviously, anything purchased in the United States may have been manufactured in a foreign country. Therefore, one should not assume that anything is manufactured in the United States unless the U.S. manufacturer issues a statement saying that it was, indeed, made in the United States.

If an importer files a Customs entry that claims an exemption based upon part of the importation being of U.S. manufacture and it is later determined that the part claimed as "U.S." is not "U.S.," is the importer subject to a penalty? The answer is yes—in order to have claimed the exemption, the law would have required the importer to certify that certain goods were of U.S. manufacture. In light of the later facts, this would be a false certification and would subject the importer to a monetary penalty.

THE ROLE OF THE CUSTOMS BROKER

Customs brokers are discussed here, in the chapter dealing with the Customs Service, for two reasons. First, it is appropriate to discuss the function of the broker before the reader has forgotten what was said regarding voluntary compliance. Second, the customs broker has been regarded for many years as a quasi-governmental official, even though not employed by the government. The broker is so regarded because he or she must be licensed by the Customs Service to perform brokerage services. In addition, before a person can obtain a license, he or she must pass a written proficiency examination administered by Customs and withstand a confidential background investigation. Customs takes these precautions to ensure that its licensees have the requisite skills and moral rectitude to serve the public at large.

From a practical standpoint, a customs broker is indispensable to most importers. Although no figures are available, experience indicates that about 99% of all Customs entries are filed by licensed brokers. The reasons for this are clear. Brokers are knowledgeable and experienced in the filing of all forms of Customs documentation. Moreover, the fees charged for the services performed are extremely reasonable. As a consequence, almost every importer uses the services of a customs broker.

Despite the wide use of brokers, most importers are uninformed regarding the legal relationship they have with their brokers. All too frequently, brokers complain that their clients do not understand the broker's role in import transactions. It seems that many importers mistakenly believe their customs brokers shield them from the law. Nothing could be more wrong.

The relationship between an importer and his or her broker is governed by the law of agency. The importer is called the principal and the broker is known as the agent. In such a relationship, it is the responsibility of the principal to direct the activities of the agent to ensure compliance with the law. Liability always runs from the agent to the principal, and the principal (importer) is held liable even for the negligent mistakes of the agent (broker).

In plain language, it is not the broker's legal duty to ensure that import transactions are reported to U.S. Customs in compliance with the laws and regulations. This is the importer's responsibility, and the employment of a broker to file Customs entries does not transfer this legal duty to the broker or shield the importer from liability. It is ultimately the importer's responsibility to determine his or her legal obligations and to comply with all laws and regulations. In other words, it is the importer, not the broker, who must be in voluntary compliance with the law.

In practice, problems arise because importers do not advise their brokers of all relevant aspects of their import transactions. For example, an importer could have certain types of reportable costs that may not be known to the broker. Without this information, the broker is unable to render assistance in the proper entering of the merchandise. Importers themselves should determine what information must be reported to U.S. Customs and then provide the necessary details to their customs brokers in order that proper disclosures are made. The broker always works best when fully informed.

SUMMARY OF PROCEDURES AND
EXAMINATION OF MERCHANDISE

All imported merchandise, and the documentation filed with Customs to clear it, undergoes certain processing steps that lead to the completion of the Customs transaction. The goods are first examined; then they are classified and appraised. Finally, the entry is liquidated to bring about the completion of the Customs decision-making process. Once liquidation occurs, all decisions become final and binding, unless the importer is dissatisfied, in which case a formal protest may be filed to contest any aspect of Customs' legal determinations. Knowledge of the formal procedures used by Customs helps the importer protect his or her rights and comply with Customs' expectations.

The examination of merchandise entails the actual, physical viewing of the goods. Examination of imported merchandise can be extremely important because most decisions regarding the classification and value of the goods are based primarily on what the entry documents say, without reference to external facts. The only chance to compare the documents with the actual merchandise occurs at the time of examination.

Imported items are subject to whatever type of examination Customs wishes to perform. Goods may be passed without examination or the entire shipment may be laid bare and each piece examined individually.

The nature of the exam is specifically determined for each shipment on a case-by-case basis. Examination can include testing in the Customs laboratory. For this purpose, samples are taken.

An examination of imported merchandise can be made by any customs officer. Most examinations, however, are accomplished by inspectors and import specialists. Inspectors conduct cargo examinations at airport warehouses, docks, piers, bonded warehouses, foreign trade zones, and container stations. Examinations at these locations constitute approximately 95% of the total.

Import specialists conduct most of their cargo examinations in the public stores or in their offices. When the import specialist desires to view a portion of a shipment, he or she may have one or more cartons or crates brought by truck to a Customs location near the customshouse known as the public stores. There the cartons or crates are opened and viewed.

Alternatively, the import specialist may request that a sample be taken from a shipment by an inspector and sent to his or her office for examination. Samples may also be obtained from the importer after release of the goods by mailing the importer a formal request for a sample.

Examination can also be conducted by special arrangement at the importer's premises or other special locations. For example, shipments of antiques or other delicate cargo may be released directly to the importer's own warehouse facility or place of business for final examination. When this occurs, the entire shipment or a designated portion of it must be held unopened and intact until the arrival of the inspector or the import specialist who will examine the goods. After this viewing occurs, the importer is then free to dispose of the merchandise in normal commercial channels.

Some merchandise may be temporarily released to the importer for erection or installation prior to examination. Certain heavy desulphurization equipment, for instance, was examined by Customs after the items had been erected and built into a steel processing plant owned by the importer.

Physical examination of goods serves several purposes. First, it can be determined whether the items are properly marked to show the country of origin and other required marks or information. Second, the contents of the packages can be inspected for the presence of contraband, such as narcotics or prohibited cultural artifacts. Third, the examination reveals the validity of the documentation presented to Customs.

The validity or accuracy of the invoices and other documents filed with the entry papers is tested by reference to the following questions, which can be answered when the goods are viewed:

1. Is the value shown for each item on the invoice reasonable, or might the goods be undervalued?

2. Is the invoiced description of the merchandise sufficiently accurate to permit proper classification?
3. Does the package contain the proper quantity of items as invoiced, or is there excess merchandise?
4. Does the package contain exactly those items the packing list or invoice says it should contain, and no others?

During the physical viewing, the examining officer makes handwritten notations on the entry documents to provide a record of what was seen. These notations may subsequently be relied on by Customs to support the various legal determinations it makes regarding the duties owed. Moreover, entry documents containing serious discrepancies may be rejected as inadequate. When this occurs, the goods can be detained or even seized.

Chapter 2

Classification of Merchandise

One part of calculating the duties owing on imported goods involves the classification of the goods. Classification is the step-by-step process of determining what particular tariff number in the Tariff Schedule of the United States applies to any given item. The Tariff Schedule is published in an 8-by-11½-inch format and is approximately three inches thick. It contains about 600 pages of tariff descriptions and corresponding tariff numbers. The schedule has 22 major subdivisions or sections, numbered from I to XXII. These sections each contain one or more subsections which are called chapters. In all, there are 99 chapters in the schedule. The entire schedule has about 8,500 tariff descriptions and tariff numbers at the eight-digit rate level. Appendix A illustrates the format of the Harmonized Tariff Schedule of the United States.

Theoretically, for any imaginable item, there is one and only one tariff description that is legally the most correct. One finds the correct tariff description by applying a somewhat complex set of rules or classification principles which are stated in the Tariff Schedule and which are discussed below. The rules require a careful reading of the section notes, chapter notes, headings, and subheadings. Though often time-consuming, a patient, methodical use of the rules will lead to a final conclusion regarding the proper tariff description.

Once the correct description in the tariff has been ascertained, the rate of duty becomes fixed because every tariff description at the eight-digit rate level has its own particular general rate of duty. When the rate of duty has been identified, Customs merely multiplies the rate by the quantity imported to determine the duties owing.

There are three types of duty rates found in the tariff. First, there is the specific rate—for example, 1.1 cents per kilogram, 10 cents per gross, 0.5 cents per liter, and $2.12 per cubic meter.

Second, there is the *ad valorem* rate. *Ad valorem* is a Latin term meaning a part or a percentage of the value. Other familiar types of *ad valorem* assessments are state and local sales taxes and most property taxes. These are calculated as a percentage of the value. Examples of *ad valorem* rates are 5.7%, 17%, and 29.8%.

The third type of duty rate is called a compound rate, and it is a combination of a specific rate and an *ad valorem* rate. Examples are 33.1 cents per kilogram, plus 7.4%, and 50 cents each, plus 7.7%.

THE HARMONIZED TARIFF SCHEDULE

The system of tariff classification currently in use by the United States is the Harmonized Tariff Schedule of the United States (HTSUS). This system became effective for goods entered in the United States on and after January 1, 1989. The U.S. Tariff Schedule is derived with some modification from the Harmonized Commodity Description and Coding System which was developed over many years by the Customs Cooperation Council (CCC) in Brussels, Belgium. The U.S. tariff system will continue to evolve because of classification opinions issued by the Harmonized System Committee of the CCC.

The Harmonized System is international in nature and forms the basis for the tariff schedules of most industrialized nations. Thus, the tariff classification applied to any given commodity by the U.S. Customs Service should be the same as that used by the major trading partners of the United States. Indeed, a primary consideration that led to the adoption of the Harmonized System by many nations, including the United States, was the desire to have a uniform system of tariff classification throughout the world.

As previously mentioned, the U.S. Tariff Schedule consists of 22 sections containing 99 chapters. Classification of specific products or commodities is accomplished by interpreting and applying certain legal language that is contained in the Tariff Schedule itself. These intrinsic materials are the General Rules of Interpretation, the section notes, the chapter notes, and the tariff headings, including subheadings. Certain other materials extrinsic to the Tariff Schedule itself may be used as aids to interpretation. These materials are the following:

1. The Explanatory Notes to the Harmonized Commodity Description and Coding System published by the CCC
2. Classification opinions of the Harmonized System Committee of the CCC
3. Classification rulings by the U.S. Customs Service
4. Classification decisions by the U.S. Court of International Trade
5. Classification decisions by the U.S. Court of Appeals for the Federal Circuit

The starting point for every discussion of classification under the HTSUS must be the General Rules of Interpretation (GRI), because these rules explain the significance of the section notes, chapter notes, and tariff headings. In addition to the six General Rules of Interpretation, the U.S. Tariff Schedule contains Additional U.S. Rules of Interpretation, currently consisting of one rule in four parts. The General Rules of Interpretation and the Additional U.S. Rules of Interpretation are set forth below.

General Rules of Interpretation

Classification of goods in the tariff schedule shall be governed by the following principles:

1. The table of contents, alphabetical index, and titles of sections, chapters and sub-chapters are provided for ease of reference only; for legal purposes, classification shall be determined according to the terms of the headings and any relative section or chapter notes and, provided such headings or notes do not otherwise require, according to the following provisions:
2. (a) Any reference in a heading to an article shall be taken to include a reference to that article incomplete or unfinished, provided that, as entered, the incomplete or unfinished article has the essential character of the complete or finished article. It shall also include a reference to that article complete or finished (or falling to be classified as complete or finished by virtue of this rule), entered unassembled or disassembled.
   (b) Any reference in a heading to a material or substance shall be taken to include a reference to mixtures or combinations of that material or substance with other materials or substances. Any reference to goods of a given material or substance shall be taken to include a reference to goods consisting wholly or partly of such material or substance. The classification of goods consisting of more than one material or substance shall be according to the principles of rule 3.
3. When, by application of rule 2(b) or for any other reason, goods are, *prima facie*, classifiable under two or more headings, classification shall be effected as follows:
   (a) The heading which provides the most specific description shall be preferred to headings providing a more general description. However, when two or more headings each refer to part only of the materials or substances contained in mixed or composite goods or to part only of the items in a set put up for retail sale, those headings are to be regarded as equally specific in relation to those goods, even if one of them gives a more complete or precise description of the goods.
   (b) Mixtures, composite goods consisting of different materials or made up of different components, and goods put up in sets for retail sale, which cannot be classified by reference to 3(a), shall be classified as if they consisted of the material or component which gives them their essential character, insofar as this criterion is applicable.
   (c) When goods cannot be classified by reference to 3(a) or 3(b), they shall be

classified under the heading which occurs last in numerical order among
those which equally merit consideration.

4. Goods which cannot be classified in accordance with the above rules shall be
classified under the heading appropriate to the goods to which they are most akin.

5. In addition to the foregoing provisions, the following rules shall apply in respect
of the goods referred to therein:

   (a) Camera cases, musical instrument cases, gun cases, drawing instrument
   cases, necklace cases and similar containers, specially shaped or fitted to
   contain a specific article or set of articles, suitable for long-term use and
   entered with the articles for which they are intended, shall be classified with
   such articles when of a kind normally sold therewith. This rule does not,
   however, apply to containers which give the whole its essential character;

   (b) Subject to the provisions of rule 5(a) above, packing materials and packing
   containers entered with the goods therein shall be classified with the goods if
   they are of a kind normally used for packing such goods. However, this provision does not apply when such packing materials or packing containers are
   clearly suitable for repetitive use.

6. For legal purposes, the classification of goods in the subheadings of a heading
shall be determined according to the terms of those subheadings and any related
subheading notes and, *mutatis mutandis*, to the above rules, on the understanding that only subheadings at the same level are comparable. For the purposes of
this rule, the relative section, chapter and subchapter notes also apply, unless
the context otherwise requires.

Additional U.S. Rules of Interpretation

1. In the absence of special language or context which otherwise requires—

   (a) a tariff classification controlled by use (other than actual use) is to be determined in accordance with the use in the United States at, or immediately
   prior to, the date of importation, of goods of that class or kind to which the
   imported goods belong, and the controlling use is the principal use;

   (b) a tariff classification controlled by the actual use to which the imported
   goods are put in the United States is satisfied only if such use is intended at
   the time of importation, the goods are so used and proof thereof is furnished
   within 3 years after the date the goods are entered;

   (c) a provision for parts of an article covers products solely or principally used
   as a part of such articles but a provision for "parts" or "parts and
   accessories" shall not prevail over a specific provision for such part or
   accessory; and

   (d) the principles of section XI regarding mixtures of two or more textile
   materials shall apply to the classification of goods in any provision in which
   a textile material is named.

Each of the rules set forth above will be discussed with a brief explanation of the meaning of each rule along with actual examples of how each
rule has been applied by the U.S. Customs Service. The examples used for
illustrative purposes are actual rulings issued by Headquarters of the Customs Service in Washington, D.C. While hypothetical examples might

have been devised to show the application of the rules, the actual rulings issued by Customs and used as examples here give a much clearer picture of the complexity of the classification process as it occurs in the real world of commerce. Moreover, actual Customs rulings provide helpful experience in learning the analytical method that Customs uses in classification cases.

In most instances, a Customs ruling is identified by a six-digit number. When the Customs rulings are discussed, the six-digit reference number and date of issuance of the ruling will be given. Note that the various Customs rulings, when quoted, will exhibit somewhat different formats, writing styles, and abbreviation usage. This occurs because the rulings are written by different customs officers. The materials quoted are set forth verbatim.

Of the six General Rules of Interpretation, the first four rules must be applied in the order in which they are stated. Rules 5 and 6 may be used whenever applicable.

GENERAL RULE OF INTERPRETATION 1

GRI 1 provides that the language used in the table of contents, alphabetical index, and the titles of sections, chapters, and subchapters is to be considered for reference purposes only. As is common with most legal documents, the actual language contained in these tables, indexes, and titles do not have any legal significance and cannot be used or interpreted to assist in the classification of merchandise.

GRI 1 also provides that the primary materials to be considered in classifying goods are the tariff headings and any pertinent section or chapter notes. In fact, such headings and notes may preempt the General Rules of Interpretation because such headings or notes may require the General Rules of Interpretation to be ignored in certain situations. In cases where the headings and legal notes do not resolve a classification, the remaining rules may be used.

An example of the application of GRI 1 is Customs Ruling 083258 of November 29, 1989. This ruling involved a request by a private party for tariff classifications for several Christmas tree ornaments, including a snowman. The snowman measured approximately 6.5 inches high. The base of the upper body and the feet were Styrofoam, with wire legs connecting the feet. The base was entirely covered with textile. The item was adorned with a winter stocking cap, scarf, earmuffs, boots, and gloves. All of these items were either red and green, or green. The snowman was holding ski poles constructed of both wood and Styrofoam, and he was wearing cardboard skis. The item was lightweight and had a string attached by which it could be suspended from a Christmas tree.

According to the ruling, the issue presented was whether the snowman and the other items were classifiable under heading 9505 as Christmas ornaments. Set forth below is the relevant portion of the Tariff Schedule:

9505	Festive, carnival or other entertainment articles, including magic tricks and practical joke articles; parts and accessories thereof:	
9505.10	Articles for Christmas festivities and parts and accessories thereof:	
	Christmas ornaments:	
9505.10.1000	Of glass	6.6%
	Other:	
9505.10.1500	Of wood	5.1%
9505.10.2500	Other	5%

Customs' reasoning and decision regarding the requested classification are as follows:

Law and Analysis

Classification under the HTSUS is governed by the General Rules of Interpretation (GRI's). GRI 1 provides that classification is determined first in accordance with the terms of the heading together with any relevant Section or Chapter notes.

Heading 9505, HTSUS, provides for festive, carnival or other entertainment articles, including magic tricks and practical joke articles: parts and accessories thereof. The succeeding subheadings specifically provide for "Articles for Christmas festivities . . ." and "Christmas ornaments." All of the subject items are Christmas-like: they represent Christmas characters and themes and they are decorated in traditional Christmas colors. Moreover, they have strings/loops attached to them and they are not too large or too heavy to be suspended from a Christmas tree. The items are designed, marketed, and sold as Christmas tree ornaments. In light of these facts, the instant items are classifiable in Heading 9505.

Holding

The submitted items are classifiable in subheading 9505.10.2500, which provides for Articles for Christmas festivities and parts and accessories thereof: Christmas ornaments: Other: other. The rate of duty is 5% *ad valorem.*

In the above ruling, Customs reached its classification decision based upon the language of the tariff heading and subheadings, without the application of any section or chapter notes or any of the General Rules of Interpretation other than GRI 1. The snowman consisted of wire, Styrofoam, textiles, wood, cardboard, and string. Although GRI 2(b) states that "the classification of goods consisting of more than one material or substance shall be according to the principles of rule 3," this admonition in 2(b) was not reached because the goods were classifiable based upon the principles set forth in GRI 1. Therefore, reference to GRI 2, 3, and 4 was not required.

Another example of GRI 1 involves Customs Ruling 084207 of April 26, 1989. This ruling involved a request for a classification ruling on a barge to be leased by New York City and used to provide housing for convicted prisoners. The vessel was registered in the Bahamas and in dimension was 103 meters long, 26 meters wide, and 29 meters high.

The competing tariff provisions that were considered in this ruling are as follows:

8901	Cruise ships, excursion boats, ferry boats, cargo ships, barges and similar vessels for the transport of persons or goods:	
8901.10.0000	Cruise ships, excursion boats and similar vessels principally designed for the transport of persons; ferry boats of all kinds	Free
8901.20.0000	Tankers	Free
8901.30.0000	Refrigerated vessels, other than those of subheading 8901.20	Free
8901.90.0000	Other vessels for the transport of goods and other vessels for the transport of both persons and goods	Free
	. . . . .	
8905	Light-vessels, fire-floats, dredgers, floating cranes, and other vessels the navigability of which is subsidiary to their main function; floating docks; floating or submersible drilling or production platforms:	
8905.10.0000	Dredgers	Free
8905.20.0000	Floating or submersible drilling or production platforms	Free
8905.90	Other:	
8905.90.1000	Floating docks	3.7%
8905.90.5000	Other	Free

The importer argued that the barge should not be classified under tariff item 8901.90.0000 as a vessel for the transport of persons or goods because it was not self-propelled, had no cargo spaces, and was incapable of transporting persons or goods. The Customs Service reached its decision on the basis of GRI 1:

According to GRI 1, to be classified in heading 8905, an article must 1) be a vessel, such as a light-vessel, fire-float, dredger, floating crane, or other vessel, and 2) be the type of vessel for which navigability is subsidiary to its main function.

The barge at issue in this case meets these criteria. It qualifies as a vessel since it is capable of being used as a means of transportation in water, and its navigable function *i.e.*, its use as a means of transportation over water, is secondary to its main function. The barge will be placed in a stationary position and will function primarily as a residential facility for convicted prisoners.

The Explanatory Notes, although not legally binding, provide some guidance on the types of vessels intended for classification in heading 8905. The notes to chapter 8905 state that vessels covered in this heading normally perform their main function in a stationary position. Also, vessels used as a residence, such as houseboats are included within this heading.

. . . . .

Holding

The barge is properly classifiable as a vessel, the navigability of which is subsidiary to its main function, in heading 8905, subheading 8905.90.50, is duty free, and subject to formal Customs consumption entry requirements.

Note that Customs, following GRI 1, made its decision based solely on the language of the tariff headings. Tariff heading 8901 refers to "vessels for the transport of persons or goods," while tariff heading 8905 refers to "vessels the navigability of which is subsidiary to their main function." When the language of these two headings is compared, it is clear that the prisoner barge at issue meets the description of heading 8905 and does not meet the description of heading 8901.

The Customs ruling quoted above refers to the Explanatory Notes and indicates that these notes provide certain information with regard to the types of vessels in heading 8905 and how those vessels perform their main function. The Explanatory Notes should not be confused with the section notes and chapter notes that are contained in the U.S. Tariff Schedule. The Explanatory Notes to the Harmonized Commodity Description and Coding System are not part of the HTSUS but are separately published in four volumes by the CCC. These notes were previously mentioned as one of the extrinsic aids to interpretation of the U.S. Tariff Schedule. Other Customs rulings discussed below also refer to the explanatory materials contained in these notes.

GENERAL RULE OF INTERPRETATION 2

GRI 2 contains two parts. GRI 2(a) actually covers three types of merchandise which, taken out of order, are:

1. Complete or finished articles that are unassembled or disassembled
2. Incomplete or unfinished articles that have the essential character of the complete or finished article
3. Incomplete or unfinished articles that are unassembled or disassembled but have the essential character of the complete or finished article

GRI 2(a) states that any reference in a heading to a specific article should be taken to include a reference to any of the above three types of articles. An incomplete or unfinished article must be sufficiently complete or finished so that, as entered, it has the essential character of the complete or finished article. This rule would also apply to intermediate articles that are so far shaped or otherwise dedicated to a particular use that they can only be used for that purpose and no other. An example might be fabric that has been pattern cut into wearing apparel pieces but not sewn together. With regard to unassembled or disassembled components, the rule contemplates that these may be assembled or reassembled only by simple assembly operations. Anything beyond simple assembly would most likely put the components beyond the scope of this rule. Extra (more than necessary) parts of an article entered in addition to necessary parts of that article must be classified separately.

An example of the application of GRI 2(a) to an incomplete or unfinished article is found in Customs Ruling 085399 of December 20, 1989. The pertinent portions of the tariff schedule discussed in this ruling are as follows:

8519	Turntables, record players, cassette players and other sound reproducing apparatus, not incorporating a sound recording device:
	. . . . .
	Other sound reproducing apparatus:
8519.91.00	Cassette type 3.7%
8519.91.0020	Designed exclusively for motor vehicle installation

This ruling involved a request for a tariff classification of incomplete or unfinished automotive tape cassette modules. The merchandise in question, described as a tape mechanism, was an electronically activated tape cassette module designed as the cassette portion of an AM/FM automobile radio/cassette player. The article itself was a rectangular metal box open on three sides and the top. The box housed the module's motor, cassette mechanism, rear control board, audio control board, microprocessor, and an audio cable. The module was electronically operated and had no mechanical push buttons.

As imported, the unit was complete but was incapable of functioning independently from the radio, which was not imported with it. The play, search, fast-forward, and rewind commands were sent from the radio's microcomputer to the module's microprocessor which received and processed them. The tape module's microprocessor was designed to be compatible only with the radio microcomputer in this specific car manufacturer's automobile radios. The module's cassette mechanism received the cassette tapes and placed them in contact with the audio heads. The control board controlled all the module's electrical features, while the audio control board amplified and fine-tuned the signal from the audio heads. The audio cable sent the amplified signal through the radio to the speakers. The tape module was inserted into a cavity in the dash below the radio, secured by six screws and connected to the car radio by a plug on the audio cable. The cost or value of the imported tape module was estimated at $53, while the cost or value of the radio with which it would be used was estimated at $250.

Based on the foregoing, the issue presented was whether the tape cassette module, in its imported condition, possessed the essential character of cassette players and other sound-reproducing apparatus of the type discussed in heading 8519. In reaching its determination in this case, Customs stated:

Law and Analysis

GRI 2(a) states that any reference in a heading to an article shall be taken to include a reference to that article incomplete or unfinished, provided that, as entered, the incomplete or unfinished article has the essential character of the complete or finished article.

Heading 8519 covers turntables, record players, cassette players and other sound reproducing apparatus, not incorporating a sound recording device. The cassette module in issue is described by this heading but is incomplete because it lacks an independent power source and a command function, both of which are provided by attachment to the radio.

The factor or factors which determine essential character for purposes of GRI 2(a) will vary with the goods. Often, the nature of the imported component and its relation to the use of the completed article (in this case a fully functioning cassette player) is determinative. In this case, the cassette module, as imported, is structurally and mechanically complete. In our opinion, it possesses the aggregate of distinctive component parts that establish its identity as a cassette tape player.

Holding

In accordance with GRI 2(a), the cassette module in issue possesses the essential character of a cassette player and other sound reproducing apparatus provided for in heading 8519. It is classifiable as other cassette type sound reproducing apparatus designed exclusively for motor-vehicle installation, in subheading 8519.91.0020, HTSUSA, dutiable at the rate of 3.7 percent *ad valorem*.

Based on the foregoing, the imported cassette module, which was incapable of functioning without the automobile radio, was nevertheless held to have the essential character of a cassette player. For this reason, it was classified as though it were a complete article under subheading 8519.91.0020.(This ruling refers to the Harmonized Tariff Schedule of the United States Annotated [HTSUSA]).

Another example of the application of GRI 2(a) to incomplete items is found in Customs Ruling 086555 of April 16, 1990. This ruling involved a classification request involving certain knocked-down (incomplete) backhoe excavators. The excavators in question were to be imported without certain key components. Under alternative A, the backhoe excavator would be imported without a link-bucket, arm, and boom. The value of the missing components comprised approximately 6% of the total value of the excavator. Under alternative B, the backhoe excavator would be imported without the link-bucket, the arm, the boom, the counterweight, and the cab assembly. Under alternative B, the missing components comprised approximately 12% of the total value of the excavator.

The issue presented was whether or not these incomplete backhoe excavators could be classified as complete articles within tariff heading 8429. Heading 8429 provides in pertinent part as follows:

8429	Self-propelled bulldozers, angledozers, graders, levelers, scrapers, mechanical shovels, excavators, shovel loaders, stamping machines and road rollers:

. . . . .

8429.52.10	Backhoes, shovels, clamshells and draglines 2%

In reaching its decision on the classification of these items, Customs stated:

According to GRI 2(a), if an incomplete article has the essential character of the complete or finished article of a heading, it is classified as the complete or finished article. Little guidance is given for the determination of an article's essential character. The nature of the item, its bulk, quantity, or value may be looked to. However, such a determination varies between different types of merchandise. . . . For machinery, the nature of the item is generally determinative. For an item to have the essential character of a machine, it must be recognizable as such a machine.

In this instance, an incomplete or unfinished backhoe excavator would be classified as an excavator, if it has the essential character of an excavator. The incomplete or unfinished excavator must be easily recognizable as an excavator. Although a part may be clearly recognizable as a component of a specific machine, the part's presence does not guarantee essential character nor does its absence guarantee the lack of essential character. If certain components are absent upon importation, but the remainder has the essential character of an excavator, then the portion of the machine which is present should be classified as an excavator.

It is the propelling base of an excavator which imparts the essential character of an excavator. Alternative A, the backhoe minus the link-bucket, arm, and the boom, has the essential character of an excavator. Alternative B, the backhoe without the link-bucket, the arm, the boom, the counterweight, and the cab assembly also has the essential character of an excavator. In both situations the propelling base is substantial enough so that it has the essential character of an incomplete or unfinished excavator within the meaning of GRI 2(a). An incomplete or unfinished article, with the essential character of a complete or finished article, is to be classified as the complete or finished article. Therefore, the two alternative backhoe excavators are properly classified within subheading 8429.52.10, HTSUSA.

The above ruling is an interesting application of GRI 2(a) because Customs held that the essential character of an excavator was imparted by the propelling base, rather than by the components used to do the digging or excavation. In this regard, notice that heading 8429 begins with the term "self-propelled." For this reason, the imported incomplete excavators were held to be classifiable as complete excavators under GRI 2(a). Would alternatives *A* and *B*, entered without their engines, have been substantial enough to have the essential character of an excavator?

GRI 2(b) deals with mixtures and combinations of materials or substances and has the effect of extending the language of a heading referring to a material or a substance to include mixtures or combinations of that material or substance with other materials or substances. GRI 2(b) also deals with goods consisting of two or more materials or substances and has the effect of broadening any heading referring to goods of a given material or substance to include goods consisting partly of that material or substance. GRI 2(b), however, cannot broaden a heading to cover goods that are not, according to the terms of the heading, includable therein. The rule further provides that, when goods consist of more than one material or substance, the classification of those goods must be made in accordance with GRI 3. Keep in mind, however, that not all goods consisting of more than one material or substance will be classified in accordance with GRI 3, if those goods can be classified by reference to GRI 1. Remember the decorative snowman, discussed above in ruling 083258, which consisted of six different materials but which was classified without reference to GRI 2(b) and GRI 3.

Examples demonstrating the application of GRI 2(b) are included in two specific Customs rulings discussed below in connection with GRI 3(b).

GENERAL RULE OF INTERPRETATION 3

GRI 3 deals with goods that are, either because of the principles stated in rule 2(b) or for some other reason, classifiable under two or more headings. The rule provides that such goods will be classified in accordance with the principles set forth in either part 3(a), part 3(b), or part 3(c). These parts must be applied in the order in which they are given, so that resort may not be made to the principle of rule 3(b) if the merchandise may be classified by reference to 3(a). Rule 3(c) cannot be used unless 3(a) and 3(b) fail to provide a classification.

When goods are classifiable under two or more headings, GRI 3(a) provides that the heading that most specifically describes the goods shall be preferred to a heading that provides a more general description. A description by name is more specific than a description by class. For example, the term "glove" is more specific than the term "wearing apparel."

GRI 3(a) further provides that two or more headings are to be regarded as equally specific in relation to mixed or composite goods when each of the headings refers to only part of the materials or substances contained in those mixed or composite goods. By the same token, two or more headings that refer to some parts of the items in a set put up for retail sale but not to all parts of such sets are to be regarded as equally specific. This shall be true in both cases, even though one of the headings may give a more complete or precise description of the goods. When the above situations occur, the classification of the goods must be determined by reference to rule 3(b) or 3(c).

An example of the application of rule 3(a) is found in Customs Ruling 085296 of December 16, 1989. This ruling involved a request for a tariff classification for refrigerated freight containers. The competing headings that were considered in this ruling are set forth as follows:

8418	Refrigerators, freezers and other refrigerating or freezing equipment, electric or other; heat pumps, other than the air conditioning machines of heading 8415; parts thereof: [. . . . . . 2.9%]
8609.00.0000	Containers (including containers for the transport of fluids) specially designed and equipped for carriage by one or more modes of transport . . . . Free

The containers in issue measured 40 feet by 8 feet by 8½ feet and had an interior volume of roughly 2,000 cubic feet. The containers were made of stainless steel and aluminum, and they were insulated with polyurethane foam. They were designed to be lifted from a container ship and secured to a truck chassis or railroad flatcar bed. Installed in each container was a U.S.-made temperature control mechanism, consisting of an evaporator, a fan mounted in a hole in the container's nose, and a condenser and compressor mounted outside the front wall of the container. This temperature control apparatus blew cooled air ranging from − 20 degrees to + 80 degrees Fahrenheit into the container box. The temperature apparatus was designed primarily to cool or chill fruits, vegetables, and other perishables, and the heating feature served to warm the condenser coils when they frosted over or to equalize the temperature in containers stored above deck when the outside temperature dropped below the desired level.

The issue presented in this ruling was whether the refrigerated freight containers should be classified as containers under heading 8609 or as refrigeration and freezing equipment under heading 8418. In reaching its decision, Customs stated:

GRI 3(a), HTSUSA, provides in part that where goods are, *prima facie*, classifiable under two or more headings, the heading which provides the most specific description shall be preferred to headings providing a more general description.

. . . . .

Explanatory Notes to the Harmonized Commodity Description and Coding System provide guidance as to the scope of the HTSUS headings at the international level. These notes indicate that articles of heading 8609 are essentially packing receptacles specially designed and equipped to be carried by road or rail, among other modes of transport, and are equipped with fittings to facilitate handling and securing on the transporting vehicle. Insulated containers for perishable foods or goods are among the principal types. The notes also indicate that refrigeration equipment of heading 8418 includes apparatus for the production in a continuous cycle, of low temperatures in the region of 0 degrees C (32 degrees F) at the active cooling element (i.e., the evaporator). Apparatus of this heading is not mounted on a common base or as a self-contained unit, but operates together. It normally utilizes an evaporator in which liquid refrigerant absorbs ambient warm air at low temperature, a compressor to raise the pressure and temperature of the gaseous refrigerant, a condenser in which the refrigerant discharges its heat to the environment, and a fan for blowing the cooled air. Both heading 8418 and heading 8609 describe the merchandise in issue.

For purposes of GRI 3(a), merchandise is classifiable in the heading which provides the most narrow and specific description or which has the requirements which are most difficult to satisfy. Heading 8418 covers equipment or apparatus primarily designed to produce low temperatures without regard to any transporting capability. Heading 8609 covers insulated transport-type containers for perishable foods or goods, whether refrigerated or not. The containers here have design features which make them suitable for conveying goods from point to point, by road or rail. In addition, because they are also insulated, they have some capacity to protect perishable goods. Because the requirements of heading 8609 are more difficult to satisfy than are those of heading 8418, we conclude that for purposes of GRI 3(a) heading 8609 provides the most specific description for the merchandise in issue.

Holding

The . . . refrigerated (reefer) containers described here are provided for in heading 8609. They are classifiable as containers specially designed and equipped for carriage by one or more modes of transport, in subheading 8609.00.0000, HTSUSA, subject to entry free of duty.

GRI 3(b) is the second rule used for classification of goods that are classifiable under two or more headings. This rule relates to (1) mixtures, (2) composite goods consisting of different materials, (3) composite goods consisting of different components, and (4) goods put up in sets for retail sale. The rule provides that the subject goods are to be classified as if they consisted of the material or component that gives them their essential character. The determination of essential character can vary among different types of goods. In some instances the bulk, quantity, weight, or value may determine the essential character, while in other instances one constituent material or component may so fundamentally contribute to the use of the item as to constitute its essential character.

Composite goods made up of different components include items in which the components are attached to one another as well as items with separable components that are so mutually complementary that they would never normally be sold in separate parts. An example of an item with separable components would be an ashtray consisting of a stand incorporating a removable ash container.

In order for goods to come within the meaning of "goods put up in sets for retail sale," the following three requirements must be met:

1. There must be at least two different articles that are classifiable in different headings.
2. A set must consist of products or articles put up together to meet a particular need or to carry out a specific activity.
3. The sets are packaged in a manner that renders them salable directly to users without repacking.

If all three of the above conditions exist, the combination of items can be considered to be goods put up in sets for retail sale. For example, a tent repair kit consisting of seam sealer, canvas cement, thread, cord, needle, pole tabs, and three swatches of repair fabric, all contained in a zippered nylon pouch, would constitute goods put up in sets for retail sale.

An example of the application of GRI 3(b) is found in Customs Ruling 085102 of September 25, 1989. This ruling involved a request for classification of a heart floral box. The merchandise was a heart-shaped box, measuring approximately 4¾ inches by 5¼ inches, which was used to hold jewelry or trinkets. The bottom of the box was made of chipwood and plywood and was covered by a cushion made of textile fabric filled with textile filling and backed by cardboard. The lid of the box was made of chipwood and plywood covered by a textile heart large enough to cover the box completely and to extend approximately two inches beyond the edges. The textile heart consisted of a sponge material covered with textile fabric and decorated with nylon lace, nylon ribbon, a nylon flower, and plastic beads. The value of the components of the item taken as a whole was predominantly textile.

This case presented the issue of the classification of composite goods consisting of different materials, namely textiles and wood. Although Customs' decision is based on GRI 3(b), GRI 2(b), for which no examples were given above, is also cited and applied by Customs. In reaching its decision regarding the classification of these jewelry boxes, Customs stated:

GRI 2(b), HTSUSA, provides in part that "The classification of goods consisting of more than one material or substance shall be according to the principles of Rule 3."

GRI 3, HTSUSA, reads in pertinent part as follows:

3. When, by application of Rule 2(b) or for any other reason, goods are *prima facie* classifiable under two or more headings, classification shall be effected as follows:

. . . . .

(b) Mixtures, composite goods consisting of different materials or made up of different components, and goods put up in sets for retail sale which cannot be classified by reference to 3(a), shall be classified as if they consisted of the material or component which gives them their essential character, insofar as this criterion is applicable.

. . . . .

The Explanatory Notes for GRI 3(b) state in pertinent part as follows:

(VIII) The factor which determines essential character will vary as between different kinds of goods. It may, for example, be determined by the nature of the material or component, its bulk, quantity, weight or value, or by the role of a constituent material in relation to the use of the goods.

In this case, what is being marketed is much more than the chipwood and plywood frame of the box. There are elements of beauty, texture and good taste that provide most of the appeal of the textile-topped, textile-lined box. Although the wood frame provides structural integrity, it cannot compare with the appeal and the value of the textile top and lining. It is apparent that the aesthetic appeal and marketability of the box are dependent upon the textile elements.

In view of the foregoing, it is our opinion that the essential character of the textile-topped and lined box is imparted by the textile components. Following GRI 3(b), HTSUSA, the heart shaped box is classifiable under the provision for other made up textile articles: other: other: other, in subheading 6307.90.9050, HTSUSA, dutiable at the rate of 7 percent *ad valorem.*

Another example of the application of GRI 3(b) is found in Customs Ruling 083970 of July 14, 1989. This ruling involved a request for a tariff classification on a double-edged wiper blade which was part of an automobile windshield wiper. The wiper blade was approximately 18 inches long and consisted of a double-edged rubber wiper blade portion attached at the top to a plastic spine or frame with a steel retainer clip on one end. The article was designed to function as the blade portion of an automotive windshield wiper.

The wiper blade consisted of rubber, plastic, and steel, thus constituting another example of composite goods consisting of different materials. Heading 8512 of the Tariff Schedule provides for windshield wipers and parts thereof, among other things. A specific issue in this case was therefore whether the merchandise was classifiable under heading 8512. This ruling also constitutes an example of the application of GRI 2(b) discussed above. In reaching its decision regarding the classification of the wiper blades, Customs stated:

In accordance with General Rule of Interpretation (GRI) 1, HTSUSA, for legal purposes, classification shall be determined according to the terms of the headings and any relative section or chapter notes. Heading 8512, HTSUSA, covers electrical lighting or signaling equipment (excluding articles of heading 8539), windshield wipers, defrosters and demisters, of a kind used for cycles or motor vehicles; parts thereof.

Section XVI, Note 2(b), HTSUSA, which governs classification of merchandise in Chapter 85, states that parts suitable for use solely or principally with a particular kind of machine, or with a number of machines of the same heading are to be classified with the machines of that kind. However, Note 2(b) is subject to Note 1(a) to Section XVI. Note 1(a) excludes from Section XVI articles of a kind used in machinery or mechanical or electrical appliances or for other technical uses, of vulcanized rubber other than hard rubber (heading 4016). Automotive windshield wiping mechanisms are mechanical or electrical appliances for the purposes of Note 1(a), and the wiper blades [are] articles of a kind used in such appliances. The wiper blades of [vulcanized] rubber are therefore excluded from classification in heading 8512.

GRI 2(b) states that any reference in a heading to a material or substance shall be taken to include a reference to mixtures or combinations of that material or substance with other materials or substances, and that the classification of goods consisting of more than one material or substance shall be according to the principles of rule 3. The wiper blade consists of the rubber wiping portion, a plastic spine, and steel retaining clip. Articles of rubber are classifiable in heading 4016, articles of plastics are classifiable in heading 3926, and articles of iron or steel are classifiable in heading 7326.

GRI 3(a) states that when two or more headings each refer to part only of the materials or substances contained in mixed or composite goods, those headings are to be regarded as being equally specific in relation to those goods. GRI 3(b) states that composite goods made up of different components which cannot be classified by reference to 3(a), shall be classified as if they consisted of the material or component which gives them their essential character. The wiper blade is designed to clean automotive windshields. In our opinion, it is the rubber portion of the article that performs the wiping function. The rubber portion therefore imparts the essential character to the wiper blade. The wiper blade is classifiable in heading 4016, and, therefore, is excluded by Note 1(a) to Section XVI from classification as a part of a windshield wiper in heading 8512.

Holding

The wiper blades in question are classifiable as other articles of vulcanized rubber other than hard rubber, in subheading 4016.99.5050. The rate of duty is 5.3 percent *ad valorem*.

As noted in the discussion of GRI 1, classification must proceed according to the terms of the headings and any pertinent section or chapter notes. Observe here that the windshield wiper blade was precluded from classification as parts of windshield wipers under heading 8512 because of an exclusion contained in note 1(a) of section XVI. This is a good example of the significance that the section and chapter notes can have when read in conjunction with the headings during the classification process.

GRI 3(c) is the last of the three rules under GRI 3 that are to be used when goods are classifiable under two or more headings. GRI 3(c) simply states that, when goods cannot be classified using rule 3(a) or 3(b), as a last resort the merchandise will be classified in the tariff heading that occurs last in numerical order among the headings considered. Stated differently, taking the headings that equally apply to an item, the heading with the highest tariff number will be selected.

For example, if a composite article consisting of different materials could be classified in chapter 39, chapter 40, or chapter 62, and rules 3(a) and 3(b) were not determinative of the classification, then in accordance with rule 3(c), the merchandise would be classified in the heading of chapter 62, since this is the heading that occurs last in the Tariff Schedule.

An example of the application of GRI 3(c) is found in Customs Ruling 085148 of November 9, 1989. This ruling involved a request for the tariff classification of a trunk-shaped, textile-covered cardboard box. The box was approximately 6 inches high, 6½ inches wide, and 4 inches deep. It had two parts, a lower portion and a lid, both constructed of cardboard or paperboard, covered with foam padding and a man-made satin textile material. The lid was attached to the bottom by two ribbons of textile material which acted as hinges. The foam and textile were adhered to the cardboard by an adhesive. The textile-covered cardboard was formed into the shape of a box and then secured at the seams by glue. The top and edges of the box were decorated with a lace trim of textile material. The top of the box was also decorated with flowers and ribbons, both of textile material. By value, the major components of the box were stated to be 42% cardboard, 30% textile material, 14% textile trim, and 7% foam padding.

The issue presented, again, was the proper classification of composite goods consisting of different materials. In reaching its decision, Customs stated in pertinent part:

In the instant case, we find no headings within the nomenclature whose terms would specifically include boxes such as these. In addition, they are not addressed by any Legal Notes, at either the Section or Chapter level. Because GRI 1 is, therefore, inconclusive, the boxes must be classified by determining essential character on the basis of component materials. . . . We have eliminated from consideration the "material-related" headings which classify goods made up of the foam and glue components, since they constitute a relatively insignificant portion of the merchandise. Two headings, then, suggest themselves for classification purposes. The first is heading 4823, HTSUSA, other articles of paper or paperboard, and the second is heading 6307, HTSUSA, other made up articles of textiles.

As noted above, neither heading 4823 nor 6307, HTSUSA, by their terms or relevant Legal Notes, includes paperboard boxes of this type. Since classification cannot be made by GRI 1, the remaining GRIs, taken in order, are used. Under GRI 2, any reference to a material or an article made of a material includes goods made wholly or in part of that material. GRIs 3(a) & (b) hold that goods such as these which are *prima facie* classifiable under two or more headings are classified by determining which of the component materials provides the goods with its essential character. The Explanatory Notes to GRI 3(b) indicate that there are no hard and fast rules for determining essential character. Each case involves an individual evaluation of such factors as weight, value, bulk, marketability, etc. In this case, the sample box is a composite good which should be classifiable as a product of either textile or paper, depending upon which material gives the product its essential character.

In this case, however, we are of the opinion that the classification of these boxes cannot be determined by essential character. None of the factors, either as a group or individually, provide sufficient support for essential character of paperboard or of textiles. Although paperboard is apparently predominant by weight, by bulk, and by value, it is the textile which distinguishes this box from ordinary cardboard boxes. The textile greatly enhances the marketability of the item, but also relies upon the cardboard frame for support and rigidity.

Failing classification by GRI 3(b), GRI 3(c) states that, among eligible headings, classification shall occur under that which is last in numerical order among those under consideration. In this case, that subheading would be 6307.90.9050, HTSUSA, Other made up articles: Other: Other: Other.

In this case, neither the paperboard nor the textile materials imparted the essential character of the boxes, unlike the heart-shaped jewelry boxes that were the subject of Customs Ruling 085102, discussed above. In that ruling, it was held that the textile components imparted the essential character of the boxes; it was stated, however, that the value of the boxes was predominantly textile. In this case, on the other hand, the value of the components was 42% cardboard, 30% textile material, 14% textile trim, and 7% foam padding. In total, the textile portion was 44% of the value, while the cardboard was 42% of the value. Thus, the cardboard and textile portions were more or less equal in value. This might help explain why neither the cardboard nor the textile portion in this case was held to constitute the essential character of the boxes.

Another example of the application of GRI 3(c) is found in Customs Ruling 085356 of November 20, 1989. This ruling involved a request for tariff classification of three school supply kits. The first kit consisted of one lead pencil, one ruler, one eraser, and one pencil sharpener. These items were packaged in a blue sheet plastic pouch, closed by a zipper.

The second kit consisted of one ballpoint pen, one pencil sharpener, one eraser, one pencil, one ruler, and a gray-and-white plastic pouch, closed by a snap at the top. All these items were packaged in a cellophane package.

The third kit consisted of one ruler, one pencil, one eraser, one sharpener, and a green plastic pouch, closed by a zipper. These items were packaged in a clear plastic bag.

The issue presented in this case involved the classification of goods put up in sets for retail sale. In reaching its classification decision, Customs stated:

General Rule of Interpretation (GRI) 3(a), HTSUSA, states that the most specific heading shall apply, but that when two or more headings refer to part only of the items in a set put up for retail sale, those headings are to be regarded as equally specific. GRI 3(a) does not apply to the instant kits.

GRI 3(b), HTSUSA, states that goods put up in sets for retail sale shall be classified according to that component which gives them their essential character.

The Explanatory Notes for GRI 3(b) state that goods put up in sets for retail sale must consist of at least two different articles which are classifiable in different headings. Each kit contains a pencil classified in Heading 9609 and an eraser classified in Heading 4016, so this requirement is met. The Explanatory Notes also state that retail sets must consist of articles put up together to carry out a particular function. All of the items involved would help a student do school writing, so the second requirement is met. Finally the Explanatory Notes state that retail sets must be put up in a manner suitable for sale directly to users without repacking. The instant kits meet this final requirement, so they do constitute goods put up in sets for retail sale.

The Explanatory Notes for GRI 3(b) state that:

> The factor which determines essential character will vary as between different kinds of goods. It may, for example, be determined by the nature of the material or component, its bulk, quantity, weight or value, or by the role of a constituent material in relation to the use of the goods.

In the case of the instant school supply kits, no one particular component stands out. No single component is of such distinctive bulk, nature, quantity, weight or value as to give the kit its essential character. Nor does any component play such a role in relation to the use of the goods as to be determinative of essential character. Inasmuch as no essential character can be determined, GRI 3(b) does not apply.

GRI 3(c) says that, if neither GRI 3(a) nor GRI 3(b) applies, merchandise shall be classified in the heading which occurs last in numerical order among those equally meriting consideration. All items within the kits appear to merit equal consideration. If entered separately, the plastic pouches are classifiable in Heading 4202, the pencils are classifiable in Heading 9609, the rulers are classifiable in Heading 9017, the pencil sharpeners are classifiable in Heading 8214, the erasers are classifiable in Heading 4016, and the ball point pen is classifiable in Heading 9608. By virtue of GRI 3(c), all three school supply kits are classifiable in Heading 9609 [pencils], which occurs last in numerical order [because each kit contains a pencil].

. . . . .

The three school supply kits are goods put up in sets for retail sale. They are classified in subheading 9609.10.00, HTSUSA, by virtue of GRI 3(c), HTSUSA, and are dutiable at the rate of 4.3 percent *ad valorem* plus 14 cents per gross.

This ruling is a good example of the analytical steps that must be followed when considering the classification of goods put up in sets for retail sale. Obviously, in a case where one of the components in the set imparted the essential character of the set, classification would have been made by reference to GRI 3(b).

GENERAL RULE OF INTERPRETATION 4

GRI 4 provides that when goods cannot be classified in accordance with rules 1 through 3, discussed above, they shall be classified under the heading appropriate to the goods to which they are most akin or similar. In order to determine the goods to which they are most akin, the items to be classified must be compared with all those items to which they might be akin. Kinship or similarity may depend upon such factors as description, character, purpose, function, or use. There are no hard-and-fast rules.

A rule such as GRI 4 is intended to provide a final way out when goods cannot be classified by reference to the first three rules. It must be understood that recourse to rule 4 will not be made in many instances. Moreover, classification by similitude or kinship frequently comes into play only in the later historical stages of a classification system. As years pass, manufacturing technology will eventually produce goods of an unusual description, nature, or substance, whose existence was not contemplated by the people who framed the classification system. When such new products occur, there will frequently be no heading that seems to be appropriate to classify them. It is in these cases that the principles of classification by kinship become important.

As previously stated, the four General Rules of Interpretation discussed above must be applied in sequential order. The two remaining rules, GRI 5 and GRI 6, are not applied sequentially and deal with (1) the classification of special containers, packing cases, and materials and (2) the classification principles to be applied to subheadings of a tariff heading.

GENERAL RULE OF INTERPRETATION 5

GRI 5 has two parts. GRI 5(a) deals with the classification of specially shaped or fitted cases. GRI 5(a) states that camera cases, instrument cases, gun cases, necklace cases, and similar containers, specially shaped or fitted to contain a specific article or set of articles, suitable for long-term use, and entered with the articles for which they are intended, shall be classified with (under the same heading as) such articles, provided the containers are of the type normally sold with such articles. This rule applies only if the five following requirements are met:

1. The containers are shaped or fitted to contain a specific article or set of articles. The containers need not be in the same shape as the articles but must be designed specifically to accommodate the particular articles for which they are intended.
2. The containers must be suitable for long-term use and have a durability approximately equivalent to that of the articles they are designed to accommodate.
3. The containers are presented (imported together) with the articles for which they are intended, even though packed separately from the articles for which they are intended.
4. The containers are of a type normally sold with such articles.
5. The containers do not impart to the whole its essential character.

Examples other than those specified in the rule itself would be pool cue cases, surveying instrument cases, typewriter cases, and coin collection cases.

Containers that impart the essential character to the whole article are excluded from the application of rule 5(a). For example, a travel bar consisting of a shaker, strainer, measuring cup, glasses, and liquor bottles contained in a locking case with a handle would not fall within the ambit of rule 5(a).

GRI 5(b) deals with the classification of packing materials and packing containers of a type normally used for packing the articles with which they are imported. The rule provides that such packing materials and containers are to be classified with (under the same heading as) the goods with which they are imported. In order to be subject to classification under this rule, the packing materials or containers must not be suitable for repetitive use. For example, aluminum beer kegs and metal soda cylinders of the type used in bars are suitable for reuse and are classified separately from their contents.

An example of the application of GRI 5(a) is found in Customs Ruling 083436 of December 22, 1989. This ruling involved a request for the tariff classification of a personal weighing scale with canvas case. The scale weighed five pounds and was in the shape of a flat square box. It contained a remote display including an adapter. The scale was described as a portable electronic scale designed for diet club members to carry back and forth from home to their club in the canvas case. The canvas case was manufactured in the shape of the scale and had a carrying strap. The scale and case were imported and packaged together for retail sale.

The question presented in this case was whether the scale and case were classifiable as a set under GRI 3(b), as a scale and its case under GRI 5(a), or as a scale and its packing material under GRI 5(b). In reaching its determination, Customs stated:

The scale without the case is classified as a personal weighing scale in 8423.10.00, HTSUSA. The case without the scale, even if considered to be an accessory to the scale, would be classified in a heading other than 8423, HTSUSA. (While parts of scales are described by Heading 8423, accessories to scales are not.) There are no Section or Chapter notes which control the classification of the merchandise when imported and packaged together for retail sale.

GRI 5(a) provides specific rules for the classification of "camera cases, musical instrument cases, gun cases . . . and similar containers." GRI 5(a) provides that articles which satisfy the criteria for cases or other containers under GRI 5(a) are not classified as one of the goods in a GRI 3(b) set (e.g. GRI 5(a) provides for the classification of cases which ". . . contain a specific article or set of articles . . .")

In order for an article to be a GRI 5(a) container, it must satisfy five requirements:

1. be specially shaped to contain a specific article, and

2. be suitable for long-term use, and

3. be presented with the articles for which they are intended, and

4. be of a kind normally sold with such articles, and

5. not give the whole its essential character.

The canvas case clearly satisfies requirements 1-3, and 5. The issue of whether it satisfies requirement 4 is less clear. Canvas cases are not normally sold with personal weighing scales. The scale under consideration is unique in that it is lightweight in design and is intended to be routinely carried to and from various locations. The basic canvas case can reasonably be accepted as a kind of case normally sold with a portable scale, and thus satisfies requirement 4 of GRI 5(a).

The case cannot be classified as packing material under GRI 5(b) because it is suitable for repetitive use. It cannot be classified as an article of a set under GRI 3(b) because it satisfies the criteria for cases under GRI 5(a).

The scale and canvas case are classified together, as a personal weighing scale with its case, in 8423.10.00, HTSUSA.

In order to clarify somewhat that portion of the above ruling that discusses sets under GRI 3(b), the following should be considered. In order for goods to qualify as "goods put up in sets for retail sale," one of the three requirements is that there must be at least two different articles that are *prima facie* (that is, for a certainty) classifiable under two or more headings. Since the carrying case at issue here meets the requirements of rule 5(a), it is capable of classification under the same heading as the scale, so there are not two different articles that are *prima facie* classifiable under two or more headings. Therefore, the scale and case do not meet the first of the three requirements for "goods put up in sets for retail sale."

An example of the application of GRI 5(b) is found in Customs Ruling 086611 of May 17, 1990. This ruling involved a request for tariff classification of certain textile drawstring pouches. The textile drawstring pouch was constructed of a cotton backed, man made fiber velour material and measured approximately four inches by five inches. The man-made fiber textile material formed the outer surface of the pouch. The pouch was used to contain a small bottle of liqueur known as a "miniature."

With regard to the classification of the pouch, either imported separately or along with a miniature of liqueur, Customs stated:

GRI 5(a) provides that containers specially shaped or fitted to contain specific articles, suitable for long-term use and entered with the articles, shall be classified with such articles when of a kind normally sold therewith. In addition, pursuant to GRI 5(b), packing materials and packing containers are also classified with the goods. However, the provision does not apply if the packing materials and packing container are clearly suitable for repetitive use. For the purposes of GRI 5(b), the term "repetitive use" is interpreted to mean use with goods of the kind presented in the packing container. It is Customs position that the subject textile bags are general purpose bags not specially shaped or fitted as provided for in GRI 5(a). With regard to classification under GRI 5(b), it is Customs opinion that the pouch is not designed for repetitive use. Although capable of further use with various small articles, such uses are considered fugitive and, therefore, not within the meaning of GRI 5(b).

The . . . liqueur, imported with the textile pouch at issue, is classifiable under heading 2208, HTSUSA, which provides for undenatured ethyl alcohol of an alcoholic strength by volume of less than 80 percent vol.; spirits, liqueurs and other spirituous beverages. . . . The textile bag, if imported separately, is classifiable in heading 6307, HTSUSA, which provides for other made up articles. It is Customs position that the textile pouch is a packing container within the meaning of GRI 5(b). Therefore, the subject . . . liqueur and textile bag are classifiable in heading 2208, HTSUSA.

. . . . .

The merchandise at issue is classifiable under subheading 2208.90.4530, HTSUSA, which provides for undenatured ethyl alcohol . . . , other, cordials, liqueurs, kirschwasser and ratafia, in containers each holding not over 4 liters. The rate of duty is 13.2 cents per proof . . . liter.

Note in this case that the result of classifying the textile pouch with the liqueur as packing, in accordance with GRI 5(b), has the effect of rendering the pouch nondutiable, inasmuch as the rate of duty for the liqueur is 13.2 cents per proof liter. This is a specific rate of duty based on the volume and strength of the liquid in the shipment. The same amount of duty would be paid on the liqueur, with or without the textile pouch, and therefore there is no additional duty by reason of the presence of the textile pouch.

GENERAL RULE OF INTERPRETATION 6

In discussing the previous General Rules of Interpretation, tariff headings consisting of four digits have been dealt with. For example, headings 9505, 8905, 8519, 8429, and other four-digit tariff headings were discussed in the rulings. GRI 6 deals with the classification of merchandise in the six-digit and eight-digit subheadings. GRI 6 provides that classification of goods in such subheadings shall be determined according to the terms of the subheadings and any relative subheading notes. GRI 6 further provides that classification at subheading levels is subject, *mutatis mutandis*, to GRIs 1 through 5. *Mutatis mutandis*, the Latin expression contained in GRI 6, means "with the necessary changes in points of detail"—that is, matters or things are generally the same but are to be altered when necessary with respect to certain words. For example, when a rule refers to the word "heading," it should be replaced with the word "subheading." Therefore, classification of goods in the subheadings of a heading are subject to General Rules of Interpretation 1 through 5, with the necessary changes made in those rules. Further, when goods are being classified under subheadings, the first four General Rules of Interpretation apply in their given order in determining classification under subheadings.

The rule also provides that only subheadings of equal level are comparable. This means that six-digit subheadings must be compared only with other six-digit subheadings and not with eight-digit subheadings. GRI 6 also states that the section notes and chapter notes apply when classification at the subheading level is considered, unless the subheadings themselves or the subheading notes require otherwise.

The classification of any product in its appropriate subheading can only be considered after the product involved has already been properly classified in the proper four-digit heading. It is only after selecting the proper four-digit heading that reference can be made to various six-digit subheadings under the four-digit heading selected. Also, it is only after picking the appropriate six-digit subheading that consideration can be given to eight-digit subheadings under the six-digit subheading selected as the correct one.

Finally, it is important to remember that the scope of an eight-digit subheading cannot be greater than the scope of the six-digit subheading under which it falls, and the scope of a six-digit subheading cannot be greater than the scope of the four-digit heading under which it falls.

An example of the application of GRI 6 is found in Customs Ruling 083532 of August 28, 1989. This ruling involved a request for tariff classification of four textile articles. However, only two of the articles are germaine to the application of GRI 6, and for this reason only these two sample items will be discussed. Both textile samples were numbered Style

No. 3080 and each contained four placemats and four napkins. In one sample, the placemats and napkins were composed of fabric that was 65% polyester and 35% cotton by weight. In the other sample, the placemats and napkins were made from fabric that was 55% polyester and 45% cotton by weight. In both instances, the placemats and napkins were packaged together and sold as sets at retail.

The specific issue involved in this ruling was whether the napkins and placemats that were packaged together and sold as sets at retail constituted "goods put up in sets for retail sale" within the meaning of GRI 3 or whether the napkins and placemats were classifiable as separate articles. In order to facilitate, to the greatest extent possible, the reader's understanding of the classification discussion in this ruling, the appropriate excerpts from the Tariff Schedule have been set forth below:

6302	Bed linen, table linen, toilet linen and kitchen linen:	
6302.40	Table linen, knitted or crocheted:	
	Other table linen:	
6302.51	Of cotton:	
6302.52	Of flax:	
6302.53.00	Of man-made fibers	12.8%
	Tablecloths and napkins:	
6302.53.0010	Damask	
6302.53.0020	Other	
6302.53.0030	Other	

In reaching its classification determination, Customs stated:

Classification of merchandise under the HTSUSA is in accordance with the General Rules of Interpretation (GRI's), taken in order. The term "sets" is discussed in GRI 3. In order to have a "set" under GRI 3, the set must contain goods which are, *prima facie*, classifiable under two or more headings. The term "heading" is not defined in the nomenclature, but it is clear it refers to the four digit level. . . . [B]oth style numbers 3080 are packaged together for retail sale, so we have to determine whether they are classified as a set.

The placemats and napkins are classifiable in the same four digit heading. Heading 6302, HTSUSA, provides for bed linen, table linen, toilet linen and kitchen linen. Relying on GRI 3, no guidance is given as to how goods are to be classified together or separately below the four digit level.

GRI 6 provides that for legal purposes, "classification of goods in the subheadings of a heading shall be determined according to the terms of those subheadings and any related subheading Notes, and *mutatis mutandis*, to the above rules, on the understanding that only subheadings at the same level are comparable." GRI 6 thus incorporates GRI's 1 through 5 in classifying goods at the subheading level. Since GRI 6 uses the phrase "for legal purposes" the preceding GRI's are to be applied at the level necessary for the final legal classification of the goods for tariff purposes. GRI 6 requires the use of GRI 3 at the eight digit level in the HTSUSA, since it is that level at which the classification of the merchandise is ultimately determined. Thus, in order to be classifiable as a "set," the components must be classifiable in at least two different subheadings.

With respect to the placemats and napkins, at the heading level, we do not have "goods put up in sets for retail sale" within the meaning of GRI 3. At the eight digit subheading level, we do not have articles classifiable under two different subheadings. The placemats and napkins fall under subheading 6302.53.00, HTSUSA, which provides for bed linen, table linen, toilet linen and kitchen linen, other table linen, of man-made fibers. It is only between competing ten digit statistical annotations that a disparity arises. It is our opinion that GRI 6 is not applicable in determining whether a "set" exists where the classification differences exist only at the ten digit level. Therefore, style numbers 3080 are not considered a "set" for classification purposes, and will be classified separately.

We note that it is Customs position that GRI 6 can apply at the ten digit level only where there is an existing question as to which statistical annotation applies and where no other rule will resolve the matter. We note that GRI 6 would not apply where there are annotations providing for the reporting of the goods separately.

Holding

The placemats of styles 3080 are classified under subheading 6302.53.0030, HTSUSA, which provides for bed linen, table linen, toilet linen and kitchen linen, other table linen, of man-made fibers, other, . . . and dutiable at the rate of 12.8 percent *ad valorem*.

The napkins of styles 3080 are classified under subheading 6302.53.0020, HTSUSA, which provides for bed linen, table linen, toilet linen and kitchen linen, other table linen, of man-made fibers, tablecloths and napkins, other, . . . and dutiable at the rate of 12.8 percent *ad valorem*.

Since the placemats and napkins involved here are packaged together for retail sale directly to consumers and since they are put up together to carry out a specific activity (that is, eating), they meet two of the three requirements necessary to be considered "goods put up in sets for retail sale." If it were determined that the placemats and napkins met the third requirement, then they would be "goods put up in sets for retail sale" and they would be classified together under the same 10-digit tariff number based upon the application of GRI 3(b) or 3(c). On the other hand, if it were determined that the placemats and napkins did not meet the third requirement for "goods put up in sets for retail sale," then they would be separately classifiable under their own 10-digit tariff numbers. Therefore, whether the goods are classified together as sets or separately is determined by whether the goods are, *prima facie*, classifiable under two or more headings, the third requirement for "sets."

Both the placemats and napkins fall under "heading" 6302, but not necessarily under the same subheading under heading 6302. Customs therefore poses the question whether the "sets" provision of GRI 3 is still an issue if the placemats and napkins fall under different six-digit or eight-digit subheadings under 6302. Based upon GRI 6, Customs concludes there would still be an issue. GRI 6 states that classification in the subheadings is determined according to the terms of the subheadings and, *mutatis mutandis*, to GRIs 1 through 5. Making the necessary changes in GRI 3 required by GRI 6, GRI 3 states as follows: When . . . goods are, *prima facie*, classifiable under two or more *subheadings*, classification shall be effected according to rules 3(a), 3(b), and 3(c). Based on this logic, Customs is correct that the "sets" issue is still viable.

Customs next inquires whether the placemats and napkins actually fall under different six-digit or eight-digit subheadings so as to meet the third requirement necessary for "goods put up in sets for retail sale." At this point, it is discovered that both articles fall under the eight-digit subheading 6302.53.00. At the eight-digit subheading level, the third requirement for "sets" is not met because articles classifiable under different subheadings at the eight-digit, "legal," level are not present. Therefore, the goods are not "sets," and they must be classified separately under their respective 10-digit tariff numbers, with the napkins under 6302.53.0020 as "Tablecloths and napkins . . . other," and with the placemats under 6302.53.0030 as "of man-made fibers . . . other," both at 12.8%.

Implicit in Customs' ruling is the notion that tariff numbers have "legal" significance only as far as the eight-digit level. The ninth and tenth digits of tariff numbers, taken together, establish the "statistical annotations" appended to the eight-digit numbers as suffixes. These last two numbers are viewed as having statistical significance only and no legal significance. Customs goes on to explain its position that GRI 6 (and through GRI 6, the remaining GRIs) can be employed at the 10-digit level to resolve only statistical issues, not legal issues.

It is interesting to note that GRI 6 itself did not resolve the classification issue in this case but was cited and applied to determine the meaning and application of the "sets" provision in GRI 3.

ADDITIONAL U.S. RULES OF INTERPRETATION 1

The Additional U.S. Rules of Interpretation (AUSRI) consist of one rule, set forth in four parts. The first two parts deal with tariff classifications controlled by use, the third part discusses the classification of parts, and the fourth part involves tariff provisions in which a textile material is named.

AUSRI 1 (a) provides that where a tariff classification is controlled by use, other than actual use, the use that governs is that use in the United

States at the date of importation, or immediately prior thereto, of goods of the same class or kind as the imported goods. The rule provides that the controlling use is the principal use. The principal use is the use that exceeds every other use, not all other uses. For example, where there are three uses of an item, one use may be 41% of the total use of the item. The second use may be 38% of the total, and the third use may be 21% of the total. In this situation, the use that exceeds every other use is the first use, at 41%, and this is the principal use. Note that the principal use exceeds every other use, but it is not necessary that the principal use exceed all other uses combined. Therefore, as a practical matter, the "principal use" may, in many instances, be less than 50% of the total uses possible.

Where a tariff classification is controlled by use, other than actual use, the burden of proof will be on the importer to present evidence or statistics to show the principal use of goods of the same class or kind as the imported goods at, or immediately prior to, the date of importation of the goods being classified. In many instances, the burden of proving the principal use of a product is not difficult, because it may be widely recognized that a product is predominantly used for a single purpose. On the other hand, where multiple uses are readily identifiable, the importer's burden of marshaling evidence to establish the principal use can present great practical difficulties.

An example of the application of AUSRI 1(a) is found in Customs Ruling 085541 of January 10, 1990. This ruling involved a request for tariff classification of an item called the ECM 2700, which was a large-screen (27-inch), high-resolution monitor used to display computer-generated signals. This monitor incorporated an RS170 interface unit (RS) that allowed the monitor to receive a composite video signal from a videocassette recorder (VCR). The monitor had no tuner. It achieved high resolution (0.76 millimeter dot pitch resolution) at 15.75 or 22 kilohertz horizontal frequency response. According to the information presented, the monitor was used primarily for information display purposes in airports, classrooms, and stock exchanges. The monitor was compatible with various computers, depending on the type of interface that was used.

The issue in this case was whether the monitor in question was classifiable in heading 8471, which provides for automatic data-processing machines and units thereof (that is, computer monitor), or in heading 8528, which provides for television receivers, including video monitors and video projection receivers. In reaching its decision regarding the classification of the monitor, Customs stated:

Customs recently ruled that projection units which display computer generated signals and video signals are classifiable as display units within subheading 8471.92.40. (HQ 085392, November 22, 1989). The principal use of the articles subject to HQ 085392 was to display computer generated signals. The monitors in question are also principally used to display computer generated signals. There-fore, the ECM is also classifiable as a display unit within subheading 8471.92.40.

Within the United States, goods classified by use are classified according to their principal use, and the "controlling use is the principal use." Additional U.S. Rule of Interpretation 1(a). You claim that the monitor in question is sold exclusively to industrial/commercial users for use as a computer display unit. This claim is sup-ported by the fact that the costs of these units would appear to preclude their use as television receivers based on either economic or efficiency reasons.

Classification as a computer display unit is also supported by additional factors. The ECM can only receive a composite video signal when connected to the RS interface. When connected to the other two interface models the ECM is not able to receive composite video signals. According to submitted information, use of the ECM with the RS will also be fairly limited. In addition, the primary reason for using the RS is to increase the range of computers with which the ECM can be used and not for video reception. Based on the fact that the principal use of the ECM is as a computer display unit, classification within heading 8471 is appropriate.

Holding

The ECM 2700 color monitor is classifiable within subheading 8471.92.40, HTSUSA, which provides for display units dutiable at 3.7 percent *ad valorem*.

In the above ruling the importer claimed that the monitor in question was sold exclusively to industrial/commercial users for use as a computer display unit. This claim was supported by the additional factors discussed in the last paragraph quoted above. Note, however, that certain minor facts can carry significant weight in helping to establish that an item will *not* be used for a certain purpose. Although their value was not stated, the monitors in question were apparently expensive. This effectively pre-cluded their use by ordinary people as television receivers, the other com-peting tariff provision. Sometimes a simple fact such as this can be pivotal in determining whether Customs will make a ruling based on the infor-mation it has or whether it will require the importer to submit further substantiating evidence to support the principal use.

AUSRI 1(b) provides that a tariff classification controlled by the actual use to which the imported goods are put in the United States can only be satisfied if (1) the actual use is intended at the time of importation of the goods, (2) the goods are in fact so used after importation, and (3) proof of the actual use of the goods after importation is furnished within three years after the date of entry of the goods.

An example of the application of AUSRI 1(b) is found in Customs Ruling 085308 of December 8, 1989. This ruling involved a request by the district director at the Port of Dallas/Fort Worth, Texas, for a clarifica-tion regarding actual use certificates and who may execute them. These use certificates were required in connection with tariff items 9817.00.50 and 9817.00.60, the pertinent parts of which are as follows:

9817.00.5000   Machinery, equipment and implements to be used
                 for agricultural or horticultural purposes . . . . Free

9817.00.6000   Parts to be used in articles provided for in headings 8432, 8433,
                 8434 and 8436, whether or not such parts are principally used as
                 parts of such articles and whether or not covered by a specific
                 provision within the meaning of additional U.S. rule of
                 interpretation 1(c) . . . . Free

One issue presented in this ruling was whether distributors of an importer's products were permitted to execute the actual use certificates required for subheadings 9817.00.50 and 9817.00.60. In discussing this matter, Customs stated:

On November 29, 1982 . . . guidelines were issued for determining the acceptability of certificates of actual use in situations described by you. We agree with you that Additional U.S. Rule of Interpretation 1(b) requires "actual use" and not "intended" or "probable" use. Furthermore, we agree that the requirements of the law must be satisfied even if some hardship results from the difficulty encountered when trying to obtain certificates from the actual end users.

. . . . . .

The nature of each imported article, the level of distribution, evidence that any use other than agricultural or horticultural is a fugitive use, and any other facts that the importer can demonstrate as relevant, should be considered when certification, prepared by any person other than the end user, is to be accepted. The burden of satisfying the actual-use certification requirement is on the importer. To the extent that an importer submits a certificate executed by, for example, a distributor of electric fencing supplies at the retail level, that importer must know that the distributor knows that all of the products are sold to individuals who are engaged in an agricultural or horticultural pursuit, and that they are using these products in that pursuit. Furthermore, the importer must present sufficient evidence to you so that you can make the determination that the certification falls within the guidelines.

If you, after reviewing the various products with the importer, are satisfied that a certificate executed by a distributor at the retail level (for example) is sufficient, then you should take appropriate action.

In this ruling, there is no discussion of the requirement under AUSRI 1(b) that the actual use made of the imported merchandise be "intended" at the time of importation. In the factual background discussed in the ruling, the imported merchandise was used not by the importer but by later purchasers in the United States. Under these circumstances, the only "intended" uses that could exist at the time of importation would be those probable uses contemplated by the importer, who is not the actual user of the goods. In a situation where the importer will not be the end user of the merchandise, a requirement relating to the importer's "intention" at the time of importation is not meaningful. This is apparently what Customs meant when it stated, "We agree with you that Additional U.S. Rule of Interpretation 1(b) requires 'actual use' and not 'intended' or 'probable' use."

Note that the burden of satisfying the actual use requirement is on the importer, and where an actual use certification is signed by someone other than the actual end user, other factual evidence must be presented to establish the likelihood that the final purchasers of the products are using them for agricultural or horticultural purposes.

AUSRI 1(c) states that, where the tariff discusses "parts of an article," that provision covers products solely or principally used as a part of such articles. However, a provision for "parts" or "parts and accessories" cannot be used where there is a more specific tariff provision covering such part or accessory. A "part" is something that cannot be used on its own but must be used in conjunction with other items to form an article capable of fulfilling an intended function.

"Accessories," on the other hand, are articles that are not needed to enable the goods with which they are used to fulfill their intended function. Accessories, however, must be identifiable as being intended for use with a specific article. Based on the foregoing, once it has been determined that an article comes within the purview of "parts" or "parts and accessories," then it is necessary to determine whether there is a specific provision in the Tariff Schedule that might cover the article. If a heading is identified that specifically covers the article in question, then the heading would prevail over a provision for "parts" or "parts and accessories."

An example of the application of AUSRI 1(c) is found in Customs Ruling 083729 of May 11, 1989. This ruling involved a request for reconsideration by Headquarters of the Customs Service of a classification ruling issued by the Port of New York. The goods involved in the ruling issued by New York were certain items known as bicycle tire rim strips. Bicycle tire rim strips are flat, circular strips of material that are placed around the bicycle tire rim to fit between the rim and the inner tube. These rim strips prevent the spoke ends, which protrude through the tire rim, from puncturing the inner tube. Rim strips are usually made of rubber and are known in Europe as "tire flaps." Because bicycles are covered by heading 8712, New York had classified the bicycle tire rim strips in subheading 8714.99.90, which provides for parts and accessories of vehicles of headings 8711 to 8713. The importer requested reconsideration of New York's ruling and suggested that the merchandise might be more properly classifiable under heading 4012, the pertinent parts of which are as follows:

4012	Retreaded or used pneumatic tires of rubber; solid or cushion tires, interchangeable tire treads and tire flaps, of rubber:	
4012.10	Retreaded tires:	
	. . . . .	
4012.20	Used pneumatic tires:	
	. . . . .	
4012.90	Other:	
4012.90.10	Solid or cushion tires	Free

	Other:	
4012.90.20	Of natural rubber	4.2%
4012.90.50	Other	5.3%

In reaching its decision regarding the importer's request for reconsideration of the classification assigned by New York, Headquarters of the Customs Service stated:

Law and Analysis

General Rule of Interpretation (GRI) 3(a), HTSUSA, says, in part, "The heading which provides the most specific description shall be preferred to headings providing a more general description." Applying GRI 3(a) to the provisions mentioned above, it is obvious that the two provisions for solid or cushion tires, interchangeable tire treads and tire flaps are more specific than the provision for parts and accessories of vehicles of headings 8711 to 8713. We further note that Additional U.S. Rule of Interpretation 1(c), provides in the absence of special language or context which otherwise requires, a provision for parts of an article covers products solely or principally used as a part of such article but a provision for "parts" or "parts and accessories" shall not prevail over a specific provision for such part or accessory. Following both GRI 3(a) and Additional U.S. Rule of Interpretation 1(c), HTSUSA, we find that the instant bicycle tire rim strips are classified in subheading 4012.90.20 if they are of natural rubber or in subheading 4012.90.50 if they are of synthetic rubber. New York letter 835808 is modified accordingly.

It might be that the classification originally assigned by Customs in New York resulted from a lack of awareness of the meaning of the words "tire flaps" as set forth in heading 4012. If one does not know that bicycle "tire rim strips" are known in Europe as "tire flaps," then it would be a simple matter to overlook the more specific description of the merchandise in heading 4012. This does, however, point out a problem that Americans face when using the current Tariff Schedule. It is derived from a European source, and many of its terms are based upon words and expressions used in Europe to describe merchandise. It is important to keep this in mind when classifying merchandise under the HTSUS.

AUSRI 1(d) indicates that where any provision in the Tariff Schedule includes the name of a textile material, the principles of section XI regarding mixtures of two or more textile materials shall apply. The principles referred to are found in the legal notes to section XI, and these include notes 2(A), (B), and (C) and subheading notes 2(A) and (B), which state as follows:

Notes

2. (A) Goods classifiable in chapters 50 to 55 or in heading 5809 or 5902 and of a mixture of two or more textile materials are to be classified as if consisting wholly of that one textile material which predominates by weight over each other single textile material.

(B) For the purposes of the above rule:
  (a) Gimped horsehair yarn (heading 5110) and metalized yarn (heading 5605) are to be treated as a single textile material the weight of which is to be taken as the aggregate of the weights of its components; for the classification of woven fabrics, metal thread is to be regarded as a textile material;
  (b) The choice of appropriate heading shall be effected by determining first the chapter and then the applicable heading within that chapter, disregarding any materials not classified in that chapter;
  (c) When both chapters 54 and 55 are involved with any other chapter, chapters 54 and 55 are to be treated as a single chapter;
  (d) Where a chapter or a heading refers to goods of different textile materials, such materials are to be treated as a single textile material.
(C) The provisions of paragraphs (A) and (B) above apply also to the yarns referred to in notes 3, 4, 5 or 6 below.   . . . . . .

Subheading Notes

2. (A) Products of chapters 56 to 63 containing two or more textile materials are to be regarded as consisting wholly of that textile material which would be selected under note 2 to this section for the classification of a product of chapters 50 to 55 consisting of the same textile materials.
  (B) For the application of this rule:
    (a) Where appropriate, only the part which determines the classification under general interpretative rule 3 shall be taken into account;
    (b) In the case of textile products consisting of a ground fabric and a pile or looped surface no account shall be taken of the ground fabric;
    (c) In the case of embroidery of heading 5810 only the ground fabric shall be taken into account. However, embroidery without visible ground shall be classified with reference to the embroidering threads alone.

Note 2(A) provides that certain goods that are a mixture of two or more textile materials are to be classified as though they consisted of only one textile material, that is, the textile material that is present in the greatest weight. For example, a fabric that consists of 40% wool, 30% cotton, and 30% man-made fibers by weight would be classified as though it were 100% wool, the textile material present in the greatest weight. Note 2(B) contains ancillary rules to be taken into account in applying note 2(A), and note 2(C) expands the coverage of notes 2(A) and 2(B) to certain yarns.

Subheading note 2(A) provides that made-up articles and wearing apparel in chapters 56 to 63, which consist of two or more textile materials, are to be classified as though they consisted wholly of that textile material that would be chosen when notes 2(A), (B), and (C) are applied to the fabrics that make up the articles or wearing apparel. Again, subheading note 2(B) contains ancillary rules to be considered when applying subheading note 2(A).

AUSRI 1(d) is a cautionary note to make it clear that the principles used for goods of mixed fiber fabrics in section XI apply throughout the Tariff Schedule in any case where a tariff provision names a textile material and the article to be classified involves a mixture of two or more textile materials. For example, subheading 4202.12.8020 of the Tariff Schedule provides for certain attaché cases, briefcases, school satchels, and similar containers with an outer surface of cotton. In determining whether such containers have an outer surface of cotton, reference must be made to the principles of section XI if the outer surface of the container involves a mixture of two or more textile materials.

Chapter 3

Appraisement of Merchandise

Appraisement is the step-by-step process used to determine the legal value of imported merchandise. When goods are dutiable at a specific rate of duty, for example, $2.12 per cubic meter, valuation is not so important. However, when the duty rate is *ad valorem*, that is, a percentage of the value, the determination of value becomes very significant.

Customs valuation is based upon a set of rules contained in a law (statute) which is highly technical and contains many precise legal terms. Understanding the fundamentals of appraisement is necessary because many potential elements of cost or value that must be reported to Customs arise from the language of the valuation law itself.

The appraisement law is set out in its entirety in appendix B. Many parts of the valuation statute rarely come into use and these more obscure sections of the law will not be dealt with here. In the discussion that follows, excerpts from the law will be quoted and explained. In order to make the legal excerpts more understandable, it is sometimes necessary to present the materials in a different order from that used in the law itself. The rearrangements that have been made in the materials are readily apparent, however, when comparison is made to the statute as set forth in appendix B.

The valuation law, which is found in Title 19, United States Code, Section 1401a, provides in part as follows:

(a) (1) Except as otherwise specifically provided for in this chapter, imported merchandise shall be appraised . . . on the basis of the following:
   (A) The transaction value provided for under subsection (b) of this section.
   (B) The transaction value of identical merchandise provided for under subsection (c) of this section, if the value referred to in subparagraph (A) cannot be determined, or can be determined but cannot be used by reason of subsection (b) (2) of this section.
   (C) The transaction value of similar merchandise provided for under sub-

section (c) of this section, if the value referred to in subparagraph (B) cannot be determined.

(D) The deductive value provided for under subsection (d) of this section, if the value referred to in subparagraph (C) cannot be determined and if the importer does not request alternative valuation under paragraph (2).

(E) The computed value provided for under subsection (e) of this section, if the value referred to in subparagraph (D) cannot be determined.

(F) The value provided for under subsection (f) of this section, if the value referred to in subparagraph (E) cannot be determined.

(2) If the value referred to in paragraph (1) (C) cannot be determined with respect to imported merchandise, the merchandise shall be appraised on the basis of the computed value provided for under paragraph (1) (E), rather than the deductive value provided for under paragraph (1) (D), if the importer makes a request to that effect to the customs officer concerned within such time as the Secretary shall prescribe. If the computed value of the merchandise cannot subsequently be determined, the merchandise may not be appraised on the basis of the value referred to in paragraph (1) (F) unless the deductive value of the merchandise cannot be determined under paragraph (1) (D).

(3) Upon written request therefor by the importer of merchandise, and subject to provisions of law regarding the disclosure of information, the customs officer concerned shall provide the importer with a written explanation of how the value of that merchandise was determined under this section.

Based on the above, there are five main ways to appraise goods, plus another that is derivative of the others. The five main ways, or bases, are the following:

1. Transaction value
2. Transaction value of identical merchandise
3. Transaction value of similar merchandise
4. Deductive value
5. Computed value

The law requires that these methods be used in the order shown above. For example, if goods can be appraised based on transaction value (1 above), then the other methods cannot be used.

One proceeds in order through these methods until the first usable method is reached. Methods 4 and 5 can be reversed, however, at the importer's option. That is, if appraisement is not possible using methods 1 through 3, the importer may elect method 5 before method 4. The last paragraph in the material quoted above provides that the importer may make a written request to Customs for a statement in writing that explains precisely how the appraised value of the importer's merchandise was arrived at under the statute. Such a statement would presumably contain every deliberative element involved in the decision-making process, except any such factual information or data whose disclosure is prohibited by law. Since appraisement decisions sometimes involve the consideration of facts about another importer's shipments, the law is written to prevent the disclosure of these private and confidential facts regarding the business affairs of another party.

All the appraisement methods shown above will be discussed, with particular emphasis on the first, transaction value.

TRANSACTION VALUE

It is frequently said that transaction value is the preferred basis of appraisement. It is preferred certainly because the law requires that it be used before the other methods. In fact, 95% or more of all importations are appraised on the basis of transaction value. It is also the simplest method to understand and, therefore, to use. With regard to transaction value, the law provides in pertinent part as follows:

(b) (1) The transaction value of imported merchandise is the price actually paid or payable for the merchandise when sold for exportation to the United States, plus amounts equal to—
  (A) the packing costs incurred by the buyer with respect to the imported merchandise;
  (B) any selling commission incurred by the buyer with respect to the imported merchandise;
  (C) the value, apportioned as appropriate, of any assist;
  (D) any royalty or license fee related to the imported merchandise that the buyer is required to pay, directly or indirectly, as a condition of the sale of the imported merchandise for exportation to the United States; and
  (E) the proceeds of any subsequent resale, disposal, or use of the imported merchandise that accrue, directly or indirectly, to the seller.
  The price actually paid or payable for imported merchandise shall be increased by the amounts attributable to the items (and no others) described in subparagraphs (A) through (E) only to the extent that each such amount (i) is not otherwise included within the price actually paid or payable; and (ii) is based on sufficient information. If sufficient information is not available, for any reason, with respect to any amount referred to in the preceding sentence, the transaction value of the imported merchandise concerned shall be treated, for purposes of this section, as one that cannot be determined.
      . . . . .
(4) For purposes of this subsection—
  (A) The term "price actually paid or payable" means the total payment

(whether direct or indirect, and exclusive of any costs, charges, or expenses incurred for transportation, insurance, and related services incident to the international shipment of the merchandise from the country of exportation to the place of importation in the United States) made, or to be made, for imported merchandise by the buyer to, or for the benefit of, the seller.

. . . . .

(h) As used in this section—

(1) (A) The term "assist" means any of the following if supplied directly or indirectly, and free of charge or at reduced cost, by the buyer of imported merchandise for use in connection with the production or the sale for export to the United States of the merchandise:

(i) Materials, components, parts, and similar items incorporated in the imported merchandise.

(ii) Tools, dies, molds, and similar items used in the production of the imported merchandise.

(iii) Merchandise consumed in the production of the imported merchandise.

(iv) Engineering, development, artwork, design work, and plans and sketches that are undertaken elsewhere than in the United States and are necessary for the production of the imported merchandise.

. . . . .

[b] (3) The transaction value of imported merchandise does not include any of the following, if identified separately from the price actually paid or payable and from any cost or other item referred to in paragraph [b] (1):

(A) Any reasonable cost or charge that is incurred for—

(i) the construction, erection, assembly, or maintenance of, or the technical assistance provided with respect to, the merchandise after its importation into the United States; or

(ii) the transportation of the merchandise after such importation.

(B) The customs duties and other Federal taxes currently payable on the imported merchandise by reason of its importation, and any Federal excise tax on, or measured by the value of, such merchandise for which vendors in the United States are ordinarily liable.

Put simply, the transaction value of imported merchandise is the price paid by the importer for the imported goods, plus the following, if not already included in that price:

1. Packing costs

2. Any commission paid to a selling agent

3. The cost or value of items provided free to the manufacturer as production assistance

4. Royalties and license fees

5. Any additional amounts that the importer is required to pay to the manufacturer or seller after the goods are resold, disposed of, or used in the United States

It should be noted that the price paid includes indirect payments by the buyer to the seller. For example, a shipment worth $1,000 is sold to the importer for $500 because the seller owes the importer $500 on another debt or transaction. The transaction value (appraised value) of this shipment would be $1,000, which includes the $500 directly paid and the $500 indirectly paid (that is, the forgiven debt). Other types of indirect payments might exist and such a possibility should be kept in mind when thinking of the price paid.

There are also certain types of costs that may be paid for separately and called another name but that are nevertheless considered part of the price paid. For example, if the importer makes a separate payment to the seller for the cost of testing the merchandise or for the cost of materials used in testing the merchandise, before it is exported to the United States, these costs are considered part of the price paid and are added to the other payments.

Another example is the situation where an importer of wearing apparel pays the foreign vendor a separate payment for securing the export allocation necessary to export a shipment of dresses to the United States. Such charges are referred to as quota charges. If the importer makes one payment to the vendor by letter of credit for the dresses and a separate payment to the vendor by check for the quota charge, the amount paid for the quota charge is still part of the price paid or payable for the dresses and is included in the transaction value of the goods. This would be true whether the quota charge was paid directly to the vendor or indirectly to the vendor through the importer's agent.

On the positive side, there may be costs included in the price paid that can be deducted to arrive at the final legal value. Such costs include (1) international freight, insurance, and transportation costs in the United States after importation; (2) costs of assembly or erection of the merchandise in the United States after arrival of the goods; and (3) duties payable by reason of the importation of the goods. These types of costs, if properly identified as to the exact dollar amounts, can be deducted from the price paid.

With regard to the five items shown above that must be added to the price paid, the following explanations may be helpful.

Packing costs means the cost of all packing, both materials and labor.

Commissions paid to a selling agent are added to the price paid, regardless of whether the agent is located in the United States or in a foreign country. When the type of commission being paid is not known, the type must be determined because "buying" commissions are not added to the price paid, even though they must be declared to Customs on each entry. In general, an agent is a buying agent if he or she is under the direction and control of the importer and does not take title to the goods. A party who is determined not to be a buying agent is usually held to be a selling agent or a seller in his or her own right, and his or her commissions are added to the price paid.

Production assistance—"assists" for short—are things that are given free of charge or at less than cost by the importer to the manufacturer for use in producing the imported items. These include:

1. Materials, components, parts, and similar items incorporated into the imported goods during manufacture or assembly
2. Tools, dies, molds, machines, and similar items used to produce the imported goods
3. Merchandise consumed in the production of the imported goods
4. Engineering, development, designs, plans, and similar work done outside the United States

Some examples of materials or components that might be given free of charge to a foreign manufacturer are the following:

1. Diodes, resistors, integrated circuits, disk drives, and other electronic components assembled into consumer electronic products
2. Lace, zippers, buttons, and other items of trim sewn into or onto wearing apparel
3. Paint, glue, chemicals, and other bulk materials used in or on the imported merchandise

Note that the above items are assists even though they may be of U.S. origin. All too often, importers assume that materials purchased in the United States and consigned to the foreign manufacturer or assembler have no relation to the Customs value of the imported merchandise. This is simply not the case. Such items are assists and must be included in the appraised value of the merchandise. The duty exemption that is allowed on U.S. goods assembled abroad is discussed in chapter 12.

The second category, tools, dies, molds, and machines, would include the following examples:

1. Tools or tooling used to stamp out metal parts or components
2. Dies for stamping or extruding metal or plastic parts or components
3. Molds for shaping metal or plastic parts or components
4. Sewing machines for stitching and assembling wearing apparel or other textile products
5. Drill presses and power saws for working solid components
6. Ovens for melting plastics or drying paint
7. Testing devices used during the production process
8. Knitting or weaving machines for textile products

The above items are representative of those things that may be consigned to a foreign vendor and used to produce imported merchandise. Some items, on the other hand, may not be assists because they are not used in the production of the goods. Such nonproduction items are illustrated by the following:

1. Fans or air conditioners for cooling the workplace
2. Adding or accounting machines used for performing administrative functions
3. Testing devices used in quality control after the goods are produced
4. Models or "soft tooling" used for analysis or evaluation only
5. Prototype or sample merchandise used for analysis or evaluation only

The above types of materials or equipment, though necessary and useful to a foreign vendor, are not used in the production process. They are, therefore, not assists.

The next category of assists involves merchandise consumed in the production of the imported goods. This category includes materials that are expended or used up during the production process but that are not incorporated into the goods themselves. Examples are the following:

1. Solvents and cleaning materials
2. Abrasives such as paste, sand paper, or grinding wheels
3. Catalysts or intermediate chemicals
4. Fuels used to run generators or machinery used in the production process

The last category of assists involves engineering, development, design work, planning, and similar efforts carried out in a foreign country. Engineering work is normally performed by engineers (civil, electrical, aeronautical, metallurgical, and so on) and the cost of such work is often referred to as a nonrecurring engineering charge or NRE. Sometimes it is necessary for a vendor to reverse-engineer a product in order to make it, and this work is included in "engineering."

Plans, designs, and artwork are also included in this category, provided the plans, designs, and artwork are more than preliminary in nature. Also, planning, designing, and performing artwork can relate to the production of product packaging in addition to the product itself. Since packing is normally included in the appraised value of the imported goods, any design work performed abroad on the packing containers would be an assist for the packaging materials.

Note that, in this category of assists, the work must be performed *outside* the United States. Hence, the cost of engineering, development, design, and planning done in the United States is not a dutiable assist. The existence of such costs, however, must be reported to U.S. Customs.

Other problems relating to assists involve the valuation of the assist and the method of apportioning that value to the imported goods. With regard to (1) components or materials incorporated into the goods and (2) merchandise consumed in producing the goods, the value of the assist is determined according to the following rules:

1. If the assist is acquired by the buyer (importer) from an unrelated party, its value is the cost of acquiring it.

2. If the assist is produced by the buyer (importer) or a party related to the buyer, its value is the cost of producing it.

Regardless of which valuation method above is used, there must be added to the cost of acquisition or the cost of production, the cost of transporting the assist to the place of foreign manufacture, that is, the place where the imported goods are produced using the assist.

The value of tools, dies, molds, and machines is determined by using the same two rules set forth above for components. Again, the cost of transporting these assists to the place of manufacture in the foreign country must be added to the assist value so determined. In addition, however, there is the possibility that tools, molds, or machines may be leased rather than acquired or produced. In this case, the value of the assist is the cost or value of the lease.

The value of tools and machines may be reduced from their original value, whether acquired, produced, or leased. If a tool or machine has been used to produce some goods, its value in the production of later goods is decreased to the extent of its previous use. For example, an importer acquires a tool for $1,000 and uses it to produce goods in the United States. Later, the importer sends the tool overseas to produce imported goods. At the time it was sent overseas, however, only half of its useful life remained. The value of the tool that is proratable to the imported goods is, therefore, $500, plus the cost of transportation to the foreign country.

Similarly, the value of tools and machines may be increased. This would occur if the assist is repaired or modified.

Once the value of the assist has been determined, the value must be apportioned to the imported merchandise. With incorporated components or consumed merchandise, apportionment is easy because it occurs on a direct one-for-one basis, the only question being how much material or merchandise was incorporated into, or used to produce, one unit of imported product. With tools, molds, and machines, however, the apportionment is more complicated because these types of assists are capable of producing more goods than are usually imported on one Customs entry. A tool, for instance, might be capable of producing 100,000 units, but its value must be apportioned to a much smaller number of imported goods.

Normally, the complete value of the assist must be captured in the apportionment, absent facts that would permit otherwise. The most common methods of apportionment are the following:

1. Total assist value apportioned to the number of units in the first importation
2. Total assist value apportioned to the number of units produced overseas at the time of the first importation
3. Total assist value apportioned to the total number of units reasonably expected to be produced and imported into the United States

It is best to illustrate the above methods using a hypothetical situation. Suppose an importer has purchased a tool in the United States and shipped it to his foreign vendor for production of imported goods. The cost of acquisition of the tool, plus transportation overseas, totals $10,000. The importer has placed an order and opened an irrevocable letter of credit for the production of 20,000 units, all to be exported to the United States. The first shipment to arrive consists of 1,000 units. At the time the first shipment arrives, a total of 5,000 units have been produced (that is, 4,000 units have yet to be shipped to the United States).

The methods of apportionment mentioned above yield the following results. Under method 1, $10,000 would be added to the price paid for the first shipment. The amount added would be equivalent to $10.00 per unit. Under method 2, $2,000, or $2.00 per unit, would be added to the price paid for the first shipment. To complete method 2, $2.00 per unit would be added to all future shipments until a total of 5,000 units had been imported and duty paid. Under method 3, $500, or $0.50 per unit, would be added to the price paid for the first shipment. To complete method 3, $0.50 per unit would be added to all future shipments until a total of 20,000 units had been imported and duty paid.

From the standpoint of U.S. Customs, all the above methods of apportionment result in a collection of duty on the full $10,000 assist value. From the importer's standpoint, however, methods 2 and 3 permit the importer to delay the payment of the assist duties.

Other methods of apportionment can be proposed by the importer, and the acceptance by Customs of any proposal depends almost entirely on how reasonable the proposal is in light of generally accepted accounting principles and the facts and documents presented by the importer.

Some final notes regarding assist value and apportionment are worth mentioning. An assist must be duty paid only once. If an assist, such as a tool, has been fully duty paid by an importer in connection with one lot of imported merchandise, it need not be apportioned again if it is used by the same importer to produce more imported merchandise. Also, U.S. Customs has ruled that a tool or machine that has been fully depreciated or amortized on the books of the importer has no legal value that can be apportioned, even if the assist is subsequently sent overseas to produce imported goods. Finally, the dutiable value of a tool or machine can be reduced to the extent that it is used to produce goods that are shipped to third countries other than the United States. For example, if 25% of all goods produced with an assist are exported to countries other than the United States, only 75% of the assist value would be apportioned to the items imported into the United States. Assists are discussed further in chapter 5.

Royalties and license fees are generally paid by an importer to the owner of patents, trademarks, or copyrights for the use of these protected interests. In many cases, these types of fees are not added to the price paid. Whether or not these fees are dutiable is determined by Customs on a case-by-case basis and depends upon the terms under which they are paid. If the payment of the royalty or license fee is linked in a direct way with the sale of the goods for exportation to the United States, the fee is most likely dutiable. On the other hand, if the calculation of the fee to be paid is based upon the total dollar value of sales of a particular product in the U.S. market, the fee is most likely not dutiable.

The last item that must be added to the price paid are additional moneys, or second stage payments, made by the importer to the foreign seller as a result of the way in which the imported goods are resold, disposed of, or used in the United States after importation. An example is where the importer and the seller agree on a price of $1.00 per unit as the selling price; they also agree that, if the importer can resell the goods in the United States for more than $3.00 each, he will pay the seller an additional $0.25 per unit. The extra $0.25 per unit would be added to the first $1.00 per unit paid to arrive at the legal appraised value per unit, provided the additional $0.25 per unit is actually paid to the seller. If the additional $0.25 per unit is never paid, the appraised value would be only $1.00 per unit.

To summarize, the following additional costs must be added to the price paid or payable to arrive at the total appraised value:

1. Packing costs
2. Selling commissions
3. Production assistance (assists)
4. Royalties and license fees
5. Proceeds of sale, use, or disposition in the United States (second stage payments) accruing to the seller

It is important to remember that the above costs can be added to the price paid only if such costs are based upon sufficient information. This means such costs must be capable of accurate determination. Estimation is not permitted. When the above additional costs exist but cannot be accurately determined, the transaction value of the merchandise becomes indeterminable, and appraisement must be made using a different basis of valuation.

The above discussion covers the basic fundamentals of appraisement under transaction value. Before discussing the four remaining ways of appraising imported merchandise, it is appropriate to explain why some merchandise cannot be appraised on the basis of transaction value.

WHEN TRANSACTION VALUE CANNOT BE USED

There are several instances when transaction value must be bypassed and another basis of appraisement used. These occasions have nothing to do with the goods themselves but are brought about solely because of the circumstances surrounding the sale of the goods to the importer.

The first instance involves the five items, discussed above, that must be added to the price paid. When one of these items must be added to the price paid, but the exact dollar cost for that item is not known, the law states that transaction value cannot be determined. In essence, the law does not allow the cost for that item to be estimated. Hence, resort must be made to the next basis of value. Other limitations on the use of transaction value are set forth in the law as follows:

[b] (2) (A) The transaction value of imported merchandise determined under paragraph (1) shall be the appraised value of that merchandise for the purposes of this chapter only if—
  (i) there are no restrictions on the disposition or use of the imported merchandise by the buyer other than restrictions that—
    (I) are imposed or required by law,
    (II) limit the geographical area in which the merchandise may be resold, or
    (III) do not substantially affect the value of the merchandise;
  (ii) the sale of, or the price actually paid or payable for, the imported merchandise is not subject to any condition or consideration for which a value cannot be determined with respect to the imported merchandise;
  (iii) no part of the proceeds of any subsequent resale, disposal, or use of the imported merchandise by the buyer will accrue directly or indirectly to the seller, unless an appropriate adjustment therefor can be made under paragraph (1) (E); and
  (iv) the buyer and seller are not related, or the buyer and seller are related but the transaction value is acceptable, for purposes of this subsection, under subparagraph (B).

Limitation (i) above involves restrictions placed on the buyer with regard to the disposition or use of the imported merchandise. Permitted restrictions are (I) those arising from the application of laws, (II) geographic limitations on resale of the goods, and (III) prohibitions that do not appreciably change the value of the goods to the buyer. Items (I) and (II) are fairly self-explanatory. Item (III) is not. It would appear, however, that item (III) explains the rationale for the limitations imposed by paragraph (i). The whole paragraph can be explained briefly as follows: Restrictions on the disposition or use of the imported goods by the importer are not desirable if they have the effect of lowering the selling price to the importer and, hence, the effect of lowering the appraised value of the goods. Therefore, restrictions that reduce the selling price of goods are not permitted. For public policy reasons, however, restrictions imposed by law should be permitted even if they tend to lower the price of the goods for export to the United States. Since geographic restrictions on resale have traditionally been permitted under prior laws, those restrictions should continue to be permitted, even if they lower the value that the importer is willing to pay for the goods. Except for these two types of restrictions, any other restriction must be shown not to affect the value of the goods before it can be accepted.

An example of a restriction that might not affect the value of the goods is where an importer of high-fashion (designer) apparel agrees not to sell or distribute the imported garments prior to the beginning of the traditional selling season for such goods (that is, spring, summer, winter, or holiday groups or lines of apparel). Such a restriction would probably not affect the value of the goods to the importer because the traditional selling seasons, as recognized by the industry, are to a large extent determined by the seasonal demands of consumers.

On the other hand, consider a restriction that prohibited the importer from distributing (reselling) the imported goods to retailers. Only sales of the imported goods to wholesalers would be permitted. Since it is well recognized that retailers can afford to pay more for imported goods than wholesalers, because of markup considerations, this restriction would probably tend to make the goods less desirable to the importer and, hence, to lower the price the importer is willing to pay. Such a restriction would probably be unacceptable under paragraph (i) above, and transaction value could not be used for appraisement.

Transaction value also cannot be used if the conditions in paragraph (ii) prevail. An example of paragraph (ii) occurs when the price paid by the importer to the foreign seller is determined in part upon some condition or consideration that does not have a precise money value. As an illustration, assume that the importer has agreed to pay the seller a certain price for imported goods on the condition that the seller in turn will buy a certain quantity of goods from the importer. Since the value to the importer of this arrangement cannot be precisely determined, the law does not allow the goods to be appraised under transaction value at the price paid.

The limitation in paragraph (iii) above is similar to that previously discussed with regard to the last one of the five items that must be added to transaction value. Here, again, if any part of the proceeds of resale, disposal, or use of the imported goods accrues to the seller, transaction value cannot be used for appraisement unless a necessary adjustment, based on sufficient information, can be made.

The restriction on the use of transaction value in paragraph (iv) occurs in sales between related parties. Examples of related parties are (1) a parent corporation selling goods to its wholly owned subsidiary and (2) a father selling goods to his son. There are other types of related party transactions, which will be discussed in detail later. Suffice it to say here that certain conditions must be met in related-party transactions, otherwise transaction value cannot be used.

TRANSACTION VALUE OF IDENTICAL
OR SIMILAR MERCHANDISE

The second and third methods of appraisement will be discussed together because they are the same in many respects. Method 2 is the transaction value of identical merchandise, and method 3 is the transaction value of similar merchandise. With respect to these bases of appraisement, the law provides as follows:

(c) (1) The transaction value of identical merchandise, or of similar merchandise, is the transaction value (acceptable as the appraised value for purposes of this chapter under subsection (b) of this section but adjusted under paragraph (2) of this subsection) of imported merchandise that is—
   (A) with respect to the merchandise being appraised, either identical merchandise or similar merchandise, as the case may be; and
   (B) exported to the United States at or about the time that the merchandise being appraised is exported to the United States.
   (2) Transaction values determined under this subsection shall be based on sales of identical merchandise or similar merchandise, as the case may be, at the same commercial level and in substantially the same quantity as the sales of the merchandise being appraised. If no such sale is found, sales of identical merchandise or similar merchandise at either a different commercial level or in different quantities, or both, shall be used, but adjusted to take account of any such difference. Any adjustment made under this paragraph shall be based on sufficient information. If in applying this paragraph with respect to any imported merchandise, two or more transaction values for identical merchandise, or for similar merchandise, are determined, such imported merchandise shall be appraised on the basis of the lower or lowest of such values.

. . . . .

[h] (2) The term "identical merchandise" means—
  (A) merchandise that is identical in all respects to, and was produced in the same country and by the same person as, the merchandise being appraised; or
  (B) if merchandise meeting the requirements under subparagraph (A) cannot be found . . . , merchandise that is identical in all respects to, and was produced in the same country as, but not produced by the same person as, the merchandise being appraised.

Such term does not include merchandise that incorporates or reflects any engineering, development, artwork, design work, or plan or sketch that—
      (I) was supplied free or at reduced cost by the buyer of the merchandise for use in connection with the production or the sale for export to the United States of the merchandise; and
      (II) is not an assist because undertaken within the United States.

. . . . . .

[h] (4) The term "similar merchandise" means—
  (A) merchandise that—
      (i) was produced in the same country and by the same person as the merchandise being appraised,
      (ii) is like the merchandise being appraised in characteristics and component material, and
      (iii) is commercially interchangeable with the merchandise being appraised; or
  (B) if merchandise meeting the requirements under subparagraph (A) cannot be found . . . , merchandise that—
      (i) was produced in the same country as, but not produced by the same person as, the merchandise being appraised, and
      (ii) meets the requirement set forth in subparagraph (A) (ii) and (iii).

Such term does not include merchandise that incorporates or reflects any engineering, development, artwork, design work, or plan or sketch that—
      (I) was supplied free or at reduced cost by the buyer of the merchandise for use in connection with the production or the sale for export to the United States of the merchandise; and
      (II) is not an assist because undertaken within the United States.

Based on the foregoing, imported merchandise can be appraised using the transaction value of identical or similar merchandise. The term "identical" should be understood to mean identical to the goods being appraised, while the term "similar" should be understood to mean similar to the goods being appraised.

Goods can only be identical if they are the same in every respect. For example, one gallon of reagent grade sulphuric acid is identical to every other gallon of reagent grade sulphuric acid, regardless of who manufactures it. For this reason, the law is comfortable in appraising the one based on the sales price of the other. Therefore, when imported goods are appraised based upon the transaction value of identical merchandise, they are appraised based upon the selling price, with the additions and subtractions discussed above, paid by someone for goods that are exactly the same.

Identical goods can be made by any manufacturer, so long as the country of production is the same as that of the goods being appraised. However, identical goods made by the same manufacturer must be considered before identical goods made by another manufacturer. Note that merchandise manufactured with engineering or development that is provided free of charge to the foreign vendor and that is not considered an assist because it was undertaken in the United States cannot be considered identical merchandise under this basis of appraisement.

The price used as the appraised value will in many cases be the price paid by someone other than the importer. Appraisements based upon the transaction value of identical merchandise are rare, primarily because there are so few goods that are truly identical.

Just as rare are goods appraised based upon the transaction value of similar merchandise, the third basis of appraisement. The only distinction between these two methods lies in the nature of the goods. Identical merchandise is identical in all respects, while similar merchandise is "like the merchandise being appraised in characteristics and component material, and is commercially interchangeable with the merchandise being appraised." Otherwise, the rules that apply to the transaction value of identical merchandise apply equally to the transaction value of similar merchandise. The third basis of appraisement is rarely used by Customs because even small differences in characteristics or component materials make goods legally dissimilar.

In order for identical or similar goods to be used as the basis of appraisement, the goods must have been exported to the United States at or about the same time as the goods being appraised. Also, the identical or similar goods must have been sold at the same commercial level and in comparable quantity to those of the goods being appraised. This simply means that sales to wholesalers and sales to retailers are not comparable. Similarly, a sale of 500 units cannot be used to appraise an importation of 100,000 units. In the absence of more acceptable sales, however, such sales may be used if sufficient information is available to make an appropriate adjustment to correct for the difference in commercial levels of sale or in quantities of sale.

Finally, if there are two or more sales of identical merchandise that can be used to appraise the imported goods, the appraisement must be based on the lower or the lowest price available. The same would be true for an appraisement based upon similar merchandise.

DEDUCTIVE VALUE

The next basis of appraisement, deductive value, provides for the appraisement of merchandise in two different situations. The situations are (1) imported goods that are resold in the United States in their imported condition, without being further processed before sale, and (2) imported goods that are further processed in the United States after importation and then resold in the U.S. market. The law as it relates to goods in situation (1) will be discussed, and a brief explanation of how the appraisement of goods in situation (2) varies from that of situation (1) will be given.

With regard to deductive value, the law provides as follows:

(d) (1) For purposes of this subsection, the term "merchandise concerned" means the merchandise being appraised, identical merchandise, or similar merchandise.

  (2) (A) The deductive value of the merchandise being appraised is whichever of the following prices (as adjusted under paragraph (3)) is appropriate depending upon when . . . the merchandise concerned is sold in the United States:

    (i) If the merchandise concerned is sold in the condition as imported at or about the date of importation of the merchandise being appraised, the price is the unit price at which the merchandise concerned is sold in the greatest aggregate quantity at or about such date.

    (ii) If the merchandise concerned is sold in the condition as imported but not sold at or about the date of importation of the merchandise being appraised, the price is the unit price at which the merchandise concerned is sold in the greatest aggregate quantity after the date of importation of the merchandise being appraised but before the close of the 90th day after the date of such importation.

         . . . . . .

  (B) For purposes of subparagraph (A), the unit price at which merchandise is sold in the greatest aggregate quantity is the unit price at which such merchandise is sold to unrelated persons, at the first commercial level after importation . . . at which such sales take place, in a total volume that is (i) greater than the total volume sold at any other unit price, and (ii) sufficient to establish the unit price.

  (3) (A) The price determined under paragraph (2) shall be reduced by an amount equal to—

    (i) any commission usually paid or agreed to be paid, or the addition usually made for profit and general expenses, in connection with sales in the United States of imported merchandise that is of the same class or kind, regardless of the country of exportation, as the merchandise concerned;

    (ii) the actual costs and associated costs of transportation and insurance incurred with respect to international shipments of the mer-

chandise concerned from the country of exportation to the United
States;

(iii) the usual costs and associated costs of transportation and insurance incurred with respect to shipments of such merchandise from
the place of importation to the place of delivery in the United
States, if such costs are not included as a general expense under
clause (i);

(iv) the customs duties and other Federal taxes currently payable on
the merchandise concerned by reason of its importation, and any
Federal excise tax on, or measured by the value of, such merchandise for which vendors in the United States are ordinarily
liable. . . .

. . . . . .

(B) For purposes of applying paragraph (A)—

(i) the deduction made for profits and general expenses shall be based
upon the importer's profits and general expenses, unless such profits and general expenses are inconsistent with those reflected in
sales in the United States of imported merchandise of the same
class or kind, in which case the deduction shall be based on the
usual profit and general expenses reflected in such sales, as determined from sufficient information. . . .

In general, the deductive value of imported merchandise is calculated
by starting with the price at which certain merchandise is resold in the
United States after importation. From this resale price, certain costs are
deducted to arrive at a "constructive" FOB (free on board) foreign port
value. It is the constructive FOB value that is the dutiable value of the
goods.

Note that only resales of goods to unrelated buyers in the United States
may be considered in computing deductive value. Related parties are specifically defined by the law, and this definition is set forth below in the
section dealing with related-party transactions. The law also specifies
that only resales at the first commercial level after importation may be
used. The first commercial level involves resales by the importer directly
to the buyer and not resales that are more than one buyer removed from
the importer.

The resale price used as a starting point may be the price at which (1)
the actual merchandise being appraised is resold, or it may be the price at
which (2) identical merchandise or (3) similar merchandise is resold.
There is no preference for using the resale price for (1) over the resale
prices for (2) or (3). The actual merchandise being appraised, identical
merchandise, and similar merchandise are all given equal treatment.

It is apparent, however, that the law requires that preference be given
to resales of the goods "at or about the date of importation of the merchandise being appraised," rather than to resales of goods that occur
much later. Thus, in ascertaining the resale price to be used as a starting

point for deductive value, resort must be made first to resales that occur near the date of importation of the goods being appraised.

If there are no resales of goods occurring at or about the date of importation of the goods being appraised, resales occurring later must be looked at, but not later than 90 days after the importation of the goods being appraised. If the only resales of goods available for consideration all occur more than 90 days after the importation of the goods being appraised, then deductive value cannot be determined and another basis of appraisement must be used.

In addition to the dates of the resales, the unit prices at which the resales occur and the total volume of goods resold at each unit price must be considered. The correct resale price to be used is that unit price at which the greatest aggregate quantity of goods is resold. The unit price at which the greatest aggregate quantity of goods is resold is that unit price whose total volume is greater than the total volume at any other unit price.

In the following example, all resales occur at or about the date of importation of the goods being appraised:

Individual Resales

Unit Price	Resale Quantity
$50	1,500
$45	2,500
$47	2,000
$50	1,200
$52	600
$45	3,000
$50	1,600

Aggregate Quantities

Unit Price	Resale Quantity
$45	5,500
$47	2,000
$50	4,300
$52	600

From the foregoing totals, it is clear that the total volume of resales at $45 per unit is greater than the total volume of resales at any other unit price. Therefore, $45 per unit would be the appropriate starting point for the deductive value calculation.

From the resale price established, the following items of cost are deducted:

1. Any selling commission paid, or the markup for profit and general expenses usually added for sales in the United States.

2. Costs incurred for international freight and insurance from the producing country to the United States.

3. The usual costs associated with transporting the goods from the port of importation to the place of delivery, including warehousing, inland freight and insurance, customs brokerage charges, and similar related costs, provided these costs are not included in general expenses in 1 above.

4. The Customs duties and other federal taxes incurred by reason of the importation of the merchandise, and any other federal taxes incurred by reason of resale in the United States.

After the above costs are deducted from the resale price, the dollar amount remaining is the deductive value (appraised value) of the merchandise. Set forth below is an illustration of the deductive value calculation. In this example, there is no sales commission involved, so a deduction is taken for profit and general expenses.

Deductive Value Calculation

SELLING PRICE IN UNITED STATES (PER UNIT)	$45.00
LESS:	
1. Usual profit and general expenses	$ 9.00
2. International freight and insurance from the country of exportation to the United States	$ 3.50
3. Costs incurred in the United States:	
a. All inland freight costs from place of importation to place of delivery	$ 1.00
b. Warehousing costs	$ 0.25
c. Costs of customs brokers and/or freight forwarders	$ 0.10
	$31.15
4. Duty at 10% (duties are divided out)	31.15
(1 + .10)	1.10
DEDUCTIVE VALUE (PER UNIT)	$28.32

In the above calculation, the deduction made for usual profit and general expenses is based on the importer's actual profit and general expenses unless they are inconsistent with the industry as a whole. When the importer's profit and general expenses differ significantly from those of other sellers of goods of the same class or kind, the deduction to be taken is based on that which is usual for the industry.

Also note that in step 4 above, when the deduction for duty is made, the duty is not subtracted; it is *divided out*. This is the proper way to take the duty out when the duty rate is an *ad valorem* rate. This is always accomplished by dividing the net price, which includes the duty, by one plus the duty rate expressed as a decimal. If the duty rate were 27.5%, for example, the net price including the duty would be divided by 1.275 (1 ⊦ 0.275) to arrive at the deductive value. If the duty rate is a specific rate—for example, five cents per piece—then the duty can be removed by simple subtraction. The duty is always subtracted or divided out as the last step in the calculation.

The above calculation shows how the deductive value is calculated when the imported goods are resold in the United States in their imported condition. When goods are further processed in the United States before they are resold, the procedures and calculation vary somewhat. The additional provisions in the law relating to processed goods are as follows:

[(2) (A)] (iii) If the merchandise concerned was not sold in the condition as imported and not sold before the close of the 90th day after the date of importation of the merchandise being appraised, the price is the unit price at which the merchandise being appraised, after further processing, is sold in the greatest aggregate quantity before the 180th day after the date of such importation. This clause shall apply to appraisement of merchandise only if the importer so elects and notifies the customs officer concerned of that election within such time as shall be prescribed by the Secretary.

. . . . . .

[And an additional deduction shall be taken from the resale price, as follows:]

[(3) (A)] (v) . . . the value added by the processing of the merchandise after importation to the extent that the value is based on sufficient information relating to cost of such processing.

When the goods being appraised have been further processed in the United States prior to resale, the provision quoted above applies only if there are no resales of identical or similar goods that are resold in the United States in their imported condition within 90 days of the importation of the goods being appraised. Where resales of identical or similar merchandise in their imported condition have occurred and these are acceptable under the law to form the basis of deductive value, these resales must be used and recourse cannot be made to the resale price of the processed merchandise being appraised.

Also note that when goods are appraised based on a resale after further processing, as discussed in paragraph (iii) above, it is only the resale price of the goods being appraised that comes into consideration. The law does not allow the use of the resale price of identical or similar goods that are further processed.

Paragraph (iii) cannot be used by Customs to appraise imported merchandise unless the importer concurs in this procedure. If the importer elects not to permit this method of appraisement, then the goods must be valued using a different basis of appraisement.

When goods are appraised based on their resale price after further processing, an additional deduction is taken from the resale price to eliminate the value added by the further processing, as shown above in paragraph (v). This deduction must be made before the duty is taken out because the cost of further processing occurs subsequent to the importation of the goods.

As stated earlier, the importer may choose to use computed value, the next basis of appraisement, before deductive value.

COMPUTED VALUE

Computed value is fairly straightforward and consists of a building up of costs to arrive at the appraised value. The law sets forth the components of computed value as follows:

(e) (1) The computed value of imported merchandise is the sum of—
- (A) the cost or value of the materials and the fabrication and other processing of any kind employed in the production of the imported merchandise;
- (B) an amount for profit and general expenses equal to that usually reflected in sales of merchandise of the same class or kind as the imported merchandise that are made by the producers in the country of exportation for export to the United States;
- (C) any assist, if its value is not included under subparagraph (A) or (B); and
- (D) the packing costs.

(2) For purposes of paragraph (1)—
- (A) The cost or value of materials under paragraph (1) (A) shall not include the amount of any internal tax imposed by the country of exportation that is directly applicable to the materials or their disposition if the tax is remitted or refunded upon the exportation of the merchandise in the production of which the materials were used; and
- (B) the amount for profit and general expenses under paragraph (1) (B) shall be based upon the producer's profits and expenses, unless the producer's profits and expenses are inconsistent with those usually reflected in sales of merchandise of the same class or kind as the imported merchandise that are made by producers in the country of exportation for export to the United States, in which case the amount under paragraph (1) (B) shall be based on the usual profit and general expenses of such producers in such sales, as determined from sufficient information.

The computed value of imported merchandise is the sum of:

1. The cost or value of all materials, labor, fabrication, or processing needed to produce the goods
2. An amount usually added by the producer for profit and general expenses in sales to the United States
3. The cost of any production assistance supplied by the buyer, if such cost is not included in 1 or 2 above
4. Packing costs

Thus, the elements used to calculate the computed value of imported goods are made up of all costs normally incurred in the manufacture and sale of those goods. The cost of materials, fabrication, and other processing shown in 1 above is the actual cost involved in producing the goods being appraised. If the producer was in a start-up mode when the imported goods were made, and this resulted in extraordinarily high costs of fabrication, those costs would nevertheless be the appropriate costs to include in the computed value of the goods. Note that all cost accounting under this basis of appraisement, unlike the other bases of appraisement, is predicated upon the generally accepted accounting principles that are followed in the country where the goods are produced, not those followed in the United States. Therefore, generalizations regarding costs should be approached with caution.

The law provides that internal taxes in the producer country that are directly related to materials and that are abated, refunded, or otherwise not imposed because of the exportation of the materials in the finished product are not to be included in the computed value calculation.

The amount to be added for profit and general expenses under 2 above is to be thought of as a unitary figure. That is, profit and general expenses are to be added together and considered always as a whole, rather than as individual components. The profit and general expenses of the actual manufacturer are used, unless they are not consistent with those of the industry as a whole. In that case, the profit and general expenses normally used by other producers of goods of the same class or kind would be substituted for those of the producer.

Additions for assists and packing would be handled according to the principles previously discussed.

Interestingly, computed value may be impossible to calculate because all the elements of cost required are in the possession of the foreign manufacturer. It should come as no surprise that many foreign companies will not release these cost details to the importer. Moreover, if the importer is not related to the foreign producer, the Customs Service has no means to compel the producer to come forth with the necessary cost information.

Appraisement of merchandise under computed value may give results that are significantly different from the appraisement of the same goods under transaction value. This may occur because some expense to the importer that is added to the price paid under transaction value would be excluded from the computed value. For example, a selling commission paid by the importer, which would be added to the price paid under transaction value, would not be included in computed value because it is not a cost of fabrication incurred by the producer in making the goods.

Also, where goods are purchased by the importer from a reseller in the country of export and not from the producer, the reseller's markup would be included in the dutiable price paid to the reseller under transaction value. If the same goods were appraised under computed value, however, the reseller's markup would be excluded from the dutiable value because it is only the profit and general expenses of *producers* that are taken into account under computed value. The profit and general expenses of later resellers who are not producers are irrelevant under the statute.

FINAL (DERIVATIVE) BASIS OF VALUE

At the beginning of the discussion on appraisement, it was stated that there are five main ways to appraise goods, plus another that is derivative of the others. The last, derivative basis of valuation will be discussed here. The law sets forth this last basis as follows:

(f) (1) If the value of imported merchandise cannot be determined, or otherwise used for the purposes of this chapter, under subsections (b) through (e) of this section [the first five bases], the merchandise shall be appraised for the purposes of this chapter on the basis of a value that is derived from the methods set forth in such subsections, with such methods being reasonably adjusted to the extent necessary to arrive at a value.

Basically, the law contemplates that all imported goods can be appraised on the basis of one of the five methods provided for, or on the basis of one of those methods after reasonable modification. This final basis gives Customs a clear way out if the other methods fail for technical reasons. Note that the first five methods must all be tried and eliminated before the last method can be used. When all else has failed, then this method is the last resort.

The most logical place to make a reasonable adjustment to one of the first five methods of appraisement is to eliminate the technical requirement that caused one of those methods to fail in the first place. For example, if the reason that transaction value could not be used in the first instance was that one of the five items to be added to transaction value could not be determined based on sufficient information, then consideration could be given to using a reasonable estimation for the cost to be added.

Suppose that the deductive value method failed solely because the one available resale in the United States that could be used occurred on the 120th day after the importation of the goods being appraised. In this instance, Customs could simply eliminate the 90 day requirement and proceed with the deductive value calculation. In choosing the required adjustment to one of the previous methods of appraisement, the touchstone is the reasonableness of the adjustment in light of the interests to be protected.

RELATED-PARTY TRANSACTIONS

If the importer is related to the foreign seller, this fact must be declared on each Customs entry. The law defines related parties as follows:

(g) (1) For purposes of this section, the persons specified in any of the following subparagraphs shall be treated as persons who are related:
   (A) Members of the same family, including brothers and sisters (whether by whole or half blood), spouse, ancestors, and lineal descendants.
   (B) Any officer or director of an organization and such organization.
   (C) An officer or director of an organization and an officer or director of another organization, if each such individual is also an officer or director in the other organization.
   (D) Partners.
   (E) Employer and employee.
   (F) Any person directly or indirectly owning, controlling, or holding with power to vote, 5 percent or more of the outstanding voting stock or shares of any organization and such organization.
   (G) Two or more persons directly or indirectly controlling, controlled by, or under common control with, any person.

If the foreign seller and the importer are not related in any of the above ways, the importer's goods can be appraised more easily by Customs. Where the parties are related, Customs is required by law to scrutinize the sales transaction more closely. The reason for this is fairly simple.

When the buyer of goods is not related to the seller, the sale between them is said to be an arm's-length transaction. Since the buyer will not pay more than the goods are worth to him or her, and the seller will not accept less than he or she wants, the price they agree upon will be a fair market price. On the other hand, when the buyer and seller are related to one another, they may set any price they want because their self-interests are not mutually exclusive.

For example, the parties may establish a selling price or "transfer" price between them that is either higher or lower than it would have been were they not related. If the parties want to take more profit in the foreign country, they will establish a high transfer price. Conversely, if they would like to take more profit in the United States, they will set a low transfer price. Table 3.1 illustrates this point.

As indicated in the table, by manipulating the selling price to the United States, the related parties can alter the amount of profit taken in the foreign and U.S. markets, as they choose. Many considerations might lead the parties to manipulate the price. Probably the most important of these would be income tax considerations.

Obviously, those who wrote the appraisement law were aware of the dangers inherent in related-party transactions. For this reason, certain safeguards were established. The valuation law states that the transaction value between related parties can only be used as the appraised value if certain conditions or tests are met. The most common of these tests are the following:

1. An examination of the circumstances of the sale of the imported merchandise indicates that the relationship between the buyer and the seller did not influence the price paid.
2. The transaction value of the imported merchandise closely approximates the deductive value or computed value of identical or similar merchandise.

If one of the above tests is met, the transaction value is acceptable as the appraised value. Note that only one test must be met, not both. To illustrate the first test, suppose that sales between branches of a large multinational corporation are involved and that the importer is the sister company of the exporter. In response to Customs' inquiries, the importing branch produces evidence that company policy requires each location to be a separate profit center and that, as a result, each branch negotiates its prices with all other branches as though they were not related. This

Table 3.1

	1 Cost to Make	2 Selling Price to United States	3 (2-1) Foreign Profit	4 Resale Price in United States	5 (4-2) U.S. Profit
Unrelated Parties	$5	$10	$5	$20	$10
Related Parties Example 1	$5	$15	$10	$20	$5
Related Parties Example 2	$5	$8	$3	$20	$12

evidence could establish that the first test was met and that the relationship did not influence the price paid.

Another instance is where the related parties establish their transfer price by reference to some external source. For example, related parties dealing in ores or minerals might set their prices by using the "spot prices" quoted in a daily trade publication. This procedure would clearly prove that the relationship did not influence the price.

The second test shown above is the easiest in practice to apply. If the transaction value between the parties is very close to the deductive value or the computed value of identical or similar goods previously imported by the same importer, then the transaction value can be used. All that is required is (1) to compute the deductive value or computed value of the identical or similar merchandise in the manner discussed above and (2) to compare it to the transaction value between the related parties. If these values are close, say within 5%, the transaction value is acceptable. Of course, if none of the tests as stated in the law are met, then Customs would proceed to the next basis of appraisement.

In summary, importing companies that buy from a related seller, as defined by the law, should anticipate the need to supply U.S. Customs with a substantial amount of information regarding the relationship that exists and the selling practices of the foreign entity.

Chapter 4

Beginning and Ending Formalities

Before U.S. Customs will release imported goods to the importer, a Customs entry must be filed. The entry must be accompanied by a deposit of estimated duties and proof that a bond exists to cover the entry.

ESTIMATED DUTIES

Estimated duties are the total moneys thought to be owing on the importation at the time the entry is filed, based on the entered classification and the entered value. The final duties may be higher or lower than the estimated duties paid. If higher, a bill for additional duties is issued to the importer. If lower, a refund check is sent to the importer. How can Customs collect additional duties if the goods have been released and the importer does not want to pay? Guaranteed payment is provided by the bond that must be filed with the entry.

CUSTOMS BONDS

The Customs bond is purchased by the importer from a bonding company known as a surety. The importer must pay a fee or premium to the surety to obtain the bond. The bond itself is essentially a legal contract involving three parties—the importer, Customs, and the surety. Like all contracts, the bond requires that everyone get something in return for giving something to someone else. The following chart shows what rights and obligations are exchanged among the parties:

	Gets	Gives
Importer	Immediate release of his or her goods from Customs	To the surety, a money fee, plus a promise to pay all sums demanded by Customs

	Gets	*Gives*
Customs	A guarantee from the surety that it will pay all moneys owed by the importer if the importer defaults on payment	Immediate release of the goods to the importer
Surety	Money fee paid by importer as premium, plus importer's promise to pay all sums demanded by Customs	A guarantee to Customs to pay importer's debts if the importer refuses to pay

This is a useful arrangement for all the parties, especially for Customs. Because of the bond, Customs does not have to chase importers around the map trying to collect additional duties.

When Customs bills remain unpaid for more than 90 days, Customs can collect the amount owed from the surety on the bond. The surety is left to pursue the importer for reimbursement of the funds. For the surety, usually an insurance company, writing Customs bonds is much like writing a form of insurance. The surety adjusts its premiums to cover the risks. Moreover, only a small percentage of entries, probably 5-10%, are liquidated with duty increases.

LIQUIDATION OF THE ENTRY

Liquidation is a legal term that indicates that all Customs decisions regarding an entry and the goods covered by it have been made. In short, the entry processing is completed in all respects. The face of the Customs entry is stamped with the word "LIQUIDATED" and the date on which it is stamped. This date becomes the date of liquidation. This is a very important date because it begins the running of the 90-day period during which the importer may file a formal protest to dispute any of the decisions that Customs has made regarding the imported merchandise. The most frequently disputed decisions involve the classification and value of the merchandise. Details regarding the filing of protests will be discussed later.

When an entry is liquidated there are three possible duty consequences. If the liquidation is a "change" liquidation, it means that the final duties owing are different from the estimated duties paid at entry, and one of two things will occur. If the final duties are more than the estimated duties, a bill is issued to the importer. If the final duties are less than the estimated duties, a refund check is issued to the importer. Finally, if the estimated and final duties are exactly the same, the entry is stamped "NO CHANGE."

The law requires that the importer be given notice of the date on which the entry is liquidated. If the importer were not notified of this important date, he or she would have no way of knowing when to file a protest. Among importers, there is a widespread misunderstanding of what constitutes the legal notice that Customs is required to give regarding the date of liquidation. The confusion surrounding this point has created some grave hardships because protest filing deadlines have been missed and large sums of money have been lost irretrievably.

There is one, and only one, legal notice of liquidation required by the law. It is contained in the Bulletin Notice of Liquidation which is posted on a bulletin board in the customshouse at the port of entry. This bulletin notice contains the name of the importer of record, the entry number, the date of liquidation, and other types of information to identify each particular Customs transaction. Any member of the general public may view this bulletin notice.

The reason there is so much confusion about something that seems so simple is explained by the fact that there are several other notices of liquidation. Unfortunately, none of the other notices have any legal significance when it comes to filing protests. To make matters worse, most importers know about the notices that do not count and know nothing about the only one that does.

Other types of notices regarding the date of liquidation are found in the refund check, in the duty bill for additional duties due, and in the courtesy notice of liquidation. In addition to the issuance date, refund checks issued by Customs usually show a date that 99% of the time is the same date as the date of liquidation. By the same token, Customs bills show a bill date that 99% of the time is the same date as the date of liquidation. Before liquidation, Customs frequently issues a courtesy notice of liquidation that tells the importer on what date Customs *expects* the entry to liquidate. The date shown on the courtesy notice is accurate 99% of the time. None of these types of notice has any legal significance. If these dates are relied on for counting days until protest deadline and the dates are wrong, the importer has no recourse if the protest is filed late.

Two other points regarding liquidation are worth mentioning. First, entries are deemed liquidated by operation of law one year from the date of entry unless Customs extends the liquidation period. If Customs does so, it must notify the importer of the extension. The time for liquidation may be extended up to *four years*. This means that the final duties owing are not determined for that length of time. This is obviously not a good situation for the importer. Second, if the importer finds that his or her entries are not routinely being liquidated within a reasonable time—that is, three to four months—or, worse yet, if the importer finds the liquidations are being extended by Customs, immediate inquiry is warranted to ascertain what is delaying the liquidations. Delay in liquidation often portends some problem involving the classification and rate of duty or the appraised value of the merchandise. It is usual for Customs to suspend liquidation of an importer's entries if he or she is under investigation for a legal violation of any sort. Therefore, it is advisable for the importer to pay attention to the status of his or her liquidations.

RELIQUIDATION OF THE ENTRY

Although liquidation completes the entry processing by Customs after all decisions regarding the goods have been made, after liquidation the decisions originally made can be reviewed during a specific period of time. If this review indicates that any errors have been made in the original liquidation, the entry can be liquidated again. The second liquidation is called a *reliquidation*.

Reliquidation of the entry may arise for two reasons. First, Customs itself may review the original liquidation and discover that an error has been made in the classification or appraisement of the merchandise. However, reviews of liquidated entries are not normally done by Customs as a matter of routine. What usually occurs is that some new information comes to light regarding a particular importer's merchandise. If this new information would have resulted in higher duties being assessed on a group of entries recently liquidated, Customs may locate those entries and reliquidate them based on the new information. A Customs-initiated reliquidation is referred to as a *voluntary reliquidation*. This type of reliquidation occurs very infrequently.

The law permits Customs on its own initiative to reliquidate an entry only within 90 calendar days of the date of the original liquidation. Not only must the error itself be discovered within 90 days, but the actual act of reliquidation must occur within the 90-day period.

A Customs-initiated (voluntary) reliquidation that takes place more than 90 days after the date of liquidation of the entry is legally invalid and cannot be judicially enforced, provided the merchandise was not fraudulently entered. If the goods were entered fraudulently, Customs has two years from the original liquidation in which to reliquidate the entry.

The second, and most common, way in which a reliquidation occurs is at the request of the importer. Such requests must be in writing, and they are referred to as protests.

PROTESTING DECISIONS MADE BY U.S. CUSTOMS

When the importer is unhappy with any decision made by Customs at the time the entry is liquidated, he or she may file a protest and have that decision reviewed. The issues most frequently raised by protest involve the classification and the appraisement of the goods. The most common type of protest is known as a formal protest.

The Formal Protest

The law that permits the filing of a formal protest is found in Title 19, United States Code, Section 1514, which states in pertinent part as follows:

Section 1514. Protest against decision of appropriate customs officer
(a) Finality of decisions; return of papers
　　Except as provided in . . . section 1501 of this title (relating to voluntary reliquidations), . . . section 1520 of this title (relating to refunds and errors), and section 1521 of this title (relating to reliquidations on account of fraud), decisions of the appropriate customs officer, including the legality of all orders and findings entering into the same, as to—
　　(1) the appraised value of merchandise;
　　(2) the classification and rate and amount of duties chargeable;
　　(3) all charges or exactions of whatever character within the jurisdiction of the Secretary of the Treasury;
　　(4) the exclusion of merchandise from entry or delivery or a demand for re-delivery to customs custody under any provision of the customs laws . . . ;
　　(5) the liquidation or reliquidation of an entry, or any modification thereof;
　　(6) the refusal to pay a claim for drawback; and
　　(7) the refusal to reliquidate an entry under section 1520(c) of this title,
shall be final and conclusive upon all persons (including the United States and any officer thereof) unless a protest is filed in accordance with this section. . . .

　　　　　　　. 　. 　. 　. 　. 　.

(c) Form, number, and amendment of protest; filing of protest
　　(1) A protest of a decision under subsection (a) of this section shall be filed in writing with the appropriate customs officer designated in regulations pre-scribed by the Secretary, setting forth distinctly and specifically each decision described in subsection (a) of this section as to which protest is made; each cate-gory of merchandise affected by each such decision as to which protest is made; and the nature of each objection and reasons therefor.

　　　　　　　. 　. 　. 　. 　. 　.

[P]rotests may be filed with respect to merchandise which is the subject of a decision specified in subsection (a) of this section by—
　　(A) the importers or consignees shown on the entry papers, or their sureties;
　　(B) any person paying any charge or exaction;
　　(C) any person seeking entry or delivery;
　　(D) any person filing a claim for drawback; or
　　(E) any authorized agent of any of the persons described in clauses (A) through (D).
　　(2) A protest of a decision, order, or finding described in subsection (a) of this section shall be filed with such customs officer within ninety days after but not before—
　　(A) notice of liquidation or reliquidation, or
　　(B) in circumstances where subparagraph (A) is inapplicable, the date of the decision as to which protest is made.

Note that in addition to protesting the classification and appraisement of the goods, the following Customs decisions may also be protested:

1. The demand for any charge or the exaction of any sum of money
2. The refusal to permit entry of merchandise
3. The refusal to deliver or release any merchandise after entry is filed
4. The liquidation or reliquidation of an entry
5. The denial of a claim for drawback
6. The refusal to reliquidate an entry under section 1520(c) of Title 19

The refund of duties under drawback provisions is discussed in Part II. Request for reliquidation under section 1520(c) is discussed later in this chapter.

A variety of persons may file protests, depending upon the type of decision complained of. The 90-day period during which a valid protest can be filed begins on the date of liquidation, the date of reliquidation, or the date upon which the objectionable decision was made.

A formal protest is usually written on Customs Form 19 and must set forth the following information, as noted on Form 19:

1. Name and address of the protesting party
2. The importer number of the protesting party
3. The entry number and date of entry
4. The date of liquidation of the entry
5. A specific description of the merchandise that was affected by the decision being protested
6. A clear statement indicating what decision is being protested and the reasons why the decision was wrong
7. A clear statement indicating what decision should have been reached and the reasons why the claimed decision is correct

The protest must be filed at the office of the district director whose decision is being protested. However, if the entry was filed at a port other than the district headquarters port, the protest may be filed with the port director at the port where the entry was filed.

The importer, like the Customs Service, has only 90 *calendar* days after liquidation within which to file a protest. Since the measure of time is calendar days, Saturdays, Sundays, and holidays are counted. This time period is extremely important because a protest filed more than 90 days past the date of liquidation is an invalid protest, and the Customs Service must deny it. This is not a discretionary matter for Customs to decide as it sees fit. There simply is no authority in the law for Customs to change a liquidation if a protest is filed late ("untimely"). It makes no difference how correct the importer's position might be with respect to the matter being protested. Past 90 days, the liquidation becomes final and binding on all parties.

It is also important to know that a protest filed *before* the date of liquidation is invalid and cannot be acted upon. There have been actual cases where the importer relied upon the liquidation date shown in the courtesy notice of liquidation to file the protest. In one such case, the entry was actually liquidated several weeks after the date shown in the courtesy notice of liquidation. As a result, the protest was filed before the entry was liquidated. The error was not discovered until more than 90 days had elapsed after the actual liquidation. Therefore, a valid protest was not filed within the proper 90-day period and the importer lost his case. For the correct method of determining the date of liquidation, refer to the section above dealing with "Liquidation of the Entry."

After the protest has been filed, it is given a number and date by Customs. The entry being protested is retrieved from the Customs record room and is attached to the protest. The protest, along with the entry, is sent to an import specialist for processing. Usually, the import specialist who reviews the protest is the same import specialist who originally classified and appraised the merchandise.

The protest reviewer will consider the arguments in the protest, along with any supporting documentation attached. If the claims in the protest appear to be correct, the protest will be approved and the entry will be reliquidated in accordance with the claims allowed. If the claims in the protest are not accepted as correct by Customs, the protest is denied. Once a protest is denied, the only means of pursuing the claims further is by filing a legal action in the Court of International Trade. Such legal actions are normally filed by attorneys.

Application for Further Review of Protest

There is an additional administrative procedure that may be used in conjunction with a protest; this procedure is known as an application for further review of protest (hereafter "further review"). Further review means that the protest will be examined by a customs officer who did not participate in the original decision being protested. Such officer is usually at a higher administrative level than the customs officer who made the objectionable decision.

A request for further review may be made on the same Customs Form 19 used for filing of the protest or may be made separately. In either case, the request must be made within the same 90-day period required for the protest. The request for further review must indicate whether the requesting party:

1. Has presently pending a request for an administrative ruling involving the same claim and the same merchandise
2. Has previously received an adverse administrative decision from Customs involving the same claim and the same merchandise
3. Has presently pending in one of the Customs courts a legal action involving the same claim and the same merchandise
4. Has previously received an adverse decision from one of the Customs courts involving the same claim and the same merchandise
5. Has made a prior request for further review involving the same claim and the same merchandise

It should be obvious that Customs may not grant further review if 1, 3, or 5 above is applicable. When 1 above applies, Customs may suspend action on the protest pending the outcome of the administrative ruling. When 3 above applies, Customs will normally deny the request for further review *and* the protest since the matter has been placed in litigation by the protesting party, who is now a legal adversary. When 5 above applies, the protesting party may request that the protest be suspended under the previous request for further review.

If either 2 or 4 above applies, Customs will deny further review unless the requesting party can convincingly show that facts exist or legal arguments are present that were not considered at the time of the previous adverse decision. When such a showing is made, a foundation is laid upon which further review may be granted.

In addition to the foregoing, a party requesting further review must affirmatively show that further review is justified. In this regard, further review is normally justified where it can be shown that the decision complained of:

1. Is inconsistent with a ruling by the Commissioner of Customs or a District Director of Customs involving substantially the same merchandise, or
2. Involves questions of fact or issues of law not previously ruled upon by Customs or the Customs courts

Where either of the above conditions apply, it is in the best interest of the Customs Service to permit a further review of the protest. If the protest is not granted in full by the district director, it is forwarded for further review to either the appropriate regional office of Customs or to Headquarters of the Customs Service in Washington, D.C. The documents are forwarded to the headquarters office if the protest raises issues involving any of the following:

1. Lack of uniformity of treatment, that is, inconsistent Customs decisions
2. An unannounced change in a prior practice that was uniformly used by Customs over an established period of time
3. The interpretation by customs officers of a court decision or a ruling by the Commissioner of Customs
4. Questions of law or fact that have not been ruled upon by the Customs courts or the headquarters office

Where none of the above circumstances exist, the protest and application for further review are forwarded for decision to the regional Customs office that serves the district in which the protest was filed. There, the protest is reviewed by regional customs officers who did not participate in the decision being reviewed.

After the appropriate further review, the protest will be granted or denied, in whole or in part. If granted, the entry papers and the protest are returned to the district director for reliquidation of the entry. If denied, the only means of pursuing the protest claims further is by filing a legal action in the Court of International Trade. Such legal actions are normally filed by attorneys.

In circumstances where further review of a protest at Headquarters of the Customs Service is justified, the importer or other protesting party should always take advantage of the opportunity for such further review. There are several reasons for this. First, further review avoids costly litigation in the Court of International Trade. Second, the review at headquarters is conducted by Customs attorneys who specialize in the areas of law raised by the issues in the protest. And third, headquarters personnel are known to be fair and objective in deciding protest issues based on the legal merits of each case.

Request for Reliquidation

The second type of protest that will be discussed permits a reliquidation of the entry to correct a clerical error, mistake of fact, or other inadvertence. The law that authorizes such protests or requests for reliquidation is found in Title 19, United States Code, Section 1520(c) (1), which provides in pertinent part as follows:

Section 1520. Refunds and errors

. . . . .

(c) Reliquidation of entry
    Notwithstanding a valid protest was not filed, the appropriate customs officer may, in accordance with regulations prescribed by the Secretary, reliquidate an entry to correct—

(1) a clerical error, mistake of fact, or other inadvertence not amounting to an error in the construction of a law, adverse to the importer and manifest from the record or established by documentary evidence, in any entry, liquidation, or other customs transaction, when the error, mistake, or inadvertence is brought to the attention of the appropriate customs officer within one year after the date of liquidation or exaction. . . .

Although frequently referred to as a protest, this legal remedy is more in the nature of a formal request. The statute permits an importer to request Customs to reliquidate an entry with a refund of duty if there has been a clerical error, mistake of fact, or other inadvertence that resulted in duties being overpaid. Such a request must be filed with Customs within one year from the date of liquidation of the entry. A request filed more than one year after liquidation is not valid and will not be granted because it is untimely.

Clerical error includes, for example, errors in transcribing numbers, errors in arithmetic, or errors in assembling documents. A mistake of fact occurs when an action is based upon a belief by a person that the material facts are other than they really are. It can be that the person is unaware of some fact or that the person believes something is a fact when in reality it is not. An inadvertence occurs when a person intends to do one thing but does something else.

In order to qualify under the law, the party requesting reliquidation must show that the error, mistake, or inadvertence:

1. Does not amount to an error in the construction of a law,

2. Is adverse to the importer, and

3. Is manifest from the record or established by documentary evidence.

These requirements are stated in the law as set forth above. The first requirement is considered with regard to the actions of customs officers. For example, if it is claimed that a customs officer erroneously or mistakenly classified or appraised certain merchandise, it must be shown that this did not occur because the customs officer misinterpreted the law. If the alleged error or mistake occurred because the officer misconstrued the law, then section 1520(c) (1) does not apply, and the entry may not be reliquidated.

The second requirement, that the error or mistake be adverse to the importer, makes this law inapplicable to errors or mistakes that are adverse to Customs. For example, a clerical error that results in a $1,000 overpayment of duty may be corrected under this law at the importer's request. If the same error, however, resulted in a $1,000 underpayment of duty, the government could not avail itself of this law to reliquidate the entry with an increase of duties. Thus, the law is advantageous only to the importer.

The third requirement deals with matters of evidence. The party requesting reliquidation must establish that the error or mistake is clear from an examination of the entry itself or the other documents relating to the transaction. The importer may not rely on evidence extrinsic to the documents to prove that an error or mistake in fact occurred.

There is no particular form of request required by law or regulation to make a claim under section 1520(c) (1). Such requests are normally contained in a letter addressed to the District Director of Customs where the entry was filed. The letter need only contain information sufficient to show that a correctable error or mistake has occurred, within the framework of the requirements discussed above. If additional information is required to perfect a claim under section 1520(c) (1), Customs will normally request it from the importer.

If Customs denies a request for reliquidation under section 1520(c) (1), such refusal to reliquidate may be protested by a formal protest under section 1514, as discussed above. The formal protest must be filed within 90 days of the date of official denial, as shown by the record. The denial notice to the importer may be in the form of a letter, a memorandum, or a form letter designed specifically for section 1520(c) (1) denials.

Controversies have existed for years about the interpretation of section 1520(c) (1), and there is a large degree of nonuniformity throughout the Customs ports in the administration of this law. Despite frequent interpretations of this statute by the Customs courts, the application of this legal remedy by the various field offices of Customs is uneven and subject to many human vagaries. Many import specialists, for example, take the position that any error or mistake involving classification or appraisement *always* results from a misconstruction of the law and, hence, is not correctable under section 1520(c) (1). Under this theory, a Customs entry for cheese that is inadvertently classified by the customs broker and the import specialist as wearing apparel could not be corrected under section 1520(c) (1), despite the appreciable evidence, manifest on its face, that someone must have been mistaken as to the facts. The uneven application of this law has proven to be very frustrating to the importing public because many of the claims involved are too small to permit them being pursued further administratively or in the courts.

The Three Most Important Legal Obligations

More than any other area of Customs law and regulation, the three requirements of invoicing, entry, and declaration of imported merchandise create the greatest problems for importers. In fact, most Customs penalties arise because of some deficiency in these areas. To a large extent, importers fail to appreciate the breadth and reach of the legal requirements involved. This chapter will attempt to explain these complex matters as simply as possible and will shed light on how invoicing, entry, and declaration merge into one legal obligation.

INVOICING OF IMPORTED MERCHANDISE

In discussing the legal requirements for invoicing of imported merchandise, two different questions need to be considered: (1) what information is required to be shown on the invoice, and (2) how should the required information be shown on the invoice? The answer to both questions will probably be surprising, but for different reasons.

What Information Must Be Shown on the Invoice

For purposes of this discussion, the pertinent part of the invoicing statute is Title 19, United States Code, Section 1481(a), which states as follows:

Section 1481. Invoice; contents
(a) All invoices of merchandise to be imported into the United States shall set forth—
(1) The port of entry to which the merchandise is destined;
(2) The time when, the place where, and the person by whom and the person to

whom the merchandise is sold or agreed to be sold, or if to be imported otherwise than in pursuance of a purchase, the place from which shipped, the time when and the person to whom and the person by whom it is shipped;

(3) A detailed description of the merchandise, including the name by which each item is known, the grade or quality, and the marks, numbers, or symbols under which sold by the seller or manufacturer to the trade in the country of exportation, together with the marks and numbers of the packages in which the merchandise is packed;

(4) The quantities in the weights and measures of the country or place from which the merchandise is shipped, or in the weights and measures of the United States;

(5) The purchase price of each item in the currency of the purchase, if the merchandise is shipped in pursuance of a purchase or an agreement to purchase;

(6) If the merchandise is shipped otherwise than in pursuance of a purchase or an agreement to purchase, the value for each item, in the currency in which the transactions are usually made, or, in the absence of such value, the price in such currency that the manufacturer, seller, shipper, or owner would have received, or was willing to receive, for such merchandise if sold in the ordinary course of trade and in the usual wholesale quantities in the country of exportation;

(7) The kind of currency, whether gold, silver, or paper;

(8) All charges upon the merchandise, itemized by name and amount when known to the seller or shipper; or all charges by name (including commissions, insurance, freight, cases, containers, coverings, and cost of packing) included in the invoice prices when the amounts for such charges are unknown to the seller or shipper;

(9) All rebates, drawbacks, and bounties, separately itemized, allowed upon exportation of the merchandise; and

(10) Any other facts deemed necessary to a proper appraisement, examination, and classification of the merchandise that the Secretary of the Treasury may require.

To understand what information must be shown on the invoice, it is best to keep in mind that there are three different requirements: (1) ordinary requirements, (2) special requirements, and (3) extraordinary requirements. The first two do not pose any particular problems. The third, however, has been troublesome to many importing companies.

Ordinary Invoicing Requirements. Ordinary invoicing requirements are the simplest part of the law because they coincide with everyday commercial practice. Basically, the law requires that the importer present with his or her Customs entry a commercial invoice. Since most sales are evidenced by a commercial invoice, this requirement is easy to meet. Next, the law generally requires that commercial invoices provide certain specific information, the most important of which are the following:

1. Time and place of sale or consignment of the goods, name of seller or consignor, and name of buyer or consignee
2. A detailed description of the merchandise, including grade, quality, quantity, and name by which each item is known

3. The purchase price of each item in the currency of purchase; or the value of each item, if consigned

4. The marks and numbers on the packages, indicating what merchandise is in each package

These items of information are precisely the sort of information that every commercial invoice contains. Therefore, almost any commercial invoice presented to Customs will be acceptable in meeting these ordinary requirements.

The invoicing law has not been amended for many years. As a consequence, some of the requirements are outdated. Information regarding the port of entry of the merchandise is no longer an essential item to be shown on the seller's invoice since that information usually appears elsewhere in the Customs entry papers. If the invoice itself does not adequately reveal the number and contents of each package or container, Customs will require the attachment to the entry of a separate packing list showing that information.

It is no longer legally necessary to show information in terms of the weights and measures of the United States or of the country of exportation, since the Harmonized Tariff Schedule of the United States generally requires all information to be reported on the entry in metric terms. With regard to the currency involved in the transaction, U.S. dollars or any foreign currency is acceptable. Where the invoice is in a foreign currency, that currency will be converted to U.S. dollars at the exchange rate in effect on the date of exportation of the merchandise from the country of exportation. The exchange rates used are published by Customs and may be a rate proclaimed by the Secretary of the Treasury or a rate certified by the Federal Reserve Bank of New York.

One area where Customs may ask for the importer's assistance on the invoices has to do with the detailed description of the merchandise. If the description of the goods is too abbreviated, it will be difficult for Customs to classify the merchandise. Therefore, the importer should ask the seller to invoice the goods by using the most complete description possible. Also, keep in mind that descriptive words that coincide with the language of the applicable tariff provisions will facilitate the classification process.

Special Invoicing Requirements. In addition to the ordinary invoicing requirements, certain types or classes of merchandise must have special descriptive information set forth in the invoice. Shown below is the list of goods that require special invoice information as set forth in the Customs Regulations:

Aluminum and alloys of aluminum

Articles manufactured of textile materials, coated or laminated with plastics or rubber

Bags manufactured of plastic sheeting

Ball or roller bearings

Beads

Bed linen and bedspreads

Chemicals

Colors, dyes, stains, and related products

Copper

Copper ores and concentrates

Cotton fabrics

Cotton raw

Cotton waste

Earthenware or crockeryware

Fish or fish livers

Footwear

Fur products and furs

Glassware and other glass products

Gloves

Grain or grain and screenings

Handkerchiefs

Hats or headgear

Hosiery

Iron or steel

Iron oxide

Machines, equipment, and apparatus

Machine parts

Machine tools

Madeira embroideries

Motion-picture films

Paper

Plastic plates, sheets, film, foil or strip

Printed matter

Pulp

Refrigeration equipment

Rolling mills

Rubber products

Screenings or scalpings of grains or seeds

Steel products (Special Summary Invoice)

Textile fiber products

Tires and tubes for tires

Tobacco

Watches and watch movements

Wearing apparel

Wood products

Wool and hair

Wool products

Woven fabric of man-made fibers

The Customs Regulations show the special information required for the above products. The special information asked for is sometimes very technical in nature and is necessary to properly classify the goods. Two examples of the special information required are set forth below:

Hosiery—(1) Indicate whether a single yarn measures less than 67 decitax. (2) Indicate whether the hosiery is full length, knee length, or less than knee length. (3) Indicate whether it contains lace or net.

Iron or steel classifiable in Chapter 72 or headings 7301 or 7307, HTSUS (T.D. 53092, 55977)—Statement of the percentages by weight or carbon and any metallic elements contained in the articles, in the form of a mill analysis or mill test certificate.

Once the importer knows what is expected, it is a fairly simple matter to comply with the regulations. Failure to have the special information on the first or second invoice presented to Customs will not, in most cases, put the importer in grave jeopardy. Customs will quickly realize that the necessary information has not been included in the invoice and will communicate this deficiency to the importer, usually through the customs broker. Therefore, these special requirements, while important, do not present great obstacles.

Extraordinary Invoicing Requirements. Most Customs penalties arise because of a failure to show "extraordinary" information on the invoice. The information is extraordinary because it normally would *not* appear on a commercial invoice. In fact, much of the information is not even known by the seller who prepares the invoice.

In addition to the ordinary information that is legally required and that is shown on most invoices, the law requires the invoice to set forth the following:

1. All charges upon the merchandise itemized by name and amount
2. Any other facts deemed necessary to a proper appraisement, examination, and classification of the merchandise that the Secretary of the Treasury may require

These are the extraordinary items that must be shown on the invoice. These requirements no doubt seem perplexing. However, an importer who is familiar with the principles of voluntary compliance, as discussed earlier, would probably know what information was meant by "all charges" and "any other facts."

To begin with, the terms "all charges upon the merchandise" and "any other facts deemed necessary" together include every cost that has been paid in connection with the imported goods. These include such costs as down payments, buying commissions, interest charges, and foreign engineering costs. One place to look for help in identifying the sort of costs that must be shown is the appraisement law.

As noted earlier, an understanding of the fundamentals of appraisement law is important because many types of costs that must be reported to Customs arise from the language of the valuation law. Below is a list of costs mentioned earlier in the discussion of appraisement:

1. Price directly paid for the goods
2. Packing costs
3. Selling and buying commissions
4. Items of production assistance, including:

   a. Materials, components, parts, and similar items incorporated into the imported goods during manufacture or assembly

   b. Tools, dies, molds, machines, and similar items used to produce the imported goods

   c. Merchandise consumed in the production of the imported goods

   d. Engineering, development, designs, plans, and similar work done outside the United States

5. Royalties and license fees
6. Indirect payments to the seller—for example, a debt that is forgiven
7. Testing costs
8. Cost of materials for testing
9. Costs of erection or assembly after importation
10. Quota charges

The above costs are certainly the sort of costs that are contemplated by the invoicing law as reportable costs. However, the above list is not exhaustive and there may be other applicable costs not mentioned in the appraisement law that should be reported on the invoice. For example, interest charges may be paid or an importer might pay a fee for the right to be an exclusive distributor. These are both examples of the extraordinary costs that must be invoiced or reported.

One of the costs most frequently omitted from the invoice involves production assistance (assists), which was discussed in connection with appraisement. Assists are tangible and intangible things that are necessary for the production of the merchandise. With regard to materials, consigned components are often overlooked as a cost incurred in production that must be invoiced. Consigned components are things such as integrated circuits, connectors, disk drives, and other physical materials that are purchased by the importer in the United States or in a third country and sent, free of charge, to the manufacturer to be incorporated into the imported product. The cost of these materials would not be included in the vendor's price, but they must be shown on the invoice.

Likewise, many products are made with tools, dies, or molds. These are either supplied free by the importer or procured by the vendor in his or her own country and separately charged to the importer on another invoice. In either case, the cost or value of these items is usually not included in the invoice price for the merchandise itself. However, these costs must be shown on the invoice for the goods.

Intangible things, such as engineering and development, that are supplied free to the vendor or contracted for separately are also part of the appraised value of the merchandise if the work is done by someone outside the United States. These costs must also be shown on the invoice for the merchandise.

With regard to the requirement to invoice any other facts deemed necessary to a proper classification and appraisement, the importer must reflect upon the transaction to see if there is anything about it that might affect the way Customs would handle the transaction. For example, might it make a difference to Customs to know that the goods purchased through the buying agent can only be bought through him and not directly from the seller? This might make a difference. There is, in reality, no limit to the type of facts that Customs might deem necessary to a proper classification and appraisement.

In discussing the extraordinary invoicing requirements, Customs has stated:

The fundamental rule to be borne in mind is that the shipper and importer must furnish the Customs officers with all pertinent information with respect to each import transaction to assist the Customs officers in determining the tariff status of the goods. (*Importing into the United States* [Washington, D.C.: U.S. Government Printing Office, 1986], 18.)

Since determining what information is "pertinent" to the transaction is obviously a problem, the best approach is to report everything and then let Customs decide what is pertinent.

In summary, (1) the invoice must contain the terms normally shown on a commercial invoice, (2) the invoice must contain certain specific information only for special classes of goods mentioned in the Customs Regulations, and (3) the invoice must show all charges paid and all costs incurred (for example, production assistance) in connection with the imported goods and any facts deemed necessary to proper classification and appraisement.

Understanding the need to report costs mentioned in the appraisement law is a good beginning for most importers. Starting with these costs as examples of reportable items, the importer may perceive other aspects of his or her transaction that should be reported.

Before moving on to an explanation of how the information should be shown on the invoice, one further point needs to be made regarding extraordinary invoicing requirements. Although Customs soon becomes aware of a failure to provide the information needed for special invoicing requirements for certain classes of merchandise, it usually does not become aware of such failures with respect to extraordinary invoicing requirements. If the importer fails to report buying commissions or foreign engineering costs on the commercial invoice, there is usually no way for Customs to be aware of the omission. These omissions, therefore, may occur repeatedly on all entries filed over an extended period of time before the problem is discovered by the importer or by Customs itself. This is why these reportable costs are so troublesome. Each omission is a separate violation of the invoicing law and each is subject to a civil penalty, whether or not Customs is deprived of any revenue as a result. Therefore, it is imperative for the importer to monitor his or her entries for compliance with all invoicing requirements.

How the Required Information Should Be Shown on the Invoice

Many of the costs required to be reported on the invoice are *not* paid to the seller of the goods. For example, buying commissions are usually paid to a third party and this cost is not known to the seller. Royalties or license fees may be paid to someone in the United States. How would the seller even be aware of these costs? Does Customs really expect the seller or shipper to type all this information on the commercial invoice? Fortunately, Customs does not expect all this information to be typed on the seller's commercial invoice.

Customs is aware that many costs required to be invoiced are paid to someone other than the seller. Therefore, Customs is very flexible regarding how these items of information are to be reported. Customs has taken the position that these extraordinary items of cost may be shown in an attachment to the invoice. Therefore, if the required information is contained in a document attached to the invoice, it meets the legal invoicing requirement. In point of fact, Customs' logic can safely be carried one step further. Since the commercial invoice is always attached to the Customs entry, any document containing the required information that is attached to the Customs entry meets the invoicing requirement. This is true even if the importer himself or herself prepares the attachment.

In conclusion, what must be reported on the invoice can be quite complicated. Fortunately, the manner of reporting it is simple.

ENTRY OF IMPORTED MERCHANDISE

The legal requirements relating to entry of imported merchandise are fairly straightforward. However, the entry statute or law is written in such a way that any violation of the invoicing law is almost always a violation of the entry law as well. The law relating to entry of merchandise is found in Title 19, United States Code, Section 1484. The pertinent parts of this law for present discussion are set forth below:

Section 1484. Entry of merchandise
(a) Requirement and time
   (1) Except as provided in sections 1490, 1498, 1552, 1553, and 1336 (j) of this title . . . one of the parties qualifying as "importer of record" . . . either in person or by an agent authorized by him in writing—
      (A) shall make entry therefor by filing with the appropriate customs officer such documentation as is necessary to enable such officer to determine whether the merchandise may be released from customs custody; and
      (B) shall file (at the time required under paragraph (2) (B) of this subsection) with the appropriate customs officer such other documentation as is necessary to enable such officer to assess properly the duties on the merchandise, collect accurate statistics with respect to the merchandise, and determine whether any other applicable requirement of law (other than a requirement relating to release from customs custody) is met.
   (2) (A) The documentation required under paragraph (1) of this subsection with respect to any imported merchandise shall be filed at such place within the customs-collection district where the merchandise will be released from customs custody as the Secretary shall by regulation prescribe.
      (B) The documentation required under paragraph (1) (B) of this subsection with respect to any imported merchandise shall be filed with the appropriate customs officer when entry of the merchandise is made. . . .
             . . . . . .
(d) Signing and contents
Such entry shall be signed by the importer of record, or his agent, and shall set forth such facts in regard to the importation as the Secretary of the Treasury may require for the purpose of assessing duties and to secure a proper examination, inspection, appraisement, and liquidation, and shall be accompanied by such invoices, bills of lading, certificates, and documents as are required by law and regulations promulgated thereunder.

The law requires that the importer shall file with the Customs entry such documentation as is necessary to enable the customs officer to assess properly the correct duties on the merchandise, to collect accurate statistics, and to determine whether other applicable requirements of law are met. Hence, if any information that would affect the appraisement is omitted, the law is not complied with. In this regard, the invoicing and entry statutes require the same thing.

The law also requires the entry to set forth such facts as may be required for assessing duties and securing proper examination, appraisement, and liquidation, and the entry must be accompanied by such invoices, certificates, and documents as are required by law and regulation. Therefore, it is apparent that the entry law is as broad in scope as the invoicing law. As a result, omitting any important fact or document from the entry papers is a violation of the entry statute. However, this law is as easily satisfied as the invoicing law because providing the necessary information anywhere in the entry papers is sufficient to comply with the law.

The discussion that follows is based largely on concepts set forth in the Customs Regulations. The word "entry" means several things when used in a Customs context. The most common meanings are (1) the entry form or document itself and (2) the act of making entry or entering the goods.

Regarding the first meaning, there are approximately seven different types of Customs entries that may be filed. Most of these types are reported on Customs Form 7501—which is commonly called the entry. All the necessary papers that must be filed with the entry are attached to it. These include the invoice, the packing list, and the bond, if a single transaction bond is used. Frequently, the entire package of documents is referred to as the entry.

By far the most common type of entry is the consumption entry. To say that goods are entered for consumption merely means that the goods, after examination and release by Customs, are given to the importer to be used by him or her for any lawful purpose. Hence, the goods are "consumed" or taken into the commerce of the United States.

Goods not entered for consumption are frequently stored in a bonded warehouse or in a foreign trade zone. The purposes achieved by filing a warehouse or foreign trade zone entry are discussed in chapter 14.

Every Customs entry has a unique entry number which serves to distinguish it from every other Customs entry. Customs always identifies an importation by the entry number. All communications from Customs to the importer will refer to this number, and Customs expects the importer to refer to this number when he or she corresponds with Customs. Without this number, Customs cannot properly identify the shipment involved. For this reason, it is advisable for the importer to establish his or her recordkeeping system by entry number, after that point in time when an entry number has been assigned. Importers who organize their documents by importing vessel name or by purchase order number always experience difficulties in communicating with Customs.

Every entry also has a date of entry. Although there are several dates that may be used, the most common legal date of entry is the date on which Customs releases the merchandise to the importer.

The party shown on the Customs entry as the "importer of record" is the party who bears all liability for duties, taxes, penalties, liquidated damages, and any other liabilities arising from the import transaction. Therefore, individuals and companies that have only a minimal or tangential interest in the goods to be imported should be wary of agreeing to act as importer of record.

The word "entry" is also used as a verb to describe an act of the importer—that is, to make entry. When an entry is filed with Customs, the goods are said to be entered. All merchandise must be entered within five working days after arrival of the importing conveyance, whether ship, airplane, or truck. However, the district director may extend the time for filing of the entry. If entry is not filed within five days, and no extension has been granted, the merchandise is usually sent to a general order (G.O.) warehouse to await the filing of the entry. Transportation charges to the G.O. warehouse and storage charges that accrue up to the time of entry become a lien upon the goods and must be paid before the goods can be released.

Most goods not entered within one year from the date of importation become subject to sale at public auction, with the proceeds of sale being used first to pay storage charges and other liens. Any moneys remaining thereafter go to the general treasury of the United States.

After the entry has been filed by the importer or the customs broker, the formal procedures of examination, classification, and appraisement begin, as described in detail above.

DECLARATION OF IMPORTED MERCHANDISE

The law relating to the declaration of imported merchandise is found in Title 19, United States Code, Section 1485, the relevant parts of which, for our discussion, are set forth as follows:

Section 1485. Declaration
(a) Requirement: form and contents
Every importer of record making an entry under the provisions of section 1484 of this title shall make and file therewith, in a form to be prescribed by the Secretary of the Treasury, a declaration under oath, stating—

(1) Whether the merchandise is imported in pursuance of a purchase or an agreement to purchase, or whether it is imported otherwise than in pursuance of a purchase or agreement to purchase;

(2) That the prices set forth in the invoice are true, in the case of merchandise purchased or agreed to be purchased; or in the case of merchandise secured otherwise than by purchase or agreement to purchase, that the statements in such invoice as to value or price are true to the best of his knowledge and belief;
(3) That all other statements in the invoice or other documents filed with the entry, or in the entry itself, are true and correct; and
(4) That he will produce at once to the appropriate customs officer any invoice, paper, letter, document, or information received showing that any such prices or statements are not true or correct.

Like the invoicing law, the statute requiring declaration of merchandise is somewhat surprising in its scope and the nature of the obligations it creates. The requirements of the law are largely contained in the declaration on the Customs entry itself, Customs Form 7501 or other entry form. Most importers who sign an entry, or have it signed for them by their customs broker, are totally unaware of the substance of the declaration made, even though it appears on the face of the entry itself. This declaration, however, is a matter of some importance and close attention to the wording is instructive.

The substance of the declaration is shown below. The numbers shown in brackets "[   ]" have been added to the quoted material for ease of discussion. These numbers and brackets do not appear in the original.

Declaration of Importer of Record (Owner or Purchaser) or Authorized Agent

I declare that I am the [check one]

_____ Importer of record and that the actual owner, purchaser, or consignee for customs purposes is as shown above.

OR   _____ owner or purchaser or agent thereof.

I further declare that the merchandise [check one]

_____ was obtained pursuant to a purchase or agreement to purchase and that the prices set forth in the invoice are true.

OR   _____ was not obtained pursuant to a purchase or agreement to purchase and the statements in the invoice as to value or price are true to the best of my knowledge and belief.

I also declare that [1] the statements in the documents herein filed fully disclose to the best of my knowledge and belief the true prices, values, quantities, rebates, drawbacks, fees, commissions, and royalties and are true and correct, and that [2] all goods or services provided to the seller of the merchandise either free or at reduced cost are fully disclosed. [3] I will immediately furnish to the appropriate customs officer any information showing a different state of facts.

By way of preliminaries, the declaration first asks whether the person signing the entry is (1) the importer of record, but not the owner or purchaser, or (2) the owner or purchaser of the merchandise or the agent of either. The declaration next asks whether the goods were obtained (1) by purchase or agreement to purchase—that is, a sale—or (2) by some means other than purchase—that is, a consignment, bequest, gift, or other means.

The last section of the declaration is the most interesting. With regard to the language covered by bracket number one [1], the declarant states that the documents filed represent and *fully disclose* the true facts regarding prices, values, quantities, rebates, drawbacks, fees, commissions, and royalties. Hence, if any facts in the entry regarding these matters are untrue or are incomplete, the declaration is false. Notice that many of the items named are also mentioned in the invoicing statute.

The material in bracket number two [2] says the declarant has fully disclosed in the entry all production assistance, that is, goods or services given to the seller free or at reduced cost. This part of the declaration is a direct reference to assists, as discussed in the appraisement law. Items of production assistance include things such as materials and components assembled into the goods; tools, dies, and molds used to produce the goods; and engineering, development, and design work done outside the United States which are necessary to make the goods.

The statement covered by bracket number three [3] is perhaps the most interesting of all the material quoted. It says that the declarant will immediately disclose to Customs any information he or she obtains that shows that something in the entry is incorrect, that is, "a different state of facts." This means that the entry must be correct at the time it is filed and at all times thereafter. If the person filing the entry discovers later that something in the document is incorrect, he or she must communicate the correct facts to Customs. Thus, the declaration creates a continuing obligation on the party who signs it.

There are at least two times when the need arises to write to Customs about an entry filed previously. These occur when (1) a fact believed to be true when the entry was filed is later discovered to have been untrue and (2) a fact that was true at the time of entry later changes.

An example of the first case is where the invoice filed with the entry states that the shipment consists of 200 dozen items. After arrival of the goods at the importer's premises, it is discovered that there are actually 210 dozen items. This is referred to as an "overage" and this excess quantity must be reported to Customs. The same would be true of shortages. An overage or shortage might result in a change in duties owing on a shipment.

An error in the invoice description of the merchandise could result in an incorrect classification and an incorrect rate of duty being applied to the goods. This also could result in an underpayment or overpayment of duties. Failure to report such an error to Customs would constitute a violation of the importer's declaration.

The second, and more interesting, case occurs where a fact that was true when the entry was filed changes subsequent to entry filing. For example, the price paid for the goods may change after the entry is filed. This may happen because of fluctuations in currency exchange rates. Frequently, an importer will agree with the seller to make certain adjustments in the price paid for the merchandise if the currency exchange rate fluctuates to the seller's disadvantage. Hence, the importer may file with the entry an invoice showing that $10,000 was paid for the shipment. After entry, however, the importer may agree to pay the seller an additional $500. When this additional sum is paid, it must be reported to Customs because the price on the invoice filed with Customs is no longer a valid or true price. Usually, in this situation additional duties will be owing to Customs.

Another example is where the importer changes the specifications for the goods, after they are ordered but before they are shipped. As a result, the price of the goods increases. Frequently, however, the seller will invoice the goods at the original price and this invoice is filed with the entry. Later, the seller will send the importer a debit note or separate invoice for the increased price of the shipment. If this subsequent charge is paid by the importer, it must be reported to Customs.

These examples show why an importer must monitor his or her import transactions even after the entry is filed with Customs. The legal obligation to report incorrect or changed facts continues for five years after the date of entry and declaration. The five-year statute of limitations will be discussed in chapter 11.

HOW INVOICE, ENTRY, AND DECLARATION MERGE

Although invoicing, entry, and declaration of merchandise have been discussed separately because there are three different laws involved, there is a sense in which the three legal requirements merge into one in many instances. One reason for this is that the declaration itself is on the face of the entry and the invoice is attached to the entry. Hence, the three requirements come together in the same package of documents. In addition, certain aspects of the three laws involved are similarly worded.

One legal act can often be described in three different ways. For example, if the importer has paid a buying agent's commission in connection with a shipment, one can ask (1) was the commission declared, (2) was the commission shown on the invoice, or (3) was the commission shown on the entry? All three questions essentially amount to the same thing. The same is true of the value of consigned components used in manufacturing (that is, production assistance). Were the components invoiced? Were the components declared? Were the components shown on the entry? One might even ask: Were the components declared on the entry? These are all ways of inquiring about the same thing.

Similarly, if one legal act is performed, the others usually will be performed as well. If consigned components are shown on an attachment to the invoice, it can be said that they are declared or entered.

In summary, whether thought of separately or in combination with one another, the three legal requirements of invoicing, entry, and declaration are the most important elements of voluntary compliance.

NOTE ON IMPORTER'S VOLUNTARY DISCLOSURE OF VIOLATIONS

When an importer discovers that invoicing, entry, or declaration errors have been made, these may be brought voluntarily to Customs' attention by the importer. Technically, this is called making a prior disclosure. Such disclosures may be made regarding other violations as well. Aside from any spiritual cleansing one may experience as a result of such disclosure, another practical benefit is a substantial reduction in penalties that may be imposed upon the importer. Whereas a violation discovered by Customs might cost the importer a $10,000 penalty, the same violation, if disclosed by the importer voluntarily, might only result in a $500 penalty. In many instances, monetary penalties can be eliminated completely. The subject of prior disclosure will be discussed in more detail in chapter 11.

Chapter 6

Country of Origin
Marking Requirements

One purpose of the marking law is to permit a purchaser of goods to determine when items are of foreign origin rather than U.S. origin. To the extent that a purchaser might have a preference for domestically produced goods, the law may tend to confer an advantage on U.S. manufacturers.

The marking statute is found in Title 19, United States Code, Section 1304, the pertinent parts of which are set forth as follows:

Section 1304. Marking of imported articles and containers
(a) Marking of articles

Except as hereinafter provided, every article of foreign origin (or its container . . .) imported into the United States shall be marked in a conspicuous place as legibly, indelibly, and permanently as the nature of the article (or container) will permit in such manner as to indicate to an ultimate purchaser in the United States the English name of the country of origin of the article. The Secretary of the Treasury may by regulations—

(1) Determine the character of words and phrases or abbreviations thereof which shall be acceptable as indicating the country of origin and prescribe any reasonable method of marking, whether by printing, stenciling, stamping, branding, labeling, or by any other reasonable method, and a conspicuous place on the article (or container) where the marking shall appear;

(2) Require the addition of any other words or symbols which may be appropriate to prevent deception or mistake as to the origin of the article or as to the origin of any other article with which such imported article is usually combined subsequent to importation but before delivery to an ultimate purchaser; and

(3) Authorize the exception of any article from the requirements of marking if—

(A) Such article is incapable of being marked;

(B) Such article cannot be marked prior to shipment to the United States without injury;

(C) Such article cannot be marked prior to shipment to the United States, except at an expense economically prohibitive of its importation;

(D) The marking of a container of such article will reasonably indicate the origin of such article;

(E) Such article is a crude substance;

(F) Such article is imported for use by the importer and not intended for sale in its imported or any other form;

(G) Such article is to be processed in the United States by the importer or for his account otherwise than for the purpose of concealing the origin of such article and in such manner that any mark contemplated by this section would necessarily be obliterated, destroyed, or permanently concealed;

. . . . .

(I) Such article was produced more than twenty years prior to its importation into the United States;

. . . . .

(K) Such article cannot be marked after importation except at an expense which is economically prohibitive, and the failure to mark the article before importation was not due to any purpose of the importer, producer, seller, or shipper to avoid compliance with this section.

. . . . .

(f) Additional duties for failure to mark

If at the time of importation any article (or its container . . .) is not marked in accordance with the requirements of this section, and if such article is not exported or destroyed or the article (or its container . . .) marked after importation in accordance with the requirements of this section . . . , there shall be levied, collected, and paid upon such article a duty of 10 per centum *ad valorem*, which shall be deemed to have accrued at the time of importation, shall not be construed to be penal, and shall not be remitted wholly or in part nor shall payment thereof be avoidable for any cause. Such duty shall be levied, collected, and paid in addition to any other duty imposed by law and whether or not the article is exempt from the payment of ordinary customs duties.

. . . . .

(h) Penalties

Any person who, with intent to conceal the information given thereby or contained therein, defaces, destroys, removes, alters, covers, obscures, or obliterates any mark required under the provisions of this chapter shall—

(1) upon conviction for the first violation of this subsection, be fined not more than $100,000, or imprisoned for not more than 1 year, or both; and

(2) upon conviction for the second or any subsequent violation of this subsection, be fined not more than $250,000, or imprisoned for not more than 1 year, or both.

The law requires every article of foreign origin (or its container) to be marked at the time of importation in a *conspicuous place* as legibly, indelibly, and *permanently* as the nature of the article (or its container) will permit, in such manner as to indicate to an *ultimate purchaser* the *English name* of the *country of origin* of the article.

The marking requirement as stated above contains a number of italicized terms, each of which has special significance. These terms will be discussed below. However, the two most important things to keep in mind regarding country of origin marking are the following: (1) every imported article must be properly marked, unless there is a specific, identifiable exception, and (2) do not assume that the foreign manufacturer or seller is aware of the proper method of marking that is required.

From the importer's standpoint, it is best to assume that the foreign maker, seller, or shipper *does not* know how the goods should be marked. Proceeding on this assumption should accomplish two things. First, the importer will do what is necessary to ensure that the foreign party understands how the goods should be marked. Second, before the importer can instruct the foreign party in proper marking, the importer himself or herself will have to ascertain what marking is proper for the merchandise involved.

Proper country of origin marking should be a high priority for every importer. The cost of marking noncomplying goods after importation can completely eliminate any profit the importer might have made on the import transaction. Remember, to mark goods properly after importation, the goods will have to be unpacked, right down to the individual item to be marked. The marking must then be applied and the goods repacked. This is very costly. Moreover, the delay caused by this procedure will frequently result in lost sales, canceled orders, or ill-will on the part of the importer's customers.

The discussion offered here about marking is intended to give the reader some insight about Customs' current regulations on marking. It is not intended, however, to be a substitute for the importer actually ascertaining for himself or herself what may be required in any given instance. For this purpose, the importer should consult with his or her customs broker or directly with customs officers. In complex cases, the broker may prefer the importer to talk directly with Customs about this important matter.

Returning now to the law itself, the special meaning of the terms set out in italics above will be explored.

Marked in a *conspicuous place* means that the ultimate purchaser in the United States is able to find the marking easily and read it without strain. What is conspicuous on one item may not be conspicuous on another item and the meaning of this term will vary according to the type of merchandise involved. It has been held that a fabric label bearing the country of origin inserted into the side seam inside a handbag in a prominent place is conspicuous. Customs reasoned that a potential buyer would open the bag and inspect the inside before buying.

Permanently marked means that the marking is sufficiently attached to the article so that it will survive normal distribution and store handling and remain on the article until the time of sale to the ultimate purchaser, unless it is deliberately removed. Therefore, if the marking can fall off or become detached in the course of normal handling, it is not permanent enough to satisfy the law.

Some items such as knives, clippers, shears, scissors, surgical instruments, pliers, pincers, calculating devices, and vacuum containers, among others, are required by the Customs Regulations to be marked by die stamping, etching, engraving, molded-in lettering, or metal plates. The methods of marking watches, clocks, and timing apparatus are particularly intensive and require special attention. Many textile items also require permanently sewn-in fabric labels. Special marking is also required by the statute on pipes and fittings, compressed gas cylinders, and manhole frames and covers.

Aside from the special classes of goods mentioned above, which are a very small percentage of imported items, most things may be marked by ink stamping, stickers, or string tags.

The *ultimate purchaser* who must be able to find the marking means the last person in the United States who will receive the article in the form in which it was imported. For articles that are to be resold at retail, the retail buyer is the ultimate purchaser. For articles that are to be distributed as gifts or promotional items, the recipient is the ultimate purchaser. If an imported article is used in manufacture, the manufacturer may be the ultimate purchaser. However, if the manufacturing process is only a minor one that leaves the article's identity intact, the final user or consumer after manufacture is the ultimate purchaser.

The *English name* means the name of the country of origin as it is spelled in English, and not some foreign variant. While "Brasil" has been accepted for "Brazil," it is best to avoid foreign spellings. Abbreviations of names and adjectival forms of names, such as "Italian" for Italy, should not be used unless they have been specifically approved by Customs. With regard to the required wording or legend that must be shown on the imported item, the terms "Made in" or "Product of" are not required except in special circumstances. It is sufficient to show the country name—for example, "Taiwan."

The *country of origin* means the country of manufacture, production, or growth of an article. Further processing or materials added to an item in another country will not create a new country of origin for that item unless the item has been substantially transformed in the second country. For example, textile fabric manufactured in the bolt in country A, but pattern cut and sewn into apparel in country B, becomes a product of country B for country of origin purposes.

Putting geographic names of places other than the country of origin on imported items can create special problems for the importer. It is common for an importer to show his or her company name and its place of residence in the United States on an imported product or its packaging—for example, "XYZ Manufacturing Co., Columbus, Ohio." When this occurs, the Customs Regulations require the name of the country of origin to be shown in close proximity to, and in letters of at least the same size as, the words "Columbus, Ohio." Moreover, the country name in this circumstance must be preceded by words such as "Made in" or "Product of." This is true even if the name of the country of origin appears elsewhere on the product. Thus, a product otherwise properly marked must be specially marked a second time if it bears any geographic place name other than the country of origin and the first marking is not close nearby. If this requirement is not met, the goods are considered to be improperly marked as to country of origin, and the problems this creates are fully as costly as those presented by no marking at all.

There are limited exceptions to the above rule, and these involve words on souvenirs or the appearance of registered trademarks and trade names. It is best to follow the general rule, however, and either eliminate competing place names or get Customs' approval of the marking to be used in conjunction with other place names.

A special problem exists with regard to unmarked items imported in bulk for repacking after importation. An example would be small toy animals shipped hundreds to a carton, unmarked, and intended to be blister-packed for individual resale after importation. In this case, and in other cases involving repacking, the Customs Regulations permit a special procedure whereby the importer may file with the entry a repacker's certificate stating that the goods are to be marked at the time of repacking, prior to sale. It is always best to obtain Customs' approval of this procedure before it is implemented.

It is a violation of law for anyone other than the ultimate purchaser to remove intentionally the country of origin marking from an imported article. This includes not only the importer but anyone else in the chain of distribution. For example, goods are imported by wholesaler A and resold to retailer B for resale to the public. Neither wholesaler A nor retailer B may tamper with the country of origin marking. The law provides that any intentional removal, defacement, or alteration of country of origin marking in order to conceal such marking may result in criminal penalties up to $250,000 and/or imprisonment for up to one year.

Merchandise that is imported unmarked will be assessed marking duties equal to 10% of the appraised value of the goods if they are not exported, destroyed, or properly marked before the liquidation of the entry. These duties are in addition to the normal duties and apply even to goods that might otherwise enter duty-free. Note that the 10% duties apply to goods unmarked at liquidation of the entry, even though the goods may be properly marked thereafter by the importer. What constitutes liquidation of the entry is explained in chapter 4. The 10% marking duties apply also to marked items bearing other geographic place names not properly attended by the country of origin as discussed above.

When imported goods are found upon examination to be unmarked, Customs normally issues to the importer Customs Form (CF) 4647, entitled "Notice of Redelivery—Markings, Etc." Customs Form 4647 is shown in appendix C. This form serves two purposes. It advises the importer (1) to properly mark the goods within 30 days or (2) to redeliver the designated merchandise to Customs. Either alternative is acceptable to Customs. Failure to mark or redeliver within 30 days will result in the assessment of liquidated damages equal to the entered value of the unmarked goods, plus the estimated duties on those goods as shown on the entry. The liquidated damages may be demanded in addition to the 10% marking duties.

If the goods cannot be properly marked or redelivered within the allotted 30 calendar days, Customs will usually grant an extension of time to accomplish either if the importer has a sufficient reason for requesting the additional time.

Frequently, the notice (CF 4647) to the importer advising him or her that the goods are not properly marked is not received by the importer until several weeks after the goods have been imported. This naturally creates a significant problem for most importers because by then the merchandise has usually been distributed to their customers. The Customs Regulations require the demand for redelivery or marking to be sent not later than 30 days after the date of entry for goods that have been physically examined prior to release by Customs. The time during which the notice (CF 4647) may be sent for goods not physically examined may be extended somewhat if a request for a sample is issued to the importer no later than 30 days after the release of the goods by Customs. Nevertheless, any notice sent within these permissible time periods is likely to reach the importer after the goods have been disposed of. When this occurs, the importer has no alternative but to advise Customs that the goods are not available for marking or redelivery. The importer must then await the liquidated damages claim and petition Customs to reduce the amount of the claim.

In summary, importing unmarked merchandise can result in monetary claims for marking duties and liquidated damages totaling at least 110% of the FOB value of the merchandise. Both the marking notice (CF 4647) and liquidated damages are further discussed in Part II.

A number of items are excepted from individual marking under the law and Customs Regulations and may be imported in an unmarked condition, so long as the outermost containers in which they reach the ultimate purchaser are marked to indicate the country of origin.

First, there are the general exceptions to marking, of which the most common are the following:

1. Articles that are incapable of being marked—for example, small transistors, pumice stones, and candy pills

2. Articles that cannot be marked prior to shipment to the United States without injury—for example, small fasteners and cotter pins

3. Articles that cannot be marked prior to shipment to the United States except at an expense that would economically prohibit their importation

4. Articles for which the marking of the containers will reasonably indicate the origin of the articles—for example, wiping cloths, zippers, and tire valves

5. Articles that are crude substances—for example, bales of rubber

6. Articles imported for use by the importer and not intended for sale in their imported form or any other form—for example, evaluation samples

7. Articles to be processed in the United States by the importer or for his or her account otherwise than for the purpose of concealing the origin of such articles and in such manner that any marking put on the goods would necessarily be obliterated, destroyed, or permanently concealed—for example, videotape to be used in cassettes

8. Articles that were produced more than 20 years prior to their importation into the United States

9. Products of possessions of the United States—for example, Guam

10. Products of the United States exported and returned

11. Articles that cannot be marked after importation except at an expense that would be economically prohibitive unless the importer, producer, seller, or shipper failed to mark the articles before importation to avoid meeting the requirements of the law

Some comments regarding item 11 may be helpful. If an importer has received unmarked items and a notice of marking has been issued by Customs, the importer may, in proper circumstances, avail himself or herself of this exception to avoid the expense of marking the goods after importation. To receive an exception from marking under this provision, the importer must be able to demonstrate to Customs' satisfaction that the cost of marking the goods would be prohibitive. For example, if the imported items are valued at 10 cents per piece and the importer can show by specific cost estimates for materials and labor that it would cost 10 cents per piece to mark the goods, then Customs might in its discretion except that particular shipment only from marking. In the exercise of its discretion, Customs will normally consider whether the importer has had problems in the past with marking.

Another exception, previously mentioned, exists for goods that are to be repacked after importation. With Customs' permission, these goods or their resale containers may be marked at the time of repacking, after release from Customs custody.

Finally, an imported article used in the United States in manufacture that results in a second article having a name, character, or use differing from that of the imported article is considered to be substantially transformed in the United States. The manufacturer or processor in the United States who combines the imported article into the final article is considered to be the ultimate purchaser and these goods are excepted from marking. The most common example of this exception involves stuffed printed circuit boards. After importation, these boards are assembled into telephones, computers, or other devices. The resulting devices all have a name, character, or use differing from that of the imported stuffed boards. Since the U.S. assembler is considered to be the ultimate purchaser, the imported boards do not have to be marked with their country of origin, even though the boards do not lose their identity after assembly.

Where goods are excepted from marking in any of the circumstances discussed above, it is normally required that the immediate container or the outermost container, depending upon the goods, be marked to show the country of origin of the imported merchandise. This requirement, however, should present no unusual difficulty or expense.

What was said above regarding marking applies only to country of origin marking. Other federal agencies also have marking requirements that must be observed. For example, the Federal Trade Commission (FTC) has specific marking requirements for fur, wool, and other textile articles. The FCC has marking requirements for radio frequency devices. The Food and Drug Administration has requirements for marking of foods, cosmetics, drugs, and medical devices. For information regarding the marking required by other federal agencies, the importer should consult his or her customs broker or U.S. Customs.

Chapter 7

Recordkeeping and Inspection of Records by Customs

The Customs statutes regarding documentation, like the other laws that have been discussed, grant broad authority to the Customs Service to gain access to internal records of the importer relating to importations.

RECORDS REQUIRED TO BE KEPT BY THE IMPORTER

The recordkeeping statute is found in Title 19, United States Code, Section 1508, which provides as follows:

Section 1508. Recordkeeping

(a) Requirements.—Any owner, importer, consignee, or agent thereof who imports, or who knowingly causes to be imported, any merchandise into the customs territory of the United States shall make, keep, and render for examination and inspection such records (including statements, declarations, and other documents) which—

(1) pertain to any such importation, or to the information contained in the documents required by this chapter in connection with the entry of merchandise; and

(2) are normally kept in the ordinary course of business.

(b) Exportations to Canada

Any person who exports, or who knowingly causes to be exported, any merchandise to Canada shall make, keep, and render for examination and inspection such records (including certifications of origin or copies thereof) which pertain to such exportations.

(c) Period of time

The records required by subsection (a) and (b) of this section shall be kept for such periods of time, not to exceed 5 years from the date of entry, as the Secretary shall prescribe.

(d) Limitation

For the purposes of this section and section 1509 of this title, a person ordering merchandise from an importer in a domestic transaction does not knowingly cause merchandise to be imported unless—

(1) the terms and conditions of the importation are controlled by the person placing the order; or

(2) technical data, molds, equipment, other production assistance, material, components, or parts are furnished by the person placing the order with knowledge that they will be used in the manufacture or production of the imported merchandise.

(e) Failure to comply with subsection (b) requirements

Any person who fails to retain records required by subsection (b) of this section or the regulations issued to implement that subsection shall be liable to a civil penalty not to exceed $10,000.

The law requires that anyone who imports merchandise into the United States shall keep records pertaining to such importations and make these records available to customs officers for examination and inspection. This requirement applies to owners, importers of record, consignees, and those acting as their agents. This requirement extends also to a person ordering merchandise from an importer, if that person controls the terms and conditions of the importation or if that person provides items of production assistance, knowing that such assists will be used to produce imported merchandise.

The records required to be kept are determined by the extent to which any given party participates in the import transaction. Thus, a consignee, an owner, an importer of record, or an agent is responsible only for those records that he or she keeps in the ordinary course of his or her business. Any person required to keep records must keep them for a period of five years from the date of entry of the merchandise in question. For storage purposes, documents may be recorded on microfilm or microfiche.

Note that the law specifically requires all records relating to the exportation of merchandise to Canada to be retained by the exporter. Failure to retain such export documents as set forth in the law and regulations can result in a civil penalty up to $10,000. The provisions relating to exports to Canada were recently added to the statute in connection with the United States–Canada Free-Trade Agreement, which is discussed in chapter 12.

The types of records an importer might normally keep would include the following:

1. Purchase orders or contracts of purchase

2. Confirmations of orders

3. Shipping documents, that is, bills of lading or air waybills

4. Customs broker billings

5. Commercial invoices

6. Customs entries and related documents

7. Applications for financing the import transactions

8. Payment documents, such as checks, wire transfers, letters of credit, sight drafts, and bank advices

9. Correspondence, such as letters, telexes, and facsimile transmissions pertaining to the imported merchandise

10. Certificates relating to inspection, origin, or other matters

11. Buying or selling agents' commission statements

12. Contracts and payment documents relating to royalties and license fees

13. Invoices relating to the purchase of items of production assistance—for example, consigned components, tools, dies, and molds

14. Documents establishing the cost or value of development, engineering, or design work done outside the United States and used to produce the goods

15. Any other documents that pertain to the importation

The above are the sort of documents that must be retained for the five-year period required by law. To reiterate, the importer is not required to make or keep any records that he or she would not normally use in the course of his or her business.

By implication, all accounting records of a consignee, owner, importer of record, or agent would also pertain to importations. These accounting records would include state, federal, and other tax returns that are necessary to complete an audit trail or verify information contained in other records.

INSPECTION OF RECORDS BY CUSTOMS OFFICERS

There are several procedures used by customs officers to obtain access to the importer's books and records. These methods are distinguished by the level of formality associated with each. The most informal method may be referred to as access by mail. This method consists of mailing the importer a request for information or documents and awaiting a response by mail. These types of mail communications will be discussed more fully in Part II. The more formal procedures for gaining access to the importer's records are found in the law.

The statutory authority granting Customs the right to examine a party's own documents and interview witnesses is contained in Title 19, United States Code, Section 1509, which provides in pertinent part as follows:

Section 1509. Examination of books and witnesses
(a) Authority.—In any investigation or inquiry conducted for the purpose of ascertaining the correctness of any entry, for determining the liability of any person for duty and taxes due or duties and taxes which may be due the United States, for determining liability for fines and penalties, or for insuring compliance with the laws of the United States administered by the United States Customs Service, the Secretary (but no delegate of the Secretary below the rank of district director or special agent in charge) may—
    (1) examine, or cause to be examined, upon reasonable notice, any record,

statement, declaration or other document, described in the notice with reasonable specificity, which may be relevant to such investigation or inquiry;

(2) summon, upon reasonable notice—

(A) the person who imported, or knowingly caused to be imported, merchandise into the customs territory of the United States,

(B) any officer, employee, or agent of such person,

(C) any person having possession, custody, or care of records relating to such importation, or

(D) any other person he may deem proper, to appear before the appropriate customs officer at the time and place within the customs territory of the United States specified in the summons (except that no witness may be required to appear at any place more than one hundred miles distant from the place where he was served with the summons), to produce records . . . [required to be kept under section 1508 of this title] . . . and to give such testimony, under oath, as may be relevant to such investigation or inquiry; and

(3) take, or cause to be taken, such testimony of the person concerned, under oath, as may be relevant to such investigation or inquiry.

(b) Service of Summons.—A summons issued pursuant to this section may be served by any person designated in the summons to serve it. Service upon a natural person may be made by personal delivery of the summons to him. Service may be made upon a domestic or foreign corporation or upon a partnership or other unincorporated association which is subject to suit under a common name, by delivering the summons to an officer, or managing or general agent, or to any other agent authorized by appointment or by law to receive service of process. The certificate of service signed by the person serving the summons is prima facie evidence of the facts it states on the hearing of an application for the enforcement of the summons. When the summons requires the production of records, such records shall be described in the summons with reasonable specificity.

Note that the law, as stated above, contains two different procedures for examining records. The second method stated involves a summons; the first does not.

The first formal procedure used to gain access to the importer's books and records involves a visit by a customs officer to the premises of the importer or to the premises of any other custodian of records that need to be examined. The Customs Regulations provide that *any* customs officer may make an appointment with any party to examine books and records (1) to determine the correctness of any Customs entry; (2) to determine the liability of any person for duties or taxes; (3) to determine the liability of any person for fines, penalties, and forfeitures; or (4) to insure compliance with Customs laws and regulations.

The request for an appointment to examine documents at the importer's place of business may be made orally or in writing, but it must provide reasonable notice of the visit and a specific description of the records to be examined. The appointment must occur during normal business hours and, to the extent possible, at a time and date that is mutually convenient to the parties.

During the appointment to examine records, the customs officer may obtain written statements, take testimony, or take testimony under oath. If testimony is taken under oath, it must be transcribed and the official transcript made available to the witness for inspection.

The second formal method employed by Customs to gain access to records involves the issuance of an official summons. The law provides in general that a summons may be issued to any party who is legally required to keep records, as discussed above, or to any officer, employee, or agent of such person. The summons is issued by the Commissioner of Customs or someone designated by him for this purpose. However, no one below the rank of district director or special agent in charge is authorized to issue summonses.

A summons is always issued to compel the appearance of a person before a customs officer. The summons by law and regulation is required to state the following:

1. The time and date of the appearance
2. The address where the person should appear
3. The name, title, and telephone number of the customs officer before whom the appearance will take place
4. The name, address, and telephone number of the customs officer issuing the summons

In addition to requiring the appearance of a person, the summons may also require the person named in the summons to bring with him or her certain records specified in the summons. These records must be identified with reasonable clarity.

During the interview compelled by the summons, the customs officer may obtain written statements, take testimony, or take testimony under oath from the person summoned. Again, testimony under oath must be transcribed and the person providing testimony must be given an opportunity to inspect the official transcript.

JUDICIAL ENFORCEMENT OF SUMMONS

The law provides that any party who fails to comply with a summons properly issued may be compelled by an order of the court to respond to the summons. This authority is found in Title 19, United States Code, Section 1510, which provides as follows:

Section 1510. Judicial enforcement

(a) Order of court.—If any person summoned under section 1509 of this title does not comply with the summons, the district court of the United States for any district in which such person is found or resides or is doing business, upon application and after notice to any such person and hearing, shall have jurisdiction to issue an order requiring such person to comply with the summons. Failure to obey such order of the court may be punished by such court as a contempt thereof.

(b) Sanctions.— (1) For so long as any person, after being adjudged guilty of contempt for neglecting or refusing to obey a lawful summons issued under section 1509 of this title and for refusing to obey the order of the court, remains in contempt, the Secretary may—

(A) prohibit that person from importing merchandise into the customs territory of the United States directly or indirectly or for his account, and

(B) instruct the appropriate customs officers to withhold delivery of merchandise imported directly or indirectly by that person or for his account.

(2) If any person remains in contempt for more than one year after the date on which the Secretary issues instructions under paragraph (1) (B) with respect to that person, the appropriate customs officers shall cause all merchandise held in customs custody pursuant to such instructions to be sold at public auction or otherwise disposed of under the customs laws.

(3) The sanctions which may be imposed under paragraphs (1) and (2) are in addition to any punishment which may be imposed by the court for contempt.

If the party who receives a summons does not comply with any or all of its terms, the customs officer who issued the summons may request the appropriate U.S. attorney to seek a U.S. district court order requiring compliance with the summons. The person who received the summons may appear in court at the hearing to defend against the action and offer testimony regarding any defects in the summons.

The district court, after a hearing on the matter, may issue an order enforcing the summons. If the person fails to comply with the court order and, in addition, if the person is adjudged guilty of contempt, the Customs Service may prohibit importation of merchandise by that person, or for his or her account, and may withhold delivery of merchandise imported by that person, or for his or her account. Such actions may continue so long as the person remains in comtempt of court. Moreover, if a person remains in contempt for more than one year, the undelivered merchandise will be considered abandoned and must be sold at public auction or otherwise disposed of. In addition to the above sanctions, which are imposed by the Secretary of the Treasury, the court itself may impose any lawful sanctions of its own against the party adjudged to be in contempt.

From the foregoing, it is clear that the Customs Service has broad authority to examine any records that can reasonably be said to pertain to any importation of merchandise.

ORGANIZATION OF REQUIRED RECORDS

The Customs laws and regulations do not require that the necessary records be organized in any particular fashion. Organization is, however, a matter of some practical importance.

The declaration made by the importer on the entry and the obligation to disclose to Customs any errors found in the entry after the entry is filed have been discussed. As a practical matter, the importer will have no opportunity to discover any errors in the entry unless the entry is examined and audited by the importer after it is filed. The process of auditing a Customs entry involves verifying all essential information contained in the invoice and entry papers and confirming the correctness of the classification and all calculations leading to the determination of the total duties owing. The steps that should be involved in auditing an entry include the following:

1. Compare the unit values for each item as found on the purchase order, confirmation of order, contract, commercial invoice, and payment instrument to insure that the unit values on the invoice filed with the entry are correct.

2. Confirm that the quantities for each item shown on the invoice are correct based upon receiving reports or other information. Compare the invoiced quantity with the purchase order.

3. Confirm that the value extensions (price times quantity) on the invoice are correct and that the total invoice value is correct.

4. Examine the description of the merchandise to insure that the items have been properly classified and the correct duty rates applied.

5. Verify that all information relating to special invoicing requirements are present. Verify that all information relating to the extraordinary invoicing requirements has been set forth in the entry papers. Such items include packing, commissions, items of production assistance, royalties or license fees, and any other facts necessary to a proper classification and appraisement of the imported goods.

6. Verify the total entered value for each separate line classification shown on the face of the entry. Verify the correctness of the duty rate applied to each entered value on the entry. Verify the total entered value shown on the entry.

7. Verify the duty extensions (entered quantity or value times duty rate) on the entry and the addition of the duty extensions to reach the total duties owing.

Any reportable errors found during the audit should be made known to Customs in writing.

Although entry audits are necessary to fulfill a legal obligation to Customs, they serve equally important business purposes. Many errors may be made by the seller in invoicing the goods. These errors may be detrimental to the importer. If the seller overcharges for an item on the invoice, this error will be detected during the entry audit. If there is an error in a classification or rate of duty used on the entry, this will come to light during the entry audit. These types of errors can easily result in an overpayment of duties if they are not detected. If duties have been overpaid on any given entry, a refund can be requested. Thus, there are sound business reasons to audit Customs entries. The importer can fulfill his or her legal obligation to Customs and serve his or her own purposes at the same time.

Regarding the issue of organizing Customs records, it should be clear, first of all, that entries cannot be efficiently audited if the necessary documents are filed at different places throughout the importer's business organization. Accordingly, the first step is to get copies of all the necessary documents into one place. Once copies of all the necessary documents are brought together in one place, the actual filing arrangement can be left to trial and error.

A starting point that seems to make sense is to have the actual Customs entries filed sequentially by entry number, since this is always the manner in which an import transaction is referred to by Customs. Another logical step is to have all documents pertaining to any given entry in the same file as the entry itself, to the extent that this is practical. Some documents such as purchase orders or letters of credit may cover more than one entry. Therefore, the importer must decide whether to file these separately or make copies for each entry file. Experience is probably the best guide in determining these details.

It is also helpful to keep unliquidated entries filed separately from liquidated entries. This tends to focus some attention on the liquidation process itself and makes it readily apparent if the importer's entries are not being liquidated by Customs. Such division of entries makes sense because unliquidated entries are active entries and liquidated entries are inactive entries.

Importers can determine for themselves what filing system works best based upon the type of documents they have and how they conduct their business. The method of organizing physical documents may be greatly affected by the use of computerized information systems. In any event, the important thing to remember is that Customs records should be organized in a way that is helpful in achieving the goals of voluntary compliance.

Chapter 8

Troubleshooting Import Transactions

In the discussion of import entry audits in chapter 7, it was stated that the auditor should "verify that all information relating to the extraordinary invoicing requirements has been set forth in the entry papers. Such items include packing, commissions, items of production assistance, royalties or license fees, and any other facts necessary to a proper classification and appraisement of the imported goods." In the audit discussion, it was assumed that the person reviewing the entries had already identified all the reportable items that must be declared at the time of entry. However, none of the methods that can be used to identify those costs were discussed. The purpose of this chapter is to provide guidance on where to look to identify reportable costs that must be declared at the time of entry.

One of the reasons that many companies are not in compliance with Customs laws and regulations regarding the proper declaration of all reportable costs is that the information that must be reported to Customs resides in many different departments within the company. Some of the necessary information may be located in the purchasing department, some in the legal department, some in the accounting department, and some in the engineering department. Therefore, it is important to know where to look for information involving reportable costs and to know what type of information may be found at the various locations. This chapter will focus on the types of documents that should be reviewed to identify costs that are reportable to Customs. Various documents will be discussed more or less in chronological order, starting with the earliest document where information regarding reportable costs may appear. The first indication that a reportable cost might be incurred will be the presence of a provision for such costs in a foreign vendor contract for the production of imported goods.

Foreign Vendor Contracts

The first step is to ascertain what imported products are manufactured under written contracts with foreign vendors. The next step is to obtain copies of all such contracts. The last step is to review carefully and systematically each contract, along with all of the exhibits and other attachments. Any written amendments to the contracts also should be reviewed.

The contractual provisions to be identified are those that involve nonproduction payments or the accumulation of costs which usually escape the Customs entry and declaration process because they are not normally identified on the commercial invoice of the foreign vendor that is filed with the Customs entry. The provisions that most frequently involve reportable costs are tools, dies, molds, and test equipment; non-recurring engineering charges; currency adjustment payments; consigned components; and price adjustments based on volume of sales.

Tools, Dies, Molds, and Test Equipment. As discussed before, tools, dies, molds, machines, and similar items are used in the production of imported goods. The foreign vendor contract may provide that these items are to be purchased by the importer directly from the tool, die, mold, or machinery maker and provided free to the foreign vendor, or the contract may state that the foreign vendor is to procure these items and bill them separately to the importer. In either case, the payment for these items normally will not be reflected in the vendor's commercial invoice for the imported goods. Therefore, special care must be taken to declare these items separately on the Customs entries for the affected goods, or the entries involved will be legally deficient and may result in a loss of revenue to Customs.

In a like manner, items of test equipment may be provided to the vendor free of charge or purchased by the vendor and separately billed to the importer for use in producing imported goods. Equal care must be taken to ensure that these items are properly declared at entry. Test equipment may include in-circuit test fixtures, functional testers, test cables, and similar items. The examples below indicate the type of wording that might be found in the foreign vendor contract.

Examples of Contract Provisions for Tooling

Example 1

The tooling charges are $172,200.00, as quoted to Buyer. All tooling paid for by Buyer shall be the property of Buyer and shall be returned to Buyer upon Buyer's request, and at Buyer's sole expense. Buyer shall pay for all tooling in three (3) separate installments as follows: fifty percent (50%) upon placement of the purchase order; twenty-five percent (25%) upon completion of first shot, which for purposes of this agreement shall mean the first model or cabinet to come out of the tool; and, twenty-five percent (25%) upon Buyer's approval of final tool samples for production.

Example 2

Buyer shall release the tool purchase order within fourteen (14) days from the date of this agreement. Buyer shall pay to Seller tooling charges in accordance with the Tool List set forth below.

Tool List

Description	Tool Type	FOB Unit Price
1. Plate Detent	Press	$2,113
2. Card Guide, Panel	Mold	$2,689
3. Lever Print Gap	Press	$2,401
4. Keeper Clutch	Press	$960
5. Brkt, Carriage Mtg	Press	$3,361
6. Carriage	Mold	$7,011

Payment of the total amount of tooling charges shall be made in two installments which shall be the amount equal to 60% and 40% of the total amount as set forth above. The first of such installments shall be made within fourteen (14) days from the date of released purchase order; the second within fourteen (14) days after Buyer's approval of actual tooling sample. Each installment shall be made in U.S. Dollars by means of bankers' checks or telegraphic transfer.

Note that, in both the examples above, the foreign vendor is going to procure the tooling and bill the importer separately for these costs. The contract states how the payments for the tooling are to be made. It is obvious that these costs will not be amortized by the vendor and will not be included in the vendor's price for the goods produced with the tools.

Also note that in the second example the importer's purchase order for the tooling is to be issued within two weeks (14 days) from the date the contract is signed. This demonstrates that tooling must be ordered, bought, and usually paid for well in advance of the importation of the affected goods. If the contract is properly reviewed as soon as it is executed, the company has ample time to ensure that the tooling is properly declared at the time of entry of the affected goods.

Nonrecurring Engineering Charges (NRE). Foreign engineering (NRE) or foreign development of any kind, including foreign costs arising from engineering changes (ECs), are considered elements of production assistance. These costs form part of the dutiable value of the imported goods and must be separately declared at the time of Customs entry filing. As discussed before, several rules may be used to prorate the cost of these assists over the total number of units to be produced. Contract provisions regarding NRE may be worded as in the following examples.

Examples of Contract Provisions for NRE

Example 1

The nonrecurring engineering charges are $55,000.00 as quoted to Buyer. Buyer shall release a purchase order for nonrecurring costs within fourteen (14) days of the date of this agreement. Buyer shall pay nonrecurring costs in two (2) installments, 50% within fourteen (14) days of the released Purchase Order and 50% within fourteen (14) days after Buyer approval of tooling samples in Taiwan, as defined on "The Milestone Chart."

Example 2

Buyer shall bear the sole responsibility of providing seller technical drawings and documents. If modification, deletion, or addition of such drawings and documents are requested by Buyer and if such modification, deletion, or addition involves additional expense to Seller, Buyer shall be responsible for and bear such expense. The extent of such expense shall be determined in concert between Buyer and Seller in view of goodwill and mutual trust. Payment of such expense shall be made within thirty (30) days after receipt of invoice from Seller.

Again, both examples state or imply that the nonrecurring charges are to be paid for separately. In example 1, such charges were known to be $55,000 at the time the contract was drafted. In example 2, however, it was not clear that the additional foreign engineering expenses would actually be incurred. Nevertheless, the contract provides that any such additional expenses will be paid for by the importer. When a contract has a provision that is contingent upon later events, it is necessary to make inquiries of knowledgeable company personnel to ascertain whether the events occurred and whether any additional payments were made to the vendor under this clause. If so, the amounts involved must be determined and declared to Customs.

Currency Adjustment Payments. Foreign vendor contracts frequently fix the unit sales prices of the imported goods to the rate of exchange for the currency used in the country of production. For example, sales prices of goods produced in Japan are tied to the exchange rate for the yen, while sales prices of goods produced in Taiwan are tied to the exchange rate for the new Taiwan dollar (NT $). These currency provisions in the contract may require the importer to make additional payments to the vendor subsequent to the importation of the goods if the exchange rate varies adversely to the vendor during the relevant period of time specified in the contract. The additional amounts owed the foreign vendor will be billed by the vendor on separate invoices or on debit notes. Regardless of the method of billing, these additional payments for the goods are part of the price paid or payable and they must be disclosed to Customs by means of a *letter* filed with Customs for that specific purpose. Since these additional payments are usually made subsequent to the actual importations, the Customs entries never reflect the increased amounts paid for the merchandise.

If the exchange rate varies adversely to the importer, the vendor may be required to refund money to the importer. Refunds received by the importer from the vendor may result in a refund of duties by U.S. Customs if the proper steps are taken to advise Customs of the contract provision that led to the vendor refunds. Thus, currency adjustment provisions sometimes work to the importer's advantage. A contract provision for currency adjustments might read like the following example.

Example of Contract Provision for Currency Adjustment: Payments to Seller (Foreign Vendor) or to Buyer (Importer)

The prices quoted are based on a U.S. dollar/new Taiwan dollar exchange rate of 31 NT dollars to one (1) U.S. dollar. A price change will occur if the exchange rates fluctuate by more than $+2$ NT dollars as determined by a three (3) calendar month moving average. The impact of exchange rate fluctuations will be shared equally (50/50 split) by Seller and Buyer.

The following formula shall be applied each time the NT fluctuates above or below the base window.

1. If the NT goes below the base window:

$$\frac{31 - NT}{NT} \times \tfrac{1}{2} \times \text{Cost of Product (CP)} = \text{Payment to Seller}$$

2. If the NT goes above the base window:

$$\frac{NT - 31}{NT} \times \tfrac{1}{2} \times \text{Cost of Product (CP)} = \text{Payment to Buyer}$$

Notes:

1. Window is defined as 31 NT dollars + or − 2 to 1 U.S. dollar.
2. Cost of Produce (CP) is equal to current price of a given model.
3. NT is the rate of the new Taiwan dollar as determined by a three (3) calendar month moving average.
4. $\tfrac{1}{2}$ is used since Buyer and Seller will split the increase/decrease equally (50/50).

The unit sales prices are to remain as stated in the contract unless the three calendar month moving average exchange rate varies by more than two new Taiwan dollars on either side of 31 NT dollars to one U.S. dollar. This defines the window. If the average exchange rate stays within the range of 29 to 33 NT dollars to one U.S. dollar, no adjustment in the contract prices will occur. If the average exchange rate falls below 29 or advances above 33 NT dollars to one U.S. dollar, then the unit sales prices as stated in the contract will be adjusted. However, the total variance will be multiplied by one-half since the burden of the change is to be split (shared) equally by the seller and buyer. For example, where the average exchange rate has advanced to 36 NT dollars to one U.S. dollar, and the unit sales price (cost of product) is U.S. $300 each, the adjustment per unit would be computed as follows:

$$\frac{36 - 31}{36} \times \frac{1}{2} \times 300 = \$20.833 \text{ per unit is owed by the seller to the buyer}$$

Conversely, where the average exchange rate has fallen to 27 NT dollars to one U.S. dollar and the unit sales price is U.S. $250 each, the adjustment per unit would be computed as follows:

$$\frac{31 - 27}{27} \times \frac{1}{2} \times 250 = \$18.519 \text{ per unit is owed by the buyer to the seller}$$

This provision in the contract was well negotiated by the seller since it contains a bias in the seller's favor. A less biased formula would exist if the first term in each computation had been stated as follows:

$$1. \ \frac{31 - NT}{31}$$

$$2. \ \frac{NT - 31}{31}$$

The currency adjustment example above is more complicated than is necessary because it requires the calculation of a three-month moving average for the exchange rate. Many contracts simply state that the exchange rate actually used by the bank for conversion of transactions will be compared to the base rate to determine when adjustments become necessary. These comparisons occur on a shipment-by-shipment basis.

Currency adjustment payments are always contingent upon events that occur after the agreement is signed. Therefore, inquiries must be made to determine if any such payments have been made or received.

Consigned Components. Vendor contracts sometimes provide that the importer will make available to the manufacturer free of charge (no charge) special components of U.S. or foreign origin to be incorporated into the imported goods. The reason for consignment of such components may be that (1) they are proprietary to the importer (for example, special integrated circuits), (2) they are unavailable to the vendor in his or her own country, or (3) they are less expensive for the importer to purchase because the importer buys them in large quantities for many other products. There may also be other reasons why the components are consigned to the vendor.

Consigned components may be large items, such as cathode ray tubes (CRTs), or small subassemblies, such as printed circuit board assemblies. Regardless of the type of item, any physical material given to the foreign vendor, whether of U.S. or foreign origin, must be invoiced or declared at the time of entry because the cost or value of these items is considered to be part of the dutiable value of the imported goods. Failure to declare these materials properly may result in a loss of revenue to Customs. A typical contract provision for consigned components might read as follows.

Example of Contract Provision for Consigned Components

The following items have been denoted as being critical parts within the current printer mechanism. Initially, these items should be either purchased from current "source controlled" vendors or "drop shipped" to Seller by Buyer.

Description	Qty Per Asm	Current Vendor	Unit Std Cost
1. Rear Carriage Bearing	1	Baxter Bearing	$ 2.47
2. Shaft Bearing	2	Simpson Ind.	$ 0.109
3. Matrix Print Hd	1	BVI - Type 3	$42.00
4. Flat Cable	3.1 ft	Universal Cable	$ 3.17/ft
5. Horizontal Motor	1	Michigan Elec	$21.00

Again, it is not absolutely certain that the consignment mentioned in the contract will occur. However, since it might occur, the company must make note of those instances when it does occur and must determine the total value of consigned components that must be declared to U.S. Customs. In the example shown, the per unit value of possible consigned components might be as high as $75.515. If all these materials were incorporated into an article dutiable at 10%, and the materials were not properly declared, the loss of revenue to Customs would be $7.55 per unit.

Price Adjustments Based on Volume of Sales. Foreign vendor contracts sometimes contain a provision that permits sales to take place at certain unit sales prices, contingent upon the buyer (importer) achieving a target purchasing volume per year or an average volume per month. For example, the importer may purchase goods at $200 per unit, provided at least 12,000 units are purchased per year. In the event that the importer does not achieve this volume in any given year, the importer would be required to pay $225 per unit. The determination of the volume achieved and the amounts owing the seller, if any, would be reconciled at the close of the year. Under this arrangement, it is clear that any additional moneys paid per unit at the end of the year would have to be reported to Customs, since the original invoices filed with the Customs entries would have reflected the lower, estimated prices used during the year before the final appropriate price became known. An example of such a contract provision is shown below.

Example of Contract Provision for Volume Discount

PRICE SCHEDULE
The price per unit paid by the Buyer is to be determined by two components: a base price and a price discount.

BASE PRICE
The Base Price at the Effective Date of this agreement is shown in the table below.

Base Price at the Effective Date

Unit Monthly Volume	Price per Unit (U.S. Dollars)
1000-1999	125
2000-2999	113
3000-3999	109
4000-4999	105
5000-6999	103
7000-over	102

Price Discounts
Price discounts are based on volume. The volume discount will be determined by the aggregate volume that Buyer buys from Seller. The table above lists the price discount based on volume purchases. Buyer may purchase units at the expected discounted price over a twelve-month period. If at the end of the twelve-month period, Buyer does not achieve the expected average monthly volume for the price discount, Seller shall be compensated according to the following procedure. Seller shall provide Buyer with the Calculated Difference defined as the difference between the total charges for the units based on the actual average monthly volume over the previous twelve-month period and the purchased price. The Calculated Difference shall be reimbursed to Seller within 45 days of receipt by Buyer. The twelve-month period shall start at the Effective Date of this agreement.

The contract example shown above permits the buyer to establish his or her own price for units purchased throughout the year based upon the average monthly volume he or she anticipates achieving over a one-year period. To the extent that the buyer's volume falls short of original expectations, he or she must pay the seller the difference at year's end.

The costs and additional payments discussed above are frequently not declared by importers because the company employees responsible for Customs compliance do not have routine access to new foreign vendor contracts for review purposes. The easiest way to prevent problems in this area is to identify these types of provisions in the foreign vendor contract as soon as it is executed by the company. This means that the upper management of the company must ensure that new contracts entered into with foreign vendors are made available to the company employees who are responsible for Customs compliance. Since contracts are involved, the upper management in this case would be the general counsel, the outside legal department, or those management officials who are authorized to sign foreign vendor contracts. When proper review of these contracts is permitted, immediate steps can be taken to ensure that the necessary declarations are made when the affected goods are imported, entered, and duty paid with U.S. Customs.

Capital Expenditure Authorizations

If production by a foreign vendor will require the importing company to make large expenditures for capital equipment, it is normal for the company to have a procedure whereby these types of anticipated costs may be recorded in a special document whose purpose is to keep the company management advised of major future expenditures. These future capital expenses are recorded on a document that is sometimes called an Authorization for Expenditure (AFE). Alternatively, this document may be called a Capital Expenditure Request (CER). Depending upon the company, other names may be utilized to identify this document. Since these types of records are used to document anticipated capital expenditures, the most likely kinds of reportable costs that will be mentioned in them will be tools, dies, molds, test equipment, production machinery, and other expensive production-related goods. The AFEs and CERs are normally numbered and kept sequentially in a logbook. The logbook can be reviewed periodically to ascertain whether any of the capital equipment listed will be used by foreign vendors to manufacture merchandise to be imported into the United States. The documents themselves will frequently have notations or remarks indicating that the capital equipment is destined for a particular foreign vendor. Of course, capital equipment to be used for domestic production will also be recorded in these logs, so care must be taken to identify only those capital expenditures that relate to foreign-produced merchandise. If an item of production equipment is identified, but it is not clear from the expenditure document where the goods will be produced, inquiries can always be made of others in the company to ascertain whether the equipment will be used domestically for production or overseas for production. In addition, if it is determined that the equipment will be used overseas, further information must be obtained to determine whether the equipment constitutes an assist within the meaning of the Customs law. If it is determined that the equipment is or will be an assist, then steps must be taken to ensure proper reporting to U.S. Customs.

Purchase Orders

Purchase orders are used in many large companies to order goods and services from vendors. Purchase orders often prove fruitful in revealing the existence of reportable charges that probably would escape proper declaration at the time of entry. Equipment and parts ordered from a company located in the United States for delivery in the United States to the company or one of its subsidiaries are normally presumed to be unrelated to Customs transactions. However, certain information shown on a purchase order may indicate that the items ordered are (1) components to be consigned to a foreign vendor for use in an imported product or (2) test equipment, tools, dies, or molds to be used offshore in the production of imported merchandise.

Where remarks or other information on the purchase order indicate that components are to be sent to a foreign vendor, there is an inference that the purchased materials may be used in the production of merchandise that will be imported. The purchase order, for example, may indicate that the domestically produced merchandise is to be drop-shipped to a specific foreign vendor. Purchase orders issued to U.S. vendors may indicate that tools, molds, dies, test equipment, or machinery will be shipped to a foreign location. This also raises an inference that these items might be used overseas to produce imported merchandise. Whenever an inference arises that purchased goods might be an assist, it is necessary to obtain additional information that is sufficient to reach a reasonable conclusion that such goods are not assists. In other words, where something might be an assist, the company has a legal obligation to Customs to satisfy itself that the item is not an assist, based upon a diligent inquiry.

Documents that are enclosed in the purchase order files or attached to the purchase orders should also be examined to determine whether any information indicates that the items ordered may be used by a foreign vendor. By and large, only a small percentage of purchase orders issued to domestic vendors will be related in any way to foreign production.

Purchase orders issued to foreign entities may be issued directly to a foreign address or issued to a subsidiary of the foreign entity located in the United States. When equipment and parts are ordered from foreign entities, there is a presumption that the merchandise will be shipped to the United States and properly entered through Customs as imported product. Again, however, there may be notations on the purchase orders or on documents attached to the purchase orders that indicate that the goods ordered are consigned components, test equipment, molds, or tooling related to imported merchandise. Where components or production equipment are ordered from one foreign vendor for shipment to another foreign vendor, there is an inference that the components or equipment may be used by the receiving foreign vendor to produce merchandise that may be imported into the United States. Where such an inference exists, it is necessary to establish that the components or equipment are not assists.

Purchase orders issued to foreign vendors may also identify freight costs relating to consigned components or charges for the modification or repair of tooling or other production equipment. As is known from the discussion of appraisement, such costs would be reportable to Customs if they relate to items used in the production of imported goods.

The above discussion involves the review of "hard copy" purchase orders. In large companies, purchase orders are often entered into computer files. Inquiries should be made to ascertain what periodic reports are printed from the computerized files. Reviewing data printouts of these files will probably be a more cost-effective way of reviewing the necessary information, provided the printout contains the pertinent facts. If not, special reports can be generated for this purpose.

Export Documentation

All companies that export merchandise to foreign countries are required to file Shipper's Export Declarations (SEDs) at the time the goods are exported. Therefore, all exporting companies have export records available for review.

All merchandise exported to a customer of the company is presumed to represent product sales. Materials exported to a foreign entity that is a source or vendor for imported goods cannot be presumed to be product sales unless that vendor is also a customer. Therefore, company export records should be reviewed to ascertain whether materials are being shipped to vendors who produce goods that are imported by the company. When such exports are identified, there is a presumption that the materials exported are being used to produce imported merchandise. Diligent inquiry is therefore necessary to establish that the exported materials are not assists.

Vendor Invoices

Reviewing vendor invoices is also a fruitful way to identify charges or costs that must be reported to Customs. Companies retain and file paid vendor invoices in many different ways. In some instances, all the invoices from one vendor may be retained in one file, or the company may batch invoices from many vendors in one file based on the date those invoices were paid. The difficulties encountered in reviewing vendor invoices are largely the result of the manner in which they are filed.

As with purchase orders, vendor invoices must be considered in two categories. The first category includes invoices from U.S. vendors for equipment and parts. Equipment and parts purchased from domestic vendors are presumed to be used by the company or its subsidiaries in the United States, unless remarks or other information on the vendor invoice indicates that the merchandise was shipped to a foreign location. When this occurs, further inquiry must be made to ascertain why the invoiced goods were shipped to a foreign country. If it is determined that the invoiced items are assists for Customs purposes, then steps must be taken to declare them properly to Customs.

The second category includes invoices from foreign vendors for materials, equipment, and parts. Materials, equipment, and parts shown on foreign vendor invoices will also be presumed to have been imported and duty paid. Again, however, notations on the foreign vendor's invoice may indicate that the invoiced goods were shipped to another foreign location or that the invoiced goods were used by that vendor himself or herself to produce other imported goods. An invoice for tooling from a foreign company that is a vendor for imported goods most likely represents an assist for the imported goods. In these situations, inquiries must be made to ascertain whether the invoiced goods are assists for Customs purposes.

Vendor Payment Records

Some companies maintain separate computerized records of payments made to all vendors with whom the company does business. Again, the vendors to whom payments are made may be domestic vendors or foreign vendors. In many instances, these payment records contain notations to indicate what the payment to the vendor was for. For example, the computer printout may indicate that a specific product was purchased, or it may contain notations such as "Tooling," "NRE," "Test fixture," "Royalty," or "License fee." Thus, the notations in these vendor payment records may help to identify payments that should be further investigated to determine whether or not the costs are reportable to Customs in connection with imported merchandise.

Debit Notes

In addition to vendor invoices, some companies maintain separate files relating to debit notes. Debit notes are much like invoices and require a payment to be made to the company that issues them. While invoices may cover both large and small charges, debit notes are frequently used to request payment for cost items of a minor nature. Nevertheless, if debit notes are received and paid by the company, they should be reviewed to see whether they reflect any reportable costs relating to imported merchandise. A cautionary word about debit notes is appropriate. Experience indicates that when a company receives and pays debit notes, very few people will know that they exist. In fact, most people asked will say that the company has never received any debit notes because they are unaware of them. Some persistence is needed to find these documents if they do exist. The effort, however, is usually well rewarded because debit notes issued by foreign vendors almost always reveal unreported dutiable charges.

If the company uses the services of a foreign buying agent, debit notes may be issued to the company by the foreign buying agent for costs related to imported goods. Some of these costs may be reportable to Customs.

Accounting Records

Company employees who are responsible for Customs compliance should gain a detailed knowledge of the company's accounting system and the records that are maintained by the accounting department. Employees in the accounting department who are knowledgeable regarding the complete chart of accounts of the company may be helpful in identifying those accounts that would be likely to contain charges that should be reported to the Customs Service. For example, tooling, test equipment, production machinery, and other reportable costs may be found in the company's fixed asset register. Or there may be specific account numbers for items such as tooling, royalties, or license fees.

If the company buys imported merchandise from a related foreign entity, such as a subsidiary, or if the company uses the services of a related foreign buying agent, questions should be asked of accounting personnel to determine whether the company has any "intercompany" accounts. Small items of cost that may be reportable to Customs can be identified in the intercompany accounts used with related foreign vendors or related foreign buying agents. These intercompany accounts are usually maintained in a way that makes them susceptible to easy review.

Accounting personnel should also be questioned regarding what types of cost accounting records exist with regard to the company's products. Where cost accounting documents exist for imported goods, the detail or backup work papers for these records may indicate the presence of costs not directly attributable to the foreign producer. For example, the accounting may show in the cost buildup the payment of royalties or license fees to other parties, as well as the payment to other parties for tooling or consigned components.

Engineering Records

If the company has an engineering department, it is often useful to discuss with engineering personnel their knowledge of the products manufactured by foreign vendors. Engineers are more likely than others in the company to be aware of the use of consigned materials in imported products. Engineering personnel will also be more aware of the existence of engineering charges paid to foreign companies.

Inquiries can be made of engineering personnel to determine whether there are bill of materials (BOM) records which are maintained for imported products. Notations on a detailed BOM for an imported product may reflect the existence of consigned material that has been purchased in the United States or in a foreign country other than the country where the goods are produced. BOM records for imported products can be discussed with engineers who are knowledgeable regarding the procurement sources for all the materials shown on the BOM.

In summary, the documents and records discussed above are all sources of information that can be used to identify assists and other appraisement-related costs that must be reported to the U.S. Customs Service in connection with imported merchandise. In most cases, these sources will not provide all the information that is necessary to make a proper declaration or disclosure to Customs regarding the reportable items. Normally, the documents and records discussed above serve as only a starting point to identify situations that require further investigation. However, these sources are excellent for bringing to light reportable costs that might otherwise go unnoticed by the department or the employees who are responsible for Customs compliance. It will frequently be the case that payments or costs, once identified, will require much painstaking research in order to obtain all the relevant information. In this regard, it is sometimes necessary to speak with employees in many different departments in order to gain a complete and accurate set of facts. However, this is the only way to ensure that the company's import transactions are properly reported to the Customs Service.

Finally, it should be noted that many items of cost related to imported goods will be identified or found more than once. For example, tooling charges mentioned in a foreign vendor contract may also appear in an AFE, CER, or other capital expenditure authorization. In most cases, the company will also issue a purchase order to a foreign vendor for the same tooling. That vendor in turn will issue an invoice for the tooling, and the payment of the vendor's invoice will be reflected in the company's vendor payment records. The same cost may appear many times, and care should be taken not to report the same cost to Customs more than once.

Also keep in mind that some of these documents will reflect estimated costs, while others will show actual costs. For example, the vendor contract, the AFE, and the purchase order will state estimated or anticipated costs for tooling and other items. The final costs for these items may be more or less than estimated. Therefore, it is important to substantiate the final amounts paid by locating later associated documents, such as vendor invoices or vendor payment records, which show the actual amounts paid for the items identified on the previous documents.

Chapter 9

Methods for Achieving Customs Compliance

The laws relating to invoicing, entry, and declaration entail the three most important obligations that an importer has to the Customs Service and they represent the areas of difficulty that result in the greatest number of problems for importers. Associated with the failure to meet these legal obligations are substantial civil penalties assessed by the Customs Service. Therefore, every importer's attention should be focused on ways in which Customs compliance may be achieved.

CUSTOMS COMPLIANCE IN GENERAL

How difficult it is for any given importer to gain a relative degree of compliance depends on several factors. The volume of Customs transactions will affect the degree of effort that is required on the part of the importer. Small importing companies, or large companies with few Customs transactions, will find it relatively easy to meet their legal obligations to report all import-related costs. On the other hand, a company with a large monthly volume of Customs transactions will find it more difficult to maintain a good compliance posture. Large companies or corporations may experience added difficulties where many different departments within the company have some role in either generating reportable costs or gathering information with regard to those costs. In these situations, achieving Customs compliance can become a formidable task.

Whether a company is small or large, success in achieving Customs compliance depends largely upon commitment and organization. It is necessary that the management of the company understands the need for Customs compliance and accepts the responsibility to ensure that compliance is achieved. In a small importing company, the necessary commitment might come from the owner of the company. In large companies, the commitment to Customs compliance must be made by corporate officers. These would include the president, the general counsel, the chief financial officer, or the controller. It is important that the acknowledgment of legal obligations is made at this level within the company because the efforts necessary to maintain acceptable compliance will require the commitment of resources within the company. Unless corporate officers stand behind the company's legal obligation to comply with the Customs laws, sufficient resources to accomplish this goal will normally not be committed. Where inadequate resources are committed to compliance by the importing company, the company's efforts will usually fall short of the mark.

It should come as no surprise that there is a cost associated with a high level of compliance. Company officers must ensure that sufficient authority is delegated to those employees who are chosen to be responsible for achieving compliance. It is necessary to see that those employees have at their disposal the cooperation of all the departments involved in resolving the problem. As mentioned before, these departments may include accounting, engineering, manufacturing, purchasing, and legal. It is also necessary to ensure that adequate resources such as clerical personnel and management information systems personnel are available to assist the responsible employees in searching files and documenting reportable charges.

What cost is required to achieve Customs compliance is largely dependent upon the degree of organization that is brought to the task. Although there may be many complexities to be dealt with, a proper analysis of the problem areas can result in the development of organized procedures for ensuring the proper reporting to Customs of all import-related costs. Different companies have different Customs problems. Depending upon the industry a company is in and the products it imports, a company will have problems unique to itself. Its problems will also vary in accordance with the way in which it conducts its business. These factors will result in one importer having a certain well-defined cluster of Customs problems, while another importer has a completely different set of concerns. Nevertheless, a careful analysis of each company's situation will reveal those areas where special procedures must be developed to ensure that Customs requirements are met. Once the necessary procedures are in place, compliance can be maintained on a cost-effective basis.

In summary, Customs compliance can be achieved only where upper management of the company (1) recognizes the legal obligations involved in importing, (2) makes a management commitment to comply with those legal obligations, and (3) provides the necessary resources to ensure that the job is carried out.

SPECIFIC METHODS FOR REPORTING COSTS TO CUSTOMS

There are different methods by which import-related costs can be reported to the Customs Service. Such costs may be reported (1) on the entry at the time of entry filing or (2) after entry by a specific letter or submission made to Customs. Which of these methods is used will depend largely upon the types of costs to be reported. The methods of reporting and the types of costs associated with each method will now be examined.

Declaration of Costs at the Time of Entry Filing

As discussed before, the importer is required by various laws to report all import-related costs for each shipment at the time the entry for the merchandise is filed. This method of declaration is desirable for those costs that are associated with a specific shipment or those costs that are known well enough in advance of entry to permit proper declaration. Examples of costs associated with each specific shipment are buying commissions and consigned components. Buying commissions are normally calculated on each shipment based on the value of the shipment. Therefore, the precise amount of commission payable is known at the time of entry of the goods. Little effort should be required to ensure that the proper commission is declared on the Customs entry. By the same token, the identity and value of any consigned materials incorporated into the imported goods at the time of manufacture is known when the merchandise is packed, ready for shipment to the United States. Therefore, there should be no difficulty in declaring these assists at the time of entry.

Other types of costs are not shipment specific but are known well enough in advance of entry filing to permit a proper declaration on the entry documents. Examples of these costs are tooling and foreign engineering. Since both tooling and foreign engineering must be utilized by the vendor to produce the merchandise, these costs are known a sufficient time in advance of entry to permit a proper determination of the value per unit to be declared. The importer, therefore, should encounter no difficulty in making the necessary declarations at the time of entry filing.

With regard to shipment-specific and known costs that are reportable to Customs, it is necessary to communicate to the customs broker the procedures that the importer wants the broker to follow. In this regard, the importer must provide specific instructions to the broker to ensure that the costs required to be reported on the entries are so reported. Because the legal obligation for reporting these costs rests upon the importer, it is important always to give the customs broker the entry instructions in writing. These instructions should be specific as to the amounts to be added at entry for each product or for each invoice. The importer should also ensure when he or she audits the entries received from the broker that the instructions given have been carried out. It is essential that there are clear communications between the importer and the customs broker regarding the exact manner in which the merchandise and related costs are to be declared at the time of entry.

Declaration of Costs after Entry by Disclosure Letter

Certain costs required to be reported to Customs are never known, or are not sufficiently known, in advance of entry to permit a proper declaration. Costs that must be declared after entry fall into two categories. First, there are those costs that will never be known at the time of entry because the costs are always incurred well after entry. Examples of these costs are currency adjustment payments, volume discount adjustment payments, and payment of royalties or license fees, where those fees are determined based on sales of products in the United States. Since the information needed to calculate these costs is never available until after the Customs entry has been filed, there is no alternative but to report these matters to Customs subsequent to entry.

Second, there are costs that either may not be known at the time of entry or may be known so shortly before entry that the required facts are not available to determine the appropriate amounts to be declared. These types of costs are usually unanticipated and not sufficiently documented at the time of entry to permit proper declaration. For example, a tool repair or modification may be approved verbally by the importer because the cost is small. The actual cost of such repair or modification is not readily identifiable until the vendor's invoice arrives and is paid. This will usually occur subsequent to the importation of the goods.

Costs associated with production emergencies are usually not verifiable until some time after the importation of the merchandise. If a material shortage develops and the importer is required to consign materials by air shipment to the vendor on an emergency basis, the information necessary to ensure proper reporting of costs may not be available when the goods arrive. This could result from uncertainty regarding which importations contain the consigned materials.

Another example is emergency engineering work that is required to correct a malfunction in the goods to be imported. Again, the response to this emergency may be quick, but the information regarding the actual costs involved may take time to develop. Therefore, these costs are ordinarily reported to Customs after filing of the entries for the goods.

Disclosures after entry are normally made to the Customs Service in the form of a letter addressing the specific costs involved.

Declaration of Costs by Periodic Report

As identified above, three types of costs must be reported to Customs: (1) costs known or anticipated at the time of entry, (2) costs that are never known at the time of entry, and (3) costs that may be known at the time of entry but whose exact value cannot be determined until later. Costs known or well anticipated at the time of entry must always be declared on the Customs entry. Since there is no reason for these costs not to be reported on the entry, it is usually unacceptable to report them after entry. On the other hand, Customs will normally entertain various proposals for the reporting of costs that are never known at the time of entry or costs that may be known but whose value cannot be readily ascertained.

Where a company encounters a large number of costs that are required to be reported subsequent to entry, it is frequently desirable that the company institute a periodic reporting procedure after discussion and approval by U.S. Customs. Having to make frequent reports of specific costs after entry can become time-consuming and inefficient. In addition, it is not necessarily cost-effective for the Customs Service to have to process numerous individual letters of explanation regarding the various costs being reported by the company in accordance with its legal obligations. Therefore, it may be in the best interests of the company and the Customs Service to develop jointly and agree upon a procedure whereby the company submits a periodic report to Customs containing all the items of cost incurred during a certain period. Since the Customs Service desires that all importers make reasonable attempts to meet their reporting obligations, Customs has proven to be very flexible in approving various proposals for the reporting of import-related costs. Periodic reporting of costs when permitted may occur on a quarterly basis or semiannually, depending upon the volume of transactions to be reported and the particular expectations of local district customs officers. Where periodic reports are to be used, there must be an agreement reached between the importer and the Customs Service as to the time of submission and the method of preparation of the reports.

If Customs is willing to entertain the submission of periodic reports from the importer, the scope of the items included in those reports may be, with Customs' permission, expanded to include certain costs that might normally be required to be reported at the time of entry. These costs are not shipment-specific costs, such as buying commissions and consigned components, but would be costs such as tooling, dies, molds, production machinery, and test equipment. Since these costs are not shipment specific but must be prorated in some manner in order to be declared at the time of entry, efficiency would suggest that the necessary declarations could occur as well on the periodic report as upon the individual entries. This has the benefit of lessening the importer's and customs broker's burden of reporting these costs on each entry. Moreover, the reporting of these items on periodic reports makes it unnecessary for Customs to review each entry to ensure that the cost has been added.

In practice, a company may agree with Customs to report at the end of one calendar quarter all reportable costs identified in the previous quarter. For example, the importer would agree to aggregate and to show on one report on June 30 all costs arising during the period January 1 to March 31 of that year. The costs shown on the report would either be duty paid with the report or carried forward to a subsequent period during which the charge would become dutiable. For example, tooling charges may be reported for the quarter in which paid, but no duty would be tendered with that report because no goods utilizing that tooling were imported. The amount so shown could be carried forward and duty paid in that quarter in which the affected goods are first imported.

Where periodic reports to Customs are utilized, a check for the appropriate amount of duties owing will normally be tendered with each report. This ensures that money owed to the Customs Service, while not received necessarily at the time of entry, is received within a short time thereafter. Customs, of course, will review each quarterly report as it is submitted and ask for any clarifications necessary.

There are significant advantages to reporting costs to Customs on a periodic basis. First, costs can be declared completely on one report without the need to set forth the same information on multiple entries. Second, the periodic report is a convenient vehicle for the declaration of those costs that, while clearly nondutiable, must nevertheless be reported. Nondutiable royalties and engineering undertaken in the United States do not have to be duty paid but must be disclosed to Customs. The periodic report provides an easy method for the presentation of this information to Customs. In addition, where the importer is in doubt whether a specific cost must be reported to Customs at all, that cost may be shown on the report with a notation that the importer believes such cost to be nondutiable. This relieves the importer from having to decide what information and facts U.S. Customs deems necessary to a proper classification and appraisement of the merchandise, a difficulty inherent in the invoicing law itself.

Finally, a good faith effort to report all costs to Customs on a periodic basis shows that the importing company takes its legal obligations seriously. Moreover, once periodic reporting has been undertaken by the company, there is less likelihood that the company and its future managers will relax the compliance effort.

HELPFUL THINGS TO KNOW ABOUT IMPORTING MERCHANDISE INTO THE UNITED STATES

Part I discussed topics that all importers must know to understand customs officers, what they do in their own particular jobs, and how imported merchandise is processed. Also explored in some depth were the major legal obligations the importer must satisfy to avoid costly problems with U.S. Customs. Part II will examine concepts and laws that are useful to know in order to communicate better with Customs, to reduce or avoid duty payments, and to obtain duty refunds under certain circumstances. Part II will also discuss what uses may be made of Customs warehouses and foreign trade zones and how an importer or other party may obtain written rulings which are binding on the Customs Service.

Chapter 10

Communications between U.S. Customs and the Importer

There are some fairly experienced importers who have never actually talked to anyone at U.S. Customs. In fact, many importers seem reluctant to communicate directly with the import specialist who processes their Customs entries. However, it is helpful for the importer to have some understanding of the way in which communications occur between the Customs Service and the importer. Certain types of specific communications, which are routinely directed to the importer by Customs, and what these communications mean will be discussed. Some general situations that give the importer an opportunity to develop a rapport with the customs officers who are responsible for processing the importer's goods will also be discussed.

SPECIFIC COMMUNICATIONS DIRECTED TO THE IMPORTER

Customs officers are required to make hundreds of decisions every day in the performance of their jobs. Many of these decisions involve the amount of duties that are owing on imported merchandise. These decisions are therefore important not only to Customs but to the importer. Most decisions made by customs officers are based solely upon information contained in the entry documents. There inevitably comes a time, however, when the documents do not contain sufficient information to permit a sound decision being made.

To obtain the further information it needs, Customs has certain forms that it sends to importers. By properly reviewing these forms and by properly responding to them, the importer can assist Customs and insure that the correct decisions are made regarding his or her imports.

The three forms most frequently received by importers directly from Customs are the Request for Information (Customs Form 28), the Notice of Action (Customs Form 29), and the Notice of Redelivery—Markings,

Etc. (Customs Form 4047). All of these forms have designated spaces that are filled in by Customs to identify the importer's transaction. Although not all of the items shown below necessarily appear on each form, the items listed are the types of identifying information Customs provides to the importer:

1. Date on which the request or notice is prepared by Customs
2. Importing carrier (vessel, airline, train, or truck)
3. Date of importation
4. Date of entry
5. Entry number
6. Name of manufacturer, seller, or shipper
7. Country of origin or country of exportation
8. Customs broker name and file reference number
9. Description of the merchandise
10. Name and address of the importer
11. Customs address where the response should be sent
12. Name and telephone number of the customs officer who issued the form

The items of information listed above will permit the importer to identify the specific import transaction to which Customs is referring. The name and telephone number of the customs officer who issued the form, as shown in item 12 above, is of special significance. This name and number are provided in the hope that the importer will telephone the customs officer to clarify any questions the importer may have regarding the notice or request.

The Request for Information

In the discussion of recordkeeping requirements, it was indicated that the most informal method of obtaining the importer's records could be referred to as "access by mail." The Request for Information (Customs Form 28) is the form used for this purpose. This form is shown in appendix D. The form contains a number of spaces where the customs officer may put a check mark to indicate the documents he or she would like submitted or the questions he or she would like answered. The documents and specific questions that the customs officer may choose are set forth below with the block number in which they appear on the form.

12A. Are you related in any way to the seller of this merchandise? If you are related, please describe the relationship, and explain how this relationship affects the price paid or payable for the merchandise.

12B. Identify and give details of any additional costs/expenses incurred in this transaction, such as:

   1. Packing

   2. Commissions

   3. Proceeds that accrue to the seller

   4. Assists

   5. Royalties and/or license fees

13A. Copy of contract, purchase order, or seller's confirmation covering this transaction, and any revisions thereto.

13B. Descriptive or illustrative literature or information explaining what the merchandise is, where and how it is used, and exactly how it operates.

13C. Breakdown of component materials or ingredients by weight and the actual cost of the components at the time of assembly into the finished article.

13D. Submit samples as indicated (article number and description).

13E. See item 14 below.

In addition, there is a large blank space in block 14 which may be used by the customs officer to elaborate on any of the information or documents requested. In block 14 the customs officer may also pose other questions or ask for documents not listed on the form, such as copies of letters of credit or payment documents. In block 15 there is a large blank space that is available for the importer's reply. In block 16, the importer must certify that the information furnished with or on the form is true and correct and that any samples provided were taken from the shipment covered by the entry designated. The importer then signs and dates the form and provides his or her title and telephone number.

The questions numbered 12 obviously relate to the appraisement law as previously discussed. Specifically, Customs is trying to ascertain whether the parties are related for Customs purposes. Also, question 12B is an attempt to identify the items of cost that may be added to the price paid for the merchandise under transaction value.

Item 13A requests that certain documents be submitted. By responding to this item, the importer has effectively provided documents and information from his or her books and records. The other items in block 13 primarily relate to information required to classify the imported merchandise.

It is important to realize that Customs would not issue the Request for Information unless there was a need to have the information to assist in classification or appraisement of the merchandise.

The Notice of Action

Another form that is frequently issued by Customs to the importer is the Notice of Action (Customs Form 29). This form is shown in appendix E. The Customs Regulations require that the importer be notified of any action taken by Customs that will result in an increase of duties of $15 or more. The Notice of Action form is designed as a convenient way for Customs to advise the importer of a duty increase, along with an explanation of why the increase is occurring. In block 12 on this form, Customs may indicate one of the two following conditions regarding the action it is taking:

1. Is *proposed*. If you disagree with this proposed action, please furnish your reasons in writing to this office within 20 days from the date of this notice. After 20 days, the entry will be liquidated as proposed.
2. Has been *taken*. The entry is in the liquidation process and is not available for review in this office.

The next section on the form indicates the type of action being taken by Customs. The items that may be specified to explain the duty increase are:

1. Rate advance
2. Value advance
3. Excess in weight or quantity
4. Other (see 13 below)

There is a large space in block 13 for an explanation of any of the matters referred to above. For example, if the action is a duty rate advance, Customs will specify in block 13 the tariff classification and rate of duty used originally on the entry and the tariff classification and rate of duty that Customs is contemplating using. By the same token, the form will indicate in block 13 the reason for any increase (advance) in the appraised value of the merchandise.

It is important to understand the difference between an action that is proposed and one that has been taken. If Customs marks the action as proposed, it is indicating one of two things. First, the customs officer may be 99% certain that the action is correct, but he or she wishes as a matter of courtesy to provide the importer with the opportunity to object to the action proposed. Of course, any objection to the proposed action must be provided within 20 days. Second, the customs officer may not be absolutely certain of the correctness of his or her decision but issues the notice trusting that the importer will provide the necessary information to support a different decision. If the form is marked to indicate that the action has been taken, there is no uncertainty on the part of the customs officer regarding the correctness of his or her decision.

The basic purpose of this form is to advise the importer that a change in classification or value will occur and that the estimated duties tendered at the time of entry filing are incorrect. The form thus indicates that there will be increased duties due in the form of a Customs bill which the importer will receive after liquidation of the entry. It is imperative that the importer carefully review any Notice of Action as soon as it is received from Customs. If the importer does not agree with any actions proposed, he or she should advise the customs officer of the reasons for disagreement.

The Request for Information and the Notice of Action are frequently used in conjunction with one another. When no response is received to a Request for Information, Customs usually has no choice but to issue a rate advance or value advance on a Notice of Action. This is but an example of the need to protect the revenue. If the importer fails to respond to the Notice of Action, an unpleasant chain of events can ensue. The actual sequence of events occurs as follows:

1. Customs issues a Request for Information.

2. The importer fails to respond to the Request for Information, either because he or she does not understand the form, it is misplaced, or it goes to the wrong department in the company.

3. Customs issues a second Request for Information regarding the same matter.

4. The importer again fails to respond to the Request for Information for any of the reasons shown in 2 above.

5. Customs then issues a Notice of Action to increase the duties on the shipment in question, with the goods being classified or appraised at the highest rate or value that might apply, given the lack of information to the contrary.

6. The importer receives the Notice of Action and fails to reply, either because he or she does not understand the meaning of the form, the form goes to the wrong person or department in the company, or the form is inadvertently filed by someone.

7. Customs liquidates the entry with an increase in duties as proposed in the Notice of Action.

8. The importer receives the increased duty bill which may be for a substantial amount of money.

9. The importer becomes extremely agitated at the prospect of having to pay the Customs Service a substantial amount of additional duties.

10. The importer contacts his customs broker or Customs directly to inquire, "What is this all about?"

11. The importer is advised by the customs broker or by Customs itself that Requests for Information were issued, followed by a Notice of Action, and that

none of these forms drew any response from the importer. As a result, the importer is advised that he has no alternative but to file a formal protest within 90 days after liquidation.

The above scenario is extremely unfortunate because a proper response to the first Request for Information would have saved considerable time and aggravation, not only for the Customs Service but for the importer as well. The importer described above is forced to file a protest to avoid paying duties that he or she might not have had to pay if he or she had provided the information requested by Customs in the first place. There is also the possibility that the importer, for one reason or another, will miss the filing date for the formal protest and, as a consequence, will have to pay the increased duties, even though those duties might not have been assessed if the importer had provided the necessary information.

In order to avoid the problems discussed above, it is important for the importer to respond properly when a Request for Information is received. In addition, any Notice of Action received from Customs should be examined to ascertain what response is expected by Customs or what response on the importer's part would be helpful in changing the customs officer's mind regarding the proposed action.

Notice of Redelivery—Markings, Etc.

The Notice of Redelivery—Markings, Etc. (Customs Form 4647) was discussed earlier with country of origin marking requirements. This form is shown in appendix C. The form is designed to notify the importer when the imported merchandise is not properly marked with the country of origin or with some other labeling or marking requirement that is indicated on the form. The form contains the following specific instructions:

TO IMPORTER—Redelivery is hereby ordered of the following shipment for the reason stated above. Deliver to Customs all merchandise which has been released to you under the terms of the entry bond. This shipment can not be released unless brought into conformity with the statute indicated. Articles not returned or properly marked within 30 days of this notice become liable for liquidated damage.

These instructions require that the goods be marked in a certain way to bring them into compliance with the law that is checked or indicated on the form. If the merchandise cannot be properly marked, then it must be redelivered to the Customs Service as required by a provision in the Customs bond. If the goods are not properly marked or redelivered, a Notice of Liquidated Damages will be issued to the importer for failure to comply with a term in the Customs bond.

The next set of instructions contained on the form is the following:

You are authorized to mark the merchandise at a place other than the public stores. When marking is accomplished complete certification below and return both copies of this form [with or without a marked sample, as indicated] to this office. Merchandise must be held until marking is verified or notification received that marking is acceptable.

These instructions require that the imported shipment be held intact at the importer's premises and not released or distributed into commercial channels until Customs has sent someone to verify the marking on the merchandise or until the form itself has been signed by Customs to indicate that the certified marking has been accepted. Therefore, the importer must do nothing with the goods until they have been marked and until the marking has been verified by Customs or certified as being acceptable. The shipment must be held until the form itself is signed at the bottom by a customs officer and dated.

With regard to the instruction that the merchandise must be held, it is important to understand that the shipment must be held intact and segregated from other merchandise of a similar nature. If the shipment is not segregated from other merchandise, it will not be possible for the visiting customs officer to identify the merchandise in question from other merchandise. Therefore, the customs officer will not be able to verify that the goods in question have been marked.

After the goods have been marked by the importer, there is a space on the form to be completed by him or her certifying that the goods have been properly marked. After signing the form, the importer returns both copies to Customs.

The importer should not certify that the merchandise has been properly marked before he or she is absolutely certain that the marking has been completed. Customs often does, in fact, send someone to verify the marking on the goods shortly after the form is returned, signed by the importer. All to frequently, the visiting customs officer discovers that the marking of the merchandise is still in progress. When this occurs, the certification signed by the importer is considered to be a false certification and the importer is subjected to monetary penalties for filing a false certification with Customs.

The Notice of Redelivery—Markings, Etc. (Customs Form 4647) is also used for purposes other than marking. In some instances, imported merchandise may be considered inadmissible unless certain documentation requirements are met. When Customs Form 4647 is used for this purpose, Customs will set forth the precise nature of the actions that must be taken by the importer to remedy the legal deficiency. Again, the instructions typed on the form by Customs should be followed explicitly.

A Word of Advice about All of the Forms Discussed Above

Each of the forms discussed above is important to Customs for different reasons. If this were not so, Customs would not take the time to send them. As indicated previously, one of the things common to the forms is that each contains a space for the customs officer to show his or her name and telephone number. Often importers attempt to respond to one of the forms without completely understanding the nature of the information requested (CF 28), the nature of the action proposed to be taken by Customs (CF 29), or the nature of the legal deficiency with the marking or the documents submitted with the entry (CF 4647). If there is anything about the form that the importer does not completely understand, he or she should call the office of the customs officer shown on the form and request a clarification of the action that must be taken. Calling Customs for a clarification is a simple thing to do. Ultimately, this can save the Customs Service and the importer a great deal of time. Customs officers prefer that the importer call and request a clarification, rather than submit information or take action that is unresponsive to the notice or request issued.

COMMUNICATIONS WITH CUSTOMS IN GENERAL

It is helpful to the importer to become acquainted with the personnel at Customs who are responsible for processing his or her entries. It is also helpful to the customs officers who handle the goods to become personally acquainted with the importer's personnel who are responsible for insuring Customs compliance.

Some importers, as a matter of routine, take time to introduce themselves to Customs personnel at a port that they will be using for the first time. Although this is not strictly necessary, such introductions do facilitate later communications between Customs and the importer. Other opportunities will present themselves to the importer to communicate directly with customs officers. The importer may solicit the opinion of customs officers regarding classification, marking, or matters of appraisement. The importer may be contemplating making some change in his or her import procedures or in the method by which he or she pays for the imported goods. Usually it is helpful to question customs officers regarding the impact that such changes may have. These types of communications between the importer and Customs Service personnel permit the development of a certain rapport whereby each becomes more comfortable in communicating with the other. The mutual trust that can be engendered by this relationship is helpful in resolving problems as they arise or in preventing problems before they arise.

HOW TO AVOID THE PROBLEM OF DISAPPEARING MAIL

Importers with large business organizations frequently encounter the problem of disappearing mail. As indicated earlier, it is important that the proper actions be taken when Customs forms are received. It is important that protests be filed in a timely manner if a Customs bill is received and the importer wants to object to the reason for the duty increase. However, it is apparent that the proper actions cannot be taken if the forms and bills mailed to the importer do not reach the proper people within the importer's organization.

The notices and forms mailed by Customs arrive with all the importer's other mail. As a consequence, those handling the mail may misdirect the forms, bills, or notices to the wrong department within the organization. Customs mail, therefore, becomes lost, inappropriately filed, or even discarded because the person handling it does not understand what it means. As a consequence, many things can go awry for the importer.

One solution to this problem is for the company to obtain a post office box at a nearby postal facility and have the customs broker use the post office box number as the official address on all entries filed with the Customs Service. When this is done, all communications issued by the Customs Service, whether bills, refunds, Requests for Information, Notices of Action, marking notices, or any other legal matter, will be sent directly to the post office box. Those in the company responsible for handling Customs matters may pick up this mail directly from the box and be absolutely certain of receiving all the correspondence issued by Customs to the importer.

Chapter 11

How U.S. Customs Redresses Its Wrongs

This chapter will examine what happens to the importer and his or her merchandise when something goes wrong and Customs discovers that the importer is not in voluntary compliance with the law. The procedures employed by the government against the importer can be extremely serious, as in the case of imprisonment or forfeiture of merchandise. Other, less drastic consequences may involve the payment of substantial fines and penalties. In any event, none of the proceedings discussed below is particularly pleasant. Knowledge of these matters, however, may encourage the importer in his or her efforts to comply voluntarily with the Customs laws and regulations.

CRIMINAL PROSECUTION

The criminal code of the United States provides that serious violations of Customs laws may be punishable by fines, imprisonment, or both. For example, the criminal law that prohibits the importation of merchandise by means of false statements provides that the importer may be punished by a fine up to $5,000, or imprisonment for up to two years, or both. Other examples of acts that may be punishable under the criminal laws are the following:

1. Entry of goods for less than legal duty
2. Illegal relanding of exported goods
3. Smuggling goods into the United States
4. Illegally removing goods from Customs' custody
5. Filing false claims for refunds of duties
6. Concealing or destroying invoices or other papers

Violations of Customs laws usually are not criminally prosecuted for one of two reasons. First, a violation, though clearly criminal in nature, may be minor or involve a small amount of money. The government in these cases usually foregoes criminal prosecution because it has bigger fish to fry. Second, many violations that may appear criminal in nature are difficult to prove because of the government's burden of showing the necessary intent to violate the law. During a criminal prosecution of a person for a violation of law, the government has the burden of proving beyond a reasonable doubt that the person had the necessary intent to commit the crime. This is generally referred to as the defendant's mental state at the time of the commission of the objectionable act. In the absence of evidence sufficient to convince a jury of the person's intent, it is very difficult to obtain a conviction under the criminal laws. In these cases, the government normally resorts to civil penalties as a means of punishment.

It is possible, however, for a person to be criminally prosecuted and subjected to civil penalties for the same act. Subjecting a party to both criminal and civil proceedings does not constitute double jeopardy, which is constitutionally prohibited. Moreover, a person who is criminally prosecuted and acquitted at trial of a criminal act may nevertheless be subjected to civil penalties for the same act. This is because the level of proof required on the part of the government is different in civil cases. In criminal proceedings, the government must prove "beyond a reasonable doubt" all the elements of the crime. This is the highest standard of proof. In civil proceedings, however, the government is only required to prove its case either by "clear and convincing evidence" or by the lesser standard known as "the preponderance of the evidence." For this reason, the person acquitted at trial in a criminal case may nevertheless be punished by civil penalties.

CIVIL PENALTIES

Although there are many laws that specify monetary penalties for Customs violations, the most commonly used statute is Title 19, United States Code, Section 1592. Frequently referred to as the "fraud" statute, this law nevertheless provides monetary penalties for merely negligent behavior as well as for intentional fraud. At the outset, it is important to know that moneys paid as Customs penalties are not tax deductible business expenses.

Recently, the American subsidiary of a large Asian industrial concern agreed to pay the U.S. Treasury $34 million in settlement of civil penalties arising from violations of the Customs law and regulations. About ten years ago, the American subsidiary of a large European industrial concern paid $5 million in lost duties and $20 million in civil penalties for Customs violations. Obviously, civil penalties can become a significant cost of doing business. Although these are extreme cases, Customs penalties of $100,000 and more are common, even for small and medium-sized companies.

Prohibited Acts under Section 1592

The penalty statute most commonly invoked by U.S. Customs is found in Title 19, United States Code, Section 1592. The prohibited conduct, contained in section (a) of the law, is set forth below:

Section 1592. Penalties for fraud, gross negligence, and negligence
(a) Prohibition.—
  (1) General rule.—Without regard to whether the United States is or may be deprived of all or a portion of any lawful duty thereby, no person, by fraud, gross negligence, or negligence—
    (A) may enter, introduce, or attempt to enter or introduce any merchandise into the commerce of the United States by means of—
      (i) any document, written or oral statement, or act which is material and false, or
      (ii) any omission which is material, or
    (B) may aid or abet any other person to violate subparagraph (A).
  (2) Exception.—Clerical errors or mistakes of fact are not violations of paragraph (1) unless they are part of a pattern of negligent conduct.

The law provides that monetary penalties may be assessed against anyone who enters merchandise into the United States by means of any document, statement, or act that is false and material. The act may consist of a material omission or failure to do something. Also, a document may be considered a false document if it fails to state some essential fact. A document, statement, act, or omission is *material* if it has the potential to alter the classification, appraisement, or admissibility of merchandise or the liability for duty. For example, if a shipment contained 400 dozen sweaters, but the invoice presented to Customs showed only 200 dozen sweaters, the invoice would be false and the falsity would be material because the value of the shipment would be understated. Hence, there would be a loss of revenue. On the other hand, a shipment of green sweaters that was invoiced as yellow sweaters would also involve a falsity, but the falsity would not be material because the misdescription would not affect the admissibility or classification of the goods or the duty owing on the merchandise.

The prohibited act or omission may be done intentionally or through negligence only. It makes no difference that the prohibited act or omission did not cause the government to lose any duties or revenue, since monetary penalties are provided for nonrevenue violations.

Section 1592 applies also to anyone who aids or abets another person to commit the prohibited acts. Clerical errors and mistakes of fact, however, are not subject to penalties unless such errors or mistakes result from a pattern or habit of negligent conduct. Clerical error means an error in the preparation, assembly, or submission of a document that results when a person intends to do one thing but does something else. It includes, for example, errors in transcribing numbers, errors in arithmetic, and the failure to assemble all the documents in a record. Mistake of fact means an action based upon a belief by a person that the material facts are other than they really are. A fact may exist but is unknown to the person, or the person may believe something is a fact when in reality it is not.

Some examples of conduct subject to monetary penalties are the following:

1. A person intentionally misdescribes merchandise on the invoice in order to obtain a lower duty rate (intentional conduct, potential loss of duties)

2. On *ad valorem* merchandise (that is, dutiable by value), a person intentionally invoices a false, lower value for the goods (intentional conduct, potential loss of duties)

3. A person negligently fails to invoice or declare the cost of materials or components given free to the manufacturer (negligent conduct, potential loss of duties)

4. A person negligently fails to invoice or declare a commission paid to a true buying agent (negligent conduct, no loss of duties)

These examples represent both intentional conduct (fraud) and negligent conduct (negligence), as well as revenue violations and nonrevenue violations.

Maximum Penalties under Section 1592

The maximum penalties that may be imposed against those who engage in prohibited conduct are contained in section (c) of Title 19, United States Code, Section 1592, as set forth below:

(c) Maximum penalties.—
    (1) Fraud.—A fraudulent violation of subsection (a) of this section is punishable by a civil penalty in an amount not to exceed the domestic value of the merchandise.
    (2) Gross Negligence.—A grossly negligent violation of subsection (a) of this section is punishable by a civil penalty in an amount not to exceed—

    (A) the lesser of—
       (i) the domestic value of the merchandise, or
       (ii) four times the lawful duties of which the United States is or may be deprived, or
    (B) if the violation did not affect the assessment of duties, 40 percent of the dutiable value of the merchandise.
  (3) Negligence.—A negligent violation of subsection (a) of this section is punishable by a civil penalty in an amount not to exceed—
    (A) the lesser of—
       (i) the domestic value of the merchandise, or
       (ii) two times the lawful duties of which the United States is or may be deprived, or
    (B) if the violation did not affect the assessment of duties, 20 percent of the dutiable value of the merchandise.

The maximum penalties that may be assessed under the law depend upon (1) the importer's degree of fault and (2) whether or not there is any loss of duties to Customs. The importer's degree of fault is usually referred to as the level of culpability.

The law recognizes three different degrees of fault or culpability. They are negligence, gross negligence, and fraud. A violation is determined to be negligent if the act or omission results from a failure to exercise reasonable care and competence in ascertaining the facts, in ascertaining the offender's obligations under the law, or in communicating information so it may be understood by the recipient. As a general rule, a violation is determined to be negligent if it results from the offender's failure to exercise reasonable care and competence to ensure that a statement made is correct.

A violation is determined to be grossly negligent if the act or omission is done with actual knowledge of, or wanton disregard for, the relevant facts and with indifference to, or disregard for, the offender's obligations under the statute.

A violation is fraudulent if the false statement, act, or omission was committed knowingly, that is, was done voluntarily and intentionally, as established by clear and convincing evidence. The intent that must be established is the intent to deceive, to mislead, or to convey a false impression.

In addition to the degree of fault, the maximum penalty also depends upon whether or not there is a loss of duties to the Customs Service. Thus, there are penalties for revenue violations (loss of duties) and nonrevenue violations (no loss of duties). The six possible penalties, along with the maximum amount permissible for each, are set forth in Table 11.1

The term "domestic value" used in Table 11.1 technically means the price at which the merchandise involved in the violation is freely offered for sale in the United States at the time and place of appraisement and in

Table 11.1
Maximum Penalties

	Revenue Violation	*Nonrevenue Violation*
Fraud	The domestic value of the goods	The domestic value of the goods
Gross Negligence	The domestic value or four times the loss of duties, whichever is less	40% of the FOB value of the goods
Negligence	The domestic value or two times the loss of duties, whichever is less	20% of the FOB value of the goods

the quantity imported. As a practical matter, the domestic value of imported merchandise normally ranges between 1½ and 2½ times the FOB purchase price of the goods.

From Table 11.1 it can be seen that the penalties permitted under section 1592 are fairly substantial, even for negligent violations, which involve the smallest degree of fault. By way of example, the maximum penalty that can be levied against an importer who negligently fails to declare a commission paid to a true buying agent (that is, a nondutiable commission; hence, no loss of revenue) would amount to 20% of the FOB value of the goods.

The Customs Service may go back five years in time and consider all entries filed by the importer for the last five years in determining the loss of duties or the value of the imported merchandise for the purpose of calculating penalties. For this reason, even negligence penalties may amount to tens of thousands of dollars.

Maximum Penalties under Section 1592 after Prior Disclosure

The importance of the "prior disclosure" provision, which reduces the amount of penalties importers must pay if they voluntarily disclose to the Customs Service any violations they may find on their own, has been discussed. The law provides for substantially reduced penalties in any case where the importer provides notice to Customs in writing concerning the circumstances of a violation that has occurred. The provision for prior (voluntary) disclosure is contained in section (c)(4) of Title 19, United States Code, Section 1592, as follows:

(c) (4) Prior Disclosure.—If the person concerned discloses the circumstances of a violation of subsection (a) of this section before, or without knowledge of, the commencement of a formal investigation of such violation, with respect to such violation, merchandise shall not be seized and any monetary penalty to be assessed under subsection (c) of this section shall not exceed—

(A) if the violation resulted from fraud—

    (i) an amount equal to 100 percent of the lawful duties of which the United States is or may be deprived, so long as such person tenders the unpaid amount of the lawful duties at the time of disclosure or within thirty days, or such longer period as the appropriate customs officer may provide, after notice by the appropriate customs officer of his calculation of such unpaid amount, or

    (ii) if such violation did not affect the assessment of duties, 10 percent of the dutiable value; or

(B) if such violation resulted from negligence or gross negligence, the interest (computed from the date of liquidation at the prevailing rate of interest applied under section 6621 of Title 26) on the amount of lawful duties of which the United States is or may be deprived so long as such person tenders the unpaid amount of the lawful duties at the time of disclosure or within 30 days, or such longer period as the appropriate customs officer may provide, after notice by the appropriate customs officer of his calculation of such unpaid amount.

The person asserting lack of knowledge of the commencement of a formal investigation has the burden of proof in establishing such lack of knowledge.

The law states that if the importer discloses a violation before Customs has begun a formal investigation of the importer or if the disclosure is made by the importer without any knowledge on his or her part that Customs has begun a formal investigation, then goods involved in a violation may not be seized and the importer is entitled to a reduction in the penalties that may be assessed. Where the importer has made a valid prior (voluntary) disclosure, the maximum penalties that may be levied are set forth in Table 11.2.

Table 11.2
Maximum Penalties After Prior Disclosure

	Revenue Violation	Nonrevenue Violation
Fraud	One times the loss of duties	10% of the FOB value
Gross Negligence	The interest on the loss of duties	No penalty
Negligence	The interest on the loss of duties	No penalty

There is no question that the amounts shown in Table 11.2 represent a dramatic reduction in the penalties assessable for violations of Customs laws and regulations. For deliberate, fraudulent revenue violations, the penalty is at most one times the loss of duties resulting from the violation. Moreover, for both types of negligent violations, the largest penalty is the interest owing on the loss of revenue during the period it was due. The interest rate used may vary, but in recent years it has been about 10%. In addition, for negligent violations with no loss of revenue, there is no penalty whatsoever. Note that the reduction in penalties is contingent upon the violator tendering to Customs any lawful duties owing within the prescribed times. Failure to pay the loss of revenue in a timely manner could jeopardize the legal status of the disclosure and, hence, the reduction in penalties, which could revert to the higher statutory maximums discussed previously.

In order for a prior disclosure to be valid, the violator must make the disclosure to Customs before Customs begins a formal investigation of the violation (that is, before Customs finds out about it or suspects it). Testing the validity of a disclosure on this basis is referred to as the objective standard. A prior disclosure may still be valid, however, even if Customs has initiated a formal investigation, if at the time the disclosure is made, the violator had no knowledge that Customs had begun a formal investigation of the violation. Testing the validity of a disclosure on this basis is referred to as the subjective standard. Naturally, a person who asserts lack of knowledge of a formal investigation has the burden of proving such lack of knowledge.

Because of the significant reduction in penalties, importers are encouraged to report to the Customs Service any violations that they might discover on their own in their import transactions. Care should be taken, however, in making a prior disclosure because certain formalities must be observed. For example, the letter sent to Customs disclosing the violation must:

1. Identify the class or kind of merchandise involved in the violation
2. Identify the importations included in the disclosure by entry number or by indicating each Customs port of entry and the approximate dates of entry
3. Specify the false statements, acts, or documents or the omissions made
4. Specify the true and accurate information or data that should have been provided in the entry documents

In addition to the above, the disclosure to Customs must be accompanied by a check for any loss of duties owing. If the loss of duties cannot be determined at the time of disclosure, it must be determined and the duties tendered within 30 days of the initial disclosure or within such reasonable extension of time as the district director may permit.

Providing Customs with a response to a Request for Information form, as discussed above, does not constitute a prior disclosure because it does not meet the formalities of such a disclosure as set forth above.

Another precaution that must be observed before a prior disclosure is made involves additional, but undisclosed, violations. Whenever a prior disclosure is made, the district director must, by regulation, refer the matter to the local Office of Enforcement for the commencement of a formal investigation of the importer. During the course of this investigation, any violations that are found and that are not included in the prior disclosure are subject to the normal statutory penalties and not to the reduced penalties associated with disclosed violations. For example, an importer who discloses only the existence of unreported buying commissions may be subject to additional regular penalties if the investigating agent discovers the existence of unreported production assistance (assists). Therefore, it is imperative for the disclosing party to perform a complete audit of his or her import transactions to ensure that all possible violations or infractions are included in the initial disclosure to Customs.

In summary, the prior disclosure provisions of the law and Customs Regulations have been instituted to encourage honesty on the part of the importing public and to assist customs officers in the performance of their jobs.

Penalty Procedures under Section 1592

The procedures that Customs must follow when imposing the penalties permitted by section 1592 are stated in section (b) of Title 19, United States Code, Section 1592, as set forth below:

(b) Procedures.—
   (1) Pre-penalty notice.—
      (A) In general.—If the appropriate customs officer has reasonable cause to believe that there has been a violation of subsection (a) of this section and determines that further proceedings are warranted, he shall issue to the person concerned a written notice of his intention to issue a claim for a monetary penalty. Such notice shall—
         (i) describe the merchandise;
         (ii) set forth the details of the entry or introduction, the attempted entry or introduction, or the aiding or procuring of the entry or introduction;
         (iii) specify all laws and regulations allegedly violated;
         (iv) disclose all the material facts which establish the alleged violation;
         (v) state whether the alleged violation occurred as a result of fraud, gross negligence, or negligence;

      (vi) state the estimated loss of lawful duties, if any; and, taking into
account all circumstances, the amount of the proposed monetary
penalty; and

    (vii) inform such person that he shall have a reasonable opportunity to
make representations, both oral and written, as to why a claim
for a monetary penalty should not be issued in the amount stated.

  (B) Exceptions.—The preceding subparagraph shall not apply if—

      (i) the importation with respect to which the violation of subsection
(a) of this section occurs is noncommercial in nature, or

    (ii) the amount of the penalty in the penalty claim issued under
paragraph (2) is $1,000 or less.

(2) Penalty claim.—After considering representations, if any, made by the
person concerned pursuant to the notice issued under paragraph (1), the
appropriate customs officer shall determine whether any violation of
subsection (a) of this section, as alleged in the notice, has occurred. If such
officer determines that there was no violation, he shall promptly issue a
written statement of the determination to the person to whom the notice
was sent. If such officer determines that there was a violation, he shall issue
a written penalty claim to such person. The written penalty claim shall
specify all changes in the information provided under clauses (i) through
(vi) of paragraph (1)(A). Such person shall have a reasonable opportunity
under section 1618 of this title to make representations, both oral and
written, seeking remission or mitigation of the monetary penalty. At the
conclusion of any proceeding under such section 1618, the appropriate
customs officer shall provide to the person concerned a written statement
which sets forth the final determination and the findings of fact and
conclusions of law on which such determination is based.

The law provides that before a penalty claim may be issued against a
party, Customs must provide the party with a pre-penalty notice
indicating the intention of the Customs Service to issue a monetary
penalty. The notice to the importer must:

1. Describe the merchandise
2. Set forth the details of the improper entry or attempted entry of the
   merchandise (entry numbers and dates of entry)
3. Specify all laws and regulations allegedly violated
4. Disclose all facts necessary to show that a violation has occurred
5. State the level of culpability as fraud, gross negligence, or negligence
6. State the estimated loss of duties and the amount of the proposed penalty
7. Inform the party of his or her right to make oral and written representations to
   show why a monetary penalty should not be issued

A pre-penalty notice as specified above is not necessary where the merchandise involved in the violation is noncommercial in nature (for example, goods imported for personal use and not for resale) or where the penalty contemplated is $1,000 or less. In these cases, the monetary claim may be made in the penalty notice, without the need to issue a pre-penalty notice.

After the issuance of the pre-penalty notice, the importer is given 30 days within which to respond and to set forth any information bearing upon the alleged violations. During this period of the administrative proceeding, Customs will examine any representations made primarily to determine whether or not there is still cause to believe that a violation has been committed. If the importer cannot convince the Customs Service that no violation has been committed, then a penalty demand (claim) will be issued to the importer.

The penalty demand will normally repeat the information contained in the pre-penalty notice, but Customs can make changes to the allegations or penalty amount as a result of the importer's response to the pre-penalty notice. After the issuance of the penalty claim, the importer is given an additional 30 days within which to submit a written statement or petition setting forth whatever facts might serve to reduce the amount of the loss of revenue claimed or to mitigate the amount of the penalty owing. The importer may also request a meeting with customs officers to make oral representations regarding the penalty claim. Normally, oral presentations are permitted only after a written petition is filed. However, any customs officer who is empowered to review and to act on petitions may, in his or her discretion, permit an oral presentation at any stage of the proceedings.

After receipt of the violator's written petition, the appropriate customs officer will review and analyze the claims and arguments for mitigation or relief set forth in the petition. During the course of this review, the customs officer looks for the existence of (1) mitigating factors, (2) aggravating factors, and (3) extraordinary factors justifying further relief. The presence or absence of these factors will be considered, and the factors themselves will be weighed against one another in reaching a decision as to the disposition of the case. Guidelines regarding the factors to be considered by Customs when reviewing a petition are set forth in sections (F), (G), and (H) of appendix B to part 171 of the Customs Regulations. These guidelines provide as follows:

(F) Mitigating Factors

The following factors shall be considered in mitigation of the penalty, provided that sufficient evidence establishes their existence. The list is not exclusive.

(1) *Contributory Customs Error.* This factor includes misleading or erroneous advice given by a Customs official only if it appears that the violator reasonably relied upon the information. If the claimed erroneous advice was not given in writing, the violator has the burden of establishing this claim by a preponderance

of the evidence. The concepts of comparative negligence may be utilized in determining the weight to be assigned to this factor. If it is determined that the Customs error was the sole cause of the violation, the penalty is to be cancelled. If the Customs error contributed to the violation, but the violator is also culpable, the Customs error is to be considered as a mitigating factor.

(2) *Cooperation with the Investigation.* In order to obtain the benefits of this factor, the violator must exhibit cooperation beyond that expected from a person under investigation for a Customs violation. Some examples of the cooperation contemplated include assisting Customs officers to an unusual degree in auditing the books and records of the violator, and assisting Customs in obtaining additional information relating to the subject violation or other violations. Merely providing the books and records of the violator may not be considered cooperation justifying mitigation.

(3) *Immediate Remedial Action.* This factor includes the payment of the actual loss of duties prior to the issuance of a penalty notice and within 30 days of the determination of the duties owed. In certain extreme circumstances, this factor may include the removal of an offending employee. The correction of organizational or procedural defects will not be considered a mitigating factor. It is expected that any importer or other involved individual will seek to remove or change any condition which contributed to the existence of a violation.

(4) *Inexperience in Importing.* Inexperience is a factor only if it contributes to the violation and the violation is not due to fraud or gross negligence.

(5) *Prior Good Record.* For the violator to benefit from this factor, the violation must have occurred as a result of negligence or gross negligence, and the violator must be able to show a consistent pattern of importations without violation of section 592, or any other statute prohibiting false or fraudulent importation practices.

(G) Aggravating Factors

Certain factors may be determined to be aggravating factors in arriving at the final mitigated penalty decision. Examples of aggravating factors include obstructing the investigation, withholding evidence, providing misleading information concerning the violation, and prior substantive violations of section 592 for which a final administrative finding of culpability has been made.

(H) Extraordinary Factors Justifying Further Relief

(1) The four factors specified below may be considered in connection with further relief. Such relief may be accorded for extraordinary factors not specified below only upon the concurrence of the Chief, Commercial Fraud and Negligence Penalties Branch, Headquarters.

   (a) *Inability to obtain jurisdiction over the violator or inability to enforce a judgment against the violator.*

   (b) *Inability to Pay the Mitigated Penalty.* The party claiming the existence of this factor must present documentary evidence in support thereof, i.e., copies of income tax returns, current financial statements, and independent audit reports.

   (c) *Extraordinary Expenses.* This factor may include such expenses as those incurred in providing one-time computer runs solely for submission to Customs to aid it in analyzing a case involving an unusual number of entries, with each entry involving several factors, i.e., violations involving subheading 9802.00.80, Harmonized Tariff Schedule of the United States. Usual accounting and legal expenses (both general and Customs), or the cost incurred in instituting remedial action would not be considered extraordinary expenses.

(d) *Customs Knowledge.* Additional relief in non-fraud cases will be granted if it is determined that Customs had actual knowledge of a violation and failed to inform the violator so that it could have taken earlier corrective action. In such cases, if a penalty is to be assessed involving repeated violations of the same kind, the maximum penalty amount for violations occurring after the date on which actual knowledge was obtained by Customs will be limited to two times the loss of revenue in revenue-loss cases or five percent of dutiable value in non-revenue-loss cases if the continuing violations were the result of gross negligence, or the lesser of one time the loss of revenue in revenue-loss cases or two percent of dutiable value in non-revenue-loss cases if the violations were the result of negligence. This factor shall not be applicable when a substantial delay in the investigation is attributable to the violator.

It should be noted that the lists of factors shown above are not to be considered exclusive. That is, there may be mitigating, aggravating, and extraordinary factors that may be present in any given case but that are not listed in the guidelines set forth above. Such additional factors may be considered by the reviewing customs officer in deciding the disposition of a case. Note, however, that consideration may not be given to additional extraordinary factors not listed in the guidelines, unless the Chief of the Penalties Branch in Washington, D.C., concurs that those additional extraordinary factors may be considered.

With regard to claims relating to favorable factors, such as mitigating factors and extraordinary factors justifying further relief, it is not sufficient for the petitioner merely to allege the existence of such factors. The petitioner must provide sufficient evidence to show that such factors exist in reality.

With regard to the mitigating factors discussed above, some additional remarks might be helpful. Contributory Customs error does not come into play very frequently. Even if an importer can be shown to have relied upon oral information received from a customs officer, it is well recognized that oral advice received from a customs officer is not binding upon Headquarters of the Customs Service. This factor might be of significance where it could be shown that the violator sought the advice of several customs officers with regard to the same subject. Under these circumstances, the violator's reliance upon erroneous advice consistently given by several customs officers would appear more compelling and carry greater weight as a mitigating factor. Where an error by Customs was not the sole cause of the violation, the violator's reliance thereon as a mitigating factor is considered only in comparison with the violator's own negligence in failing to ascertain his or her legal obligations.

Cooperation with investigators and the taking of remedial action are not given a great deal of weight unless the cooperation given or the actions taken go well beyond those normally expected of a person in similar circumstances. Claims relating to these two factors are given careful scrutiny and must be supported by unusual circumstances. Note that Customs does not usually expect a company to discharge an employee just because that employee had responsibility for Customs compliance. U.S. Customs must recognize that the discharge or retention of any employee is subject to many important considerations beyond the peripheral involvement of that employee in the conduct of the company's import transactions. When an employee, however, has acted with willful disregard of the law or with total disregard of the company's policies regarding observance of the law, discharge may be warranted.

Inexperience in importing and the violator's prior good record are factors that are always important in mitigating penalties. Note, however, that the two factors tend to be mutually exclusive. Since inexperience in importing is usually based upon a low level of import activity, a prior good record (that is, a record with no violations) would be expected. By the same token, a claim of prior good record would carry little weight where that good record was based upon a low level of import activity. Therefore, a petitioner should claim one of these factors, but not both.

A claim of inexperience may be established by different circumstances. For example, an importer who has been importing for only a short period of time, say six months, would be considered to be an inexperienced importer. However, inexperience may also exist where an importer has been importing for many years but has only five or six importations during each of those years.

The presence of aggravating factors in a penalty case is a matter of concern only to the reviewing customs officer. Obviously, a petitioner would not bring such matters to the notice of the Customs Service. Therefore, the petitioner will usually become aware of the existence of such factors only when they are stated in the written decision of the Customs Service regarding the disposition of the case. This is not strictly true, of course, where the aggravation complained of is repeated violations or offenses by the same importer. The importer would be aware of his or her own bad record. Repeated offenses by the same importer is an aggravating factor frequently raised by Customs in penalty decisions.

With regard to extraordinary factors justifying further relief, the four factors shown are to be considered exclusive, unless the Chief of the

Penalties Branch concurs that additional factors may be considered. This does not mean that the petitioner must obtain permission to claim additional factors not listed. It merely means that the reviewing officer may not grant further relief without obtaining permission to grant it.

The inability of Customs to obtain jurisdiction over a violator or the inability of Customs to enforce a judgment against a violator are matters more important to Customs' own internal administration of its penalties program than they are to the petition process. These are matters not normally raised by a petitioner as defenses to a monetary penalty claim. Rather, they are factors taken into consideration by Customs in reaching a decision not to pursue a violator beyond certain limits.

The petitioner's inability to pay a penalty or mitigated penalty is discussed below in connection with the other options that are available to the petitioner after receipt of a Customs penalty decision.

Claims regarding extraordinary expenses incurred in defending against a penalty claim are treated in much the same way as the mitigating factors of cooperation and the taking of immediate remedial action. Unless it can be shown that the petitioner has incurred expenses that run well beyond those normally incurred in defending against a penalty claim, a claim regarding expenses will not be given much weight. Only those expenses related to extraordinary efforts on the petitioner's part will be considered as justification for relief beyond that normally accorded in penalty cases.

Customs' knowledge of a violation and Customs' failure to inform the violator of the circumstances of the prohibited behavior are claims that, like contributory Customs error, must be set forth with great particularity. It is not sufficient merely to allege that Customs knew of the violations and failed to take steps to prevent future violations. An example of Customs' knowledge of a violation would be where Customs sent a Request for Information form and the importer in response set forth information revealing the existence of a violation, such as the failure to report production assistance. If the importer's response to the Request for Information was actually received by Customs and no effort was made to advise the importer that he or she was in violation of the law for not reporting the assists, then this circumstance could be taken as an extraordinary factor justifying further relief. Note that where Customs' knowledge of a violation is a factor, the further relief granted amounts only to a reduction in penalty assessment for those violations occurring after the time Customs had actual knowledge that a violation existed.

After consideration of the mitigating and aggravating factors present in a case, the reviewing customs officer will reach a decision with regard to the initial mitigation of the penalty claim. The Revised Penalty Guidelines, as set forth in appendix B to part 171 of the Customs Regulations, place limits on the mitigation of penalties below which reviewing officers should not go. As stated in the guidelines, the greatest mitigation allowable is shown in Table 11.3. The effect of the mitigation process is apparent when the information shown in Table 11.3 is compared to the statutory maximum penalties set forth in Table 11.1.

The permissible mitigation levels set forth in Table 11.3 apply to mitigation of the penalty after consideration of mitigating and aggravating factors only, but before consideration of extraordinary factors justifying further relief. Hence, the determination of mitigation is made first through a weighing of mitigating and aggravating factors. When this level of mitigation has been determined, the reviewing officer may further examine the circumstances of the case to see if there are present any extraordinary factors justifying further relief. Therefore, relief beyond the mitigation levels set forth in Table 11.3 is possible, but only where extraordinary factors are present that would justify such further relief. The penalties imposed by Customs on violators are still substantial, even after the maximum mitigation allowed.

After consideration of the importer's written petition, the Customs Service renders a written decision that either reduces the penalty amount or leaves it the same as stated in the penalty notice. This decision will state (1) the final amount of the duties determined to be owing, if any, (2) the amount of the final penalty, and (3) the date by which all amounts owing must be paid. After receipt of Customs' written decision in response to the importer's petition, the importer may choose to (1) pay the amounts owing, (2) file a supplemental petition or offer in compromise, or (3) ignore the decision and do nothing. Each of these alternatives will be explored.

The importer may pay the duties and penalties in one lump sum, or, if the payment of the amount involved would create a financial hardship on the importer, arrangements may sometimes be made with the Customs Service to pay the moneys over a period of one or two years. In order to convince the Customs Service that a hardship exists, the importer must

Table 11.3
Permissible Mitigation of Penalties Before Consideration of Extraordinary Factors Justifying Further Relief

	Revenue Violation	*Nonrevenue Violation*
Fraud	As low as five times the loss of duties	As low as 50% of the FOB value of the goods
Gross Negligence	As low as 2½ times the loss of duties	As low as 25% of the FOB value of the goods
Negligence	As low as ½ times the loss of duties	As low as 5% of the FOB value of the goods

provide specific proof in the form of financial documents or tax returns to show an inability to pay the penalty in a lump sum amount. If payment is permitted over an extended period, interest must be paid at the prevailing interest rate as specified by the law.

If the importer is dissatisfied with the decision rendered by Customs on the original petition, a second petition referred to as a supplemental petition may be filed. The supplemental petition must be filed within the time prescribed in the first Customs decision or within the time permitted by any extension of time reasonably granted by Customs.

The supplemental petition can raise new defenses or issues not previously addressed, or the petitioner can dispute claims or points of authority relied upon by Customs in its written decision on the case. If payment of the mitigated penalty amount would result in financial hardship for the petitioner, this fact can be raised in the supplemental petition. Claims of hardship, however, must be supported by documentary evidence such as tax returns, accounting statements, and net worth statements. It is important to note that the duties and mitigated penalties owing, as stated in the first Customs decision, may remain unpaid while Customs is considering the supplemental petition.

Alternatively, within the same prescribed time, or any extension granted, the importer may file an offer in compromise of claims in lieu of a supplemental petition. (Offers in compromise are discussed separately below.) After the filing of a supplemental petition or an offer in compromise, the Customs Service will render a second decision on the penalty case.

After receipt of the second decision on the case, the importer may pay the amounts determined to be finally owing, if any, or the importer may again seek further relief. If the second decision by Customs is a rejection of an offer in compromise made after the first decision, the importer may elect to file a supplemental petition. If Customs' second decision is in response to a supplemental petition, the importer may file an offer in compromise or a second supplemental petition.

The Customs Regulations state that Customs will not entertain a second supplemental petition unless the importer pays in advance all duties and penalties previously determined to be owing. For the purposes of this rule, the term "second supplemental petition" includes an offer in compromise. If Customs grants further relief after reviewing a second supplemental petition, Customs will make a refund of a portion of the duties or penalties previously paid.

The Customs Regulations also provide that second supplemental petitions will be accepted only under one of the following circumstances:

1. It is filed within two years of notice of the decision on the first supplemental petition

2. It is filed within 30 days of an administrative or judicial decision that reduces the loss of duties on the entries involved in the penalty case (thereby reducing the calculated penalty)

3. If the appropriate official decides that the acceptance of a second supplemental petition is warranted

After reviewing the second supplemental petition or offer in compromise, Customs will render a third written decision on the case. At this point, the petitioner's administrative remedies are substantially exhausted.

If the importer refuses to pay the duties and penalties owing after a decision by Customs on the original petition or first supplemental petition, or if the importer fails to petition at all, the Customs Service may institute an action in the Court of International Trade to recover all duties and penalties owing. If an action is commenced by the government in court, however, all elements of the penalty are reopened for determination by the court. For example, the court after trial may determine (1) what violations occurred, (2) what degree of fault was involved, (3) what loss of duties occurred, and (4) what the proper penalty assessment should be.

Offer in Compromise

In section 1592 penalty cases, and in other penalty cases, the importer may offer to pay the government a fixed sum of money in settlement of any and all claims. The statutory provision for offers in compromise of claims is found in Title 19, United States Code, Section 1617, which states as follows:

Section 1617. Compromise of government claims by Secretary of Treasury

Upon a report by a customs officer, United States attorney, or any special attorney, having charge of any claim arising under the customs laws, showing the facts upon which such claim is based, the probabilities of a recovery and the terms upon which the same may be compromised, the Secretary of the Treasury is authorized to compromise such claim, if such action shall be recommended by the General Counsel for the Department of the Treasury.

The amount offered to settle a claim must be tendered in full to the Commissioner of Customs, along with the written offer. The amount offered is usually less than the amount that has been demanded in the penalty claim. The importer may make such an offer in lieu of submitting a penalty petition, or the importer may make such an offer after he or she has petitioned Customs and received a decision on the petition. Such cash offers are made to induce the government to compromise its claims and release the importer from further liability.

Where the Customs Service can clearly prove a violation of the law, it will not normally entertain or accept an offer in compromise. However, when some aspect of the government's case is open to question or presents substantial risks in litigation, the government may prefer to accept a cash offer in an amount less than that claimed. The benefit to the importer is that he or she may obtain a settlement in an amount that is substantially less than that demanded by the Customs Service. If an offer is made and it is rejected by the government, the moneys tendered with the offer are returned to the party who made the offer. If the offer is accepted, the government's case with respect to that claim is closed.

Statute of Limitations Defense

A statute of limitations is a legal provision that bars the government or a party from bringing a legal action against another party after the expiration of a certain number of years. With regard to violations of section 1592, the period of limitation is contained in Title 19, United States Code, Section 1621, which states as follows:

Section 1621. Limitation of actions

No suit or action to recover any pecuniary penalty or forfeiture of property accruing under the customs laws shall be instituted unless such suit or action is commenced within five years after the time when the alleged offense was discovered: *Provided,* That in the case of an alleged violation of section 1592 of this title arising out of gross negligence or neligence, such suit or action shall not be instituted more than five years after the date the alleged violation was committed: *Provided further,* That the time of the absence from the United States of the person subject to such penalty or forfeiture, or of any concealment or absence of the property, shall not be reckoned within this period of limitation.

In the case of violations of section 1592, the Customs Service is barred by law from commencing an action in court to enforce a penalty more than five years after the date of entry of the merchandise in cases involving negligence or gross negligence. If an entry is more than five years old (from the date of entry), no penalties can be collected for violations that occurred on that entry. Where fraud is involved, no action may be commenced in court to enforce a penalty more than five years after the date upon which the fraud was discovered by Customs. Customs has five years from the date it discovers a fraudulent (intentional) violation within which it can process a penalty or file suit in court to collect lost duties and penalties. Where fraud is involved, there is no limit on how far back in time Customs can go in recovering lost duties and penalties.

The statute of limitations provides a legal defense to an importer when the government unnecessarily delays initiating or completing a negligence penalty action. In practice, when the entries involved in a negligence penalty proceeding are somewhat old to begin with, the statute of limitations may expire (run out) while the administrative penalty proceeding is still in progress. If this occurs, the administrative penalty proceeding must be terminated because any court action to recover the penalties is barred by the statute. However, the Customs Service may continue to press for the collection of any loss of revenue resulting from the violations.

In a case where administrative penalty proceedings have been instituted and the statute of limitations is about to expire, the Customs Service may request that the importer execute a waiver of the statute of limitations. In waiving the statute of limitations, the importer voluntarily relinquishes his or her right to raise the statute of limitations as a defense or bar against the government pursuing any court action beyond the date of expiration of the statute of limitations. If the importer refuses to waive the statute of limitations, the Customs Service must institute an action in the U.S. Court of International Trade to prevent the running of the statute. The institution of court proceedings tolls or stops the running of the statute during the time when such court proceedings are in progress.

Usually, it is in the importer's best interest to waive the statute of limitations when requested to do so by the Customs Service. This prevents the institution of a costly court proceeding in which the importer would have to appear and defend, and confers upon the importer the benefit of continuing the less costly administrative resolution of the penalty proceedings. For this reason, importers usually comply with a request by the Customs Service to file a written waiver of the statute of limitations.

SEIZURE AND FORFEITURE OF MERCHANDISE

There are numerous laws and regulations that permit the seizure of goods and property by U.S. Customs. Items that may be seized range in size from small personal items imported by passengers arriving in the United States to entire oceangoing vessels and commercial airliners. Time and space do not permit a complete examination of all the laws and regulations involved. Therefore, the material that follows will attempt to draw the broad outlines of those general procedures used by Customs when imported merchandise becomes subject to seizure.

When a shipment of merchandise is seized by the Customs Service, the entire shipment is physically taken into custody by Customs. The goods will normally remain in the custody of Customs pending the outcome of judicial or administrative proceedings. Seized merchandise may be subject to forfeiture to the government.

When seized merchandise is forfeited to the government, the ownership of the goods passes from the importer or rightful owner to the government. Forfeited merchandise may be sold by Customs at public auction or disposed of in any other manner permitted under the laws and regulations. Forfeiture of merchandise cannot occur without the necessary judicial or administrative proceedings required by law.

Prohibited merchandise such as pornography, immoral articles, products of convict labor, and cultural artifacts are usually forfeited and not returned to the owner or importer.

Seized merchandise that is not forfeited to the government is normally returned to the owner or importer after completion of an administrative or judicial proceeding to determine what amount of fine or penalty must be paid to prevent a forfeiture and to obtain release of the goods. In addition, any other restrictions on the merchandise that result from improper or incomplete documentation must be satisfied prior to release of the goods.

As stated earlier, there are numerous Customs laws that permit the seizure of merchandise. Many of these laws are very broadly worded and permit a seizure of any goods imported contrary to law. The policy of the Customs Service with regard to the seizure of ordinary commercial shipments has had an extremely varied history. Many of the laws that permit the seizure of goods also permit the assessment of penalties in lieu of seizure. During certain periods of time, Customs has adopted a lenient policy and assessed penalties without seizing the merchandise involved in the underlying violation. During other periods of time, Customs has become less lenient and has seized most shipments involved in Customs violations. The particular policy that may be in effect at any given time is of great importance to most importers because the seizure of merchandise and the detention of it by Customs during the seizure proceeding causes great hardship and inconvenience to the importer. Since the merchandise may be held for a number of weeks or a number of months, there is great danger that the goods will become completely worthless to the importer.

At one time, seizures of merchandise involved in section 1592 violations were very common. However, the law itself was changed by Congress to permit the seizure of merchandise only in limited circumstances. Seizures of merchandise under section 1592 are now permitted only when the district director has reasonable cause to believe that:

1. The owner or importer is insolvent.
2. The owner or importer is beyond the jurisdiction of the United States.
3. Seizure is essential to protect the revenue.
4. Seizure is essential to prevent the introduction of prohibited or restricted merchandise into the Customs territory of the United States.

If none of the above conditions apply, merchandise may not be seized for violations of section 1592.

The Customs Regulations regarding the seizure of merchandise are as broadly worded as are the laws themselves. The regulations provide that property may be seized by any customs officer who has reasonable cause to believe that any law or regulation enforced by the Customs Service has been violated and that the merchandise by reason of such violation has become subject to seizure or forfeiture. The regulations require that a receipt for seized property shall be given at the time of seizure to the person from whom the property is seized.

The Customs Regulations also provide that any conveyance used to facilitate the importation of merchandise or articles contrary to law is subject to seizure and forfeiture. The regulations state that every vessel, vehicle, animal, aircraft, or other conveyance that is used in the importation of any article contrary to law shall be seized and held for forfeiture. Such seized conveyances may be forfeited to the government after proper proceedings or released to the owner after payment of fines or penalties.

When merchandise or property is seized, a written notice of any fine, penalty, or potential forfeiture must be given to each party that has an interest in the seized property. The notice must inform each interested party of the right to apply for mitigation of penalties or cancellation of the forfeiture.

If forfeiture of property is a possibility, the written notice must inform any interested party that unless the party provides an express agreement to defer judicial or administrative forfeiture proceedings until completion of the administrative process, those proceedings will be commenced immediately. Most importers who are notified of the seizure of their merchandise do provide the Customs Service with a written agreement to defer forfeiture proceedings during the administrative process because forfeiture proceedings are costly and involve the risk of loss of the merchandise.

The notice of seizure given to the owner or importer of the merchandise must also contain the following information:

1. The provisions of law alleged to have been violated
2. A description of the specific acts or omissions forming the basis of the alleged violations
3. If the violations involve the entry of merchandise,
   a. A description of the merchandise and the circumstances of its entry
   b. The identity of each entry if specific entries are involved
4. If the violations involve a loss of revenue,
   a. The total loss of revenue and how it was computed

b. The loss of revenue attributable to each entry, if readily susceptible to calculation

After receipt of the seizure notice, the importer or owner may file a petition for the reduction of monetary penalties or for the payment of an amount necessary to cancel the forfeiture of the merchandise.

If the importer or owner of the seized goods desires to obtain release of the merchandise before the completion of the administrative proceedings, he or she may offer to pay the appraised domestic value of the seized property in order to obtain an immediate release. In certain circumstances, the Customs Service will release the seized merchandise upon payment of less than the domestic value. The amount that must be deposited as security for the release of the goods will depend upon the maximum amount that may be levied as fines or monetary penalties after completion of the administrative proceeding.

If the owner or importer of seized merchandise fails to file a petition for relief, Customs may proceed with an action to collect any fines or penalties due and begin the required judicial or administrative proceedings necessary to forfeit the merchandise.

Although seized merchandise is usually returned to the importer or owner, the procedures that must be endured prior to the release of the merchandise constitute a grave inconvenience. Also, the penalties that must be paid to obtain release of seized merchandise can often be very substantial.

LIQUIDATED DAMAGES

Unlike penalties, which result from violations of laws or regulations, liquidated damages arise from a breach of a provision in a contract. In the Customs context, the contract that gives rise to liquidated damages is the Customs bond filed at the time of entry.

The law dealing with bonds is found in Title 19, United States Code, Section 1623, which states in pertinent part as follows:

Section 1623. Bonds and other security

(a) In any case in which bond or other security is not specifically required by law, the Secretary of the Treasury may by regulation or specific instruction require, or authorize customs officers to require, such bonds or other security as he, or they, may deem necessary for the protection of the revenue or to assure compliance with any provision of law, regulation, or instruction which the Secretary of the Treasury or the Customs Service may be authorized to enforce.

(b) Whenever a bond is required or authorized by a law, regulation, or instruction which the Secretary of the Treasury or the Customs Service is authorized to enforce, the Secretary of the Treasury may—

(1) Except as otherwise specifically provided by law, prescribe the conditions and form of such bond, and fix the amount of penalty thereof, whether for the payment of liquidated damages or of a penal sum. . . .

(c) Cancellation of bond

The Secretary of the Treasury may authorize the cancellation of any bond provided for in this section, or of any charge that may have been made against such bond, in the event of a breach of any condition of the bond, upon the payment of such lesser amount or penalty or upon such other terms and conditions as he may deem sufficient. In order to assure uniform, reasonable, and equitable decisions, the Secretary of the Treasury shall publish guidelines establishing standards for setting the terms and conditions for cancellation of bonds or charges thereunder.

The provisions quoted above essentially authorize the Secretary of the Treasury to do the following things:

1. To require by regulation the taking of bonds or other security to protect the revenue and insure compliance with laws and regulations
2. To determine the form (language) of bonds, the conditions to be included therein, and the liquidated damages to be charged for the breach of the conditions in the bond
3. To cancel any liquidated damages claimed as a result of a breach, upon the payment of a lesser amount and upon such other terms and conditions as may be deemed proper

As indicated previously, the entry bond is a contract involving three parties, namely, the importer, the surety, and U.S. Customs. This written contract contains certain provisions to which the importer must adhere. For example, one of the provisions states that the importer will redeliver merchandise into Customs' custody when so requested by the Customs Service. If a request for redelivery is made and the merchandise is not redelivered, the importer has breached this provision in the bond. Other Customs bonds contain different provisions that may be breached by the party giving the bond. Some examples of claims for liquidated damages involve the following:

1. Late filing of entry summary (Customs Form 7501)
2. Violation of temporary importation bonds
3. Shortage, irregular delivery, nondelivery, or delivery directly to the consignee of in-bond merchandise
4. Failure to redeliver merchandise into Customs' custody or failure to comply with a notice of refusal of admission issued by another government agency
5. Failure to provide missing documents

6. Failure to file timely shipper's export declarations

7. Violation of warehouse proprietor's bond

8. Violation of airport security regulations

9. Violation of foreign trade zone regulations

10. Failure to hold merchandise at the place of examination

When a bond breach occurs, the Customs Service, as another party to the contract, is entitled to receive monetary damages. Since the actual monetary damages incurred by Customs because of the bond breach are difficult to ascertain, the bond contains a provision that states how damages are to be determined in the event of a breach. Such a provision is referred to as a liquidated damages clause. For this reason, liquidated damages proceedings are fundamentally different from actions to recover penalties. Liquidated damages are contractual and not considered to be penal in nature.

When the importer fails to redeliver merchandise or has breached some other provision in the bond, the Customs Service issues a notice of liquidated damages to the importer. Liquidated damage claims are issued in differing amounts, depending upon the nature of the breach. The amount of the initial claim for damages could be (1) a small sum based upon the duty owing; (2) the FOB value of the merchandise, plus the estimated duty; or (3) in some instances twice the FOB value of the merchandise.

After receipt of the liquidated damages notice, the importer or other violator may file a petition to have the amount of the claim reduced. Depending upon the nature of the merchandise involved and the conduct giving rise to the bond breach, the final amount that must be paid can vary greatly. In some instances, the claim may be settled by the Customs Service upon payment of 2% or 3% of the FOB value of the goods. In more serious cases, Customs may not be willing to settle the claim for less than the full amount stated in the initial liquidated damages notice. As with penalty proceedings, the importer or other violator may file a supplemental petition, second supplemental petition, or an offer in compromise.

Unlike penalties, moneys paid to the Customs Service as liquidated damages are tax deductible for business purposes. The Customs Service never detains or withholds release of merchandise during the processing of a liquidated damages claim. Liquidated damages that are not paid by the importer may be demanded by Customs from the surety. In the event of nonpayment by either the importer or the surety, the Customs Service may institute a court proceeding against the importer and the surety to recover the damages due.

Chapter 12

Duty Exemptions, Special Rate Programs, and Temporary Importations

This chapter will discuss products that may enter the United States duty free or with reduced duties. A special procedure by which products that would otherwise be dutiable can be entered temporarily for certain purposes and then exported without payment of duties will also be discussed.

The duty exemptions and special duty rate programs are all more or less complicated by specific eligibility and documentation requirements. Space will not permit an examination of all the rules regarding eligibility and documentation as found in the Tariff Schedule and Customs Regulations. Instead, the broad outlines of these provisions and the more general requirements will be covered. Importers who believe they can benefit from these exemptions and special programs should explore fully the exact requirements for each before setting any plans in motion. Customs brokers or customs officers should be consulted beforehand regarding the specific facts and merchandise to ensure that all qualifications are met. This is particularly important since any doubts about eligibility will be resolved in favor of the government and the revenue.

DUTY EXEMPTIONS

Duty exemptions are found in chapter 98 of the Harmonized Tariff Schedule of the United States and are referred to as special classification provisions.

American Goods Returned

American goods that are exported and returned to the United States may be entered duty free under tariff item 9801.00.10, which reads as follows:

Products of the United States when returned after having been exported, without

having been advanced in value or improved in condition by any process of
manufacture or other means while abroad...FREE

Products entered under this provision may be new or used. U.S. items
of ordinary packing such as cardboard cartons, wrappings, stuffing
materials, or string tags are classified here, even though used to pack
items of foreign origin.

Items must be returned without having undergone any enhancement or
improvement while abroad. Enhancement or improvements added
abroad that can be removed or eliminated before return to the United
States will not disqualify an item from duty free treatment. If an item is
not returned in the exact condition in which it was exported, care should
be taken to ensure that there has been no advance in value or
improvement in condition.

The documents required to be submitted with the entry for U.S. goods
returned are (1) a declaration by the foreign shipper, (2) a declaration for
free entry by the importer or owner on the top portion of Customs Form
3311, and (3) a Certificate of Exportation on the bottom portion of
Customs Form 3311. If the district director is reasonably satisfied because
of the nature of the articles or other evidence that the items meet the
requirements of 9801.00.10, he or she may waive the production of all the
required documents.

To avoid penalties for submitting false declarations, the importer
should insist that personnel authorized to sign Customs Form 3311 on
behalf of the company obtain sufficient facts to justify the declaration and
claim that the entered goods are products of the United States.

Previously Imported Articles

There are several tariff provisions that permit previously imported and
duty paid items to be reimported free of duty. Two of these involve items
sent abroad under lease or contract or items sold to foreign customers but
rejected because the items do not meet specifications. Neither of these
provisions can be used for items that were exported with benefit of
drawback. Drawback of duties is discussed in chapter 13.

Tariff item 9801.00.20 provides as follows:

Articles, previously imported, with respect to which the duty was paid upon such
previous importation or which were previously free of duty pursuant to the
Caribbean Basin Economic Recovery Act or Title V of the Trade Act of 1974, if (1)
reimported, without having been advanced in value or improved in condition by
any process of manufacture or other means while abroad, after having been
exported under lease or similar use agreements, and (2) reimported by or for the
account of the person who imported it into, and exported it from, the United
States. .... FREE

Item 9801.00.20 requires by its terms that the following conditions be met:

1. Goods were previously imported.
2. Goods were duty paid or duty free under the Caribbean Basin Economic Recovery Act or Title V of the Trade Act of 1974 (the Generalized System of Preferences)—both of which are discussed below.
3. Goods were not enhanced or improved while abroad.
4. Goods were under a use or lease agreement when they were exported from the United States.
5. Goods were previously imported by or for the account of party A.
6. Goods were exported by or for the account of party A.
7. Goods were reimported by or for the account of party A.

The above requirements are qualifying conditions and the failure to meet any one of them will result in the goods being classified under a dutiable classification in another tariff chapter. For example, if the goods were exported by or for the account of party B, they would not qualify. If the goods were exported for testing and approval by the foreign customer prior to the execution of a lease agreement, they probably do not qualify.

Item 9801.00.25 provides as follows:

Articles, previously imported, with respect to which the duty was paid upon such previous importation if (1) exported within three years after the date of such previous importation, (2) reimported without having been advanced in value or improved in condition by any process of manufacture or other means while abroad, (3) reimported for the reason that such articles do not conform to sample or specifications, and (4) reimported by or for the account of the person who imported them into, and exported them from, the United States............................FREE

Many of the qualifying conditions in this provision are the same as for 9801.00.20. Item 9801.00.25 differs from 9801.00.20 in the following ways:

1. Duty free importation on a prior occasion is immaterial.
2. The goods must be exported within three years of any previous duty paid importation.
3. The reimportation must result from the goods not conforming to sample or specifications.
4. The existence of a lease is immaterial.

As always, precise analysis is required to determine eligibility. For example, used computer equipment returned to the U.S. seller as a trade-in and down payment for more advanced equipment under the terms of a first sales agreement would not qualify under this provision. The returned equipment under these circumstances cannot be considered to be nonconforming as to sample or specifications.

The Customs Regulations require for item 9801.00.25 that the following documents be submitted in the format shown in the regulations:

1. A declaration by the person who received and is returning the merchandise to the United States
2. A declaration by the importer or owner attesting to the pertinent facts

Failure to submit the required documents at entry or later will result in a denial of the duty free claim.

Because the facts in both declarations are susceptible to verification by reference to other documents, the importer should anticipate that Customs might request (1) a copy of the previous import entry, (2) a copy of the export entry, or (3) a copy of the correspondence showing that the goods failed to meet specifications.

Articles Repaired, Altered, or Processed Abroad

The provisions discussed here allow for reduced duty payments, not duty free importation. The goods may be of U.S. or foreign manufacture originally. Once again, goods that have received the benefit of duty drawback or remission, abatement, or refunds of duty do not qualify under these provisions. The three tariff items in question read as follows:

	Articles returned to the United States after having been exported to be advanced in value or improved in condition by any process of manufacture or other means:	
	Articles exported for repairs or alterations:	
9802.00.40	Repairs or alterations made pursuant to a warranty	A duty upon the value of the repairs or alterations.
9802.00.50	Other [repairs or alterations]	A duty upon the value of the repairs or alterations.
9802.00.60	Any article of metal (as defined in U.S. note 3 (d) of this subchapter) manufac-	

tured in the United States or subjected to a process of manufacture in the United States, if exported for further processing, and if the exported article as processed outside the United States, or the article which results from the processing outside the United States, is returned to the United States for further processing . . . .   A duty upon the value of such processing outside the United States.

In all three instances, the duty paid is based upon the value of the repair, alteration, or processing (metals only) that occurs abroad. The rate of duty is determined by ascertaining what rate would apply to the goods if they did not qualify for these provisions. That is, each product would be classified normally like other imported goods to determine where they would fall in the Tariff Schedule. The duty rate for the resultant classification would then be used on the entry to calculate the duties owing on the value of the repair, alteration, or processing. For example, if an item would normally take a duty rate of 5% *ad valorem*, the duty would be 5% of the value of the repair, alteration, or processing.

In determining the value to be used for the repair, alteration, or processing, the following are considered in the order stated:

1. The cost to the importer of such change
2. If no charge is made, the value of such change

The cost to the importer would be the amount actually paid to the foreign party for services performed as set out in the invoice and entry papers and would include the cost of materials. If no charge is made for the cost of repair, alteration, or processing or if the appraising officer concludes that the charge as shown on the invoice or entry papers is insufficient, then the value of the change will be determined in accordance with the Customs valuation law.

At the time of entry, estimated duties must be deposited based upon the full cost or fair value of the repairs, alterations, or processing, and such cost or fair value shall be limited to the cost or value of the repairs, alterations, or processing actually performed abroad, which will include the cost of all domestic and foreign materials used but will not include (1) expenses incurred in the United States for engineering, plans, or specifications or (2) the cost of tools and equipment furnished to the foreign party.

Before the exportation of the articles to be repaired, altered, or processed, the owner or exporter must file a Certificate of Registration (top portion of Customs Form 4455) with Customs in sufficient time to permit Customs to examine the articles before exportation. For articles of metal to be processed abroad, the importer must include on the reverse side of Customs Form 4455 a statement regarding the origin of the metal articles, the nature of any processing performed before exportation, and the name of the party who will further process the articles after their importation.

The filing of Customs Form 4455 before exportation of the goods is very important and should not be overlooked because failure to do so may result in Customs denying classification under chapter 98, in which case full duties must be paid. Although Customs in some circumstances may waive this requirement if it was not met, the documentary proof of export which must be submitted to obtain the waiver can be extremely burdensome.

At the time of entry of the goods that were repaired, altered, or processed, the importer must file the following:

1. The Certificate of Registration (Customs Form 4455) signed by a customs officer before exportation of the goods
2. A declaration by the person who performed the repairs, alterations, or processing stating the applicable facts as required by the Customs Regulations
3. A declaration by the importer or owner of the returned articles stating the applicable facts as required by the Customs Regulations

The Customs Regulations as currently written have eliminated all the above documentary requirements (CF 4455 and declarations) for merchandise entered under 9802.00.50, nonwarranty repairs. However, this is believed to be an error that occurred when the Harmonized Tariff Schedule was amended. Therefore, it is advisable for importers to meet the documentary requirements as shown unless, or until, they are officially advised that such requirements do not apply to goods entered under item 9802.00.50.

Before any plans are put in motion to utilize the three special tariff provisions discussed here, it is essential for the importer to discuss his or her plans with customs officers. This will prevent any missteps on the importer's part that could have the effect of disqualifying the goods from these provisions. For example, goods do not qualify for repairs if they are sent abroad for testing and return or if a defective item is simply replaced with a new unit. Moreover, if testing only or replacement occurs along with repair or alteration and the goods are commingled in such a way that items cannot be identified relative to the processing that occurred, the entire claim may be disallowed. Customs has very set notions regarding what kind of lot or piece identification and control will be required for different types of goods. Therefore, the prudent plan is to discuss all these matters with Customs beforehand. This is true for all the provisions shown above.

Articles Assembled Abroad with U.S. Components

Tariff item 9802.00.80 applies to goods containing some U.S.-manufactured components. The U.S. components may be purchased and supplied to the foreign assembler by the importer or purchased by the foreign assembler directly from the U.S. maker of the parts. It is the U.S. components that are entitled to the exemption.

The language of the Tariff Schedule for this tariff item is as follows:

9802.00.80	Articles assembled abroad in whole or in part of fabricated components, the product of the United States, which (a) were exported in condition ready for assembly without further fabrication, (b) have not lost their physical identity in such articles by change in form, shape or otherwise, and (c) have not been advanced in value or improved in condition abroad except by being assembled and except by operations incidental to the assembly process such as cleaning, lubricating and painting.....................................	A duty upon the full value of the imported article, less the cost or value of such products of the United States.

The duty rate for imported goods containing U.S. components is the same rate that would be applicable to the goods if they were classified normally, without reference to chapter 98.

The dutiable value of imported goods containing U.S. components does not include the purchase price of the components or any freight costs incurred in shipping them to the port of export in the United States. The purchase price of the components, plus the freight and expenses involved in shipping the components to the port from which they are exported to the foreign country for assembly, is called the port of export (POE) value. This is the value of the U.S. components that escapes the assessment of duty. However, the dutiable value does include all freight and other expenses incurred in moving the U.S. components from the U.S. port of export to the place of assembly.

The freight and other related expenses of moving the U.S. components from the U.S. port of exportation to the final point of assembly in the foreign country may be called international expenses. These expenses are part of the dutiable value of the imported goods containing the U.S. components.

If the foreign assembler purchases the U.S. components himself or herself, the purchase price and all shipping expenses to his or her plant will be included in the price he or she charges for the final product. Thus, the dutiable value is the price paid for the goods, less the POE value of the components. For example, the assembler purchases the U.S. components himself or herself and charges a final price of $48 per unit for the assembled goods. The cost to the assembler for the U.S. components contained in the goods is $15 per unit, the freight on the components to the port of export is $1.00 per unit, and the international expenses on the components from the port of export to the assembly plant are $2.00 per unit. The dutiable value is determined as follows:

Appraised value	$48.00 ea. (price paid)
Less POE value	− 16.00 ea. ($15.00 plus $1.00)
Dutiable value	$32.00 ea.

If the U.S. importer purchases the components and ships them to the assembler free of charge, the supplied components are considered to be production assistance, the value of which must be added to the price paid to arrive at transaction value. The assist value is the purchase price of the components, plus all freight costs to the assembler's plant. In this case, the calculation of the appraised and dutiable values would be as follows:

Price paid to foreign assembler for finished product	$30.00 ea.	
Purchase price of components paid in United States by importer	$15.00 ea.	
Cost of shipping components to U.S. port of export	$1.00 ea.	POE value of components
Cost of shipping components from port of export to foreign assembly plant	$2.00 ea.	International expenses
	$30.00 ea.	price paid
	$18.00 ea.	assist value ($15.00 plus $1.00, plus $2.00)
Appraised value	$48.00 ea.	
Less POE value of components	$16.00 ea.	
Dutiable value	$32.00 ea.	

Of course, the calculations involved might be somewhat more complicated than those shown above. Other adjustments such as selling commissions, royalty payments, or other assists might have to be added to the price paid in arriving at the full appraised value. In any event, the principle remains the same: the dutiable value of imported products containing eligible U.S. components is determined by finding the full appraised value for the product and then deducting the allowable value for the U.S. components, which is their POE value.

The next items to consider are identifying what constitutes an "eligible U.S. component" and what constitutes "assembly" within the meaning of the law. To qualify for the exemption, the components must be "products of the United States" and they must be only "assembled" abroad.

An eligible U.S. component or product of the United States is an article manufactured in the United States that may consist (1) wholly of U.S. components or materials, (2) partially of U.S. and partially of foreign components or materials, or (3) wholly of foreign components or materials. If the article consists wholly or partially of foreign components or materials, the manufacturing process that takes place in the United States must substantially transform the foreign materials into a new and different article. For example, foreign metal ingots melted in the United States and manufactured into automobile bumpers or body panels would be substantially transformed into new and different articles. Thus, products manufactured in the United States are eligible U.S. components if they are (1) made wholly from U.S. materials or (2) made partially or wholly from foreign materials that are substantially transformed during manufacture in the United States.

Assembly of components is the fitting or joining together of fabricated components. Fitting or joining may be accomplished by bolting, screwing, nailing, welding, soldering, gluing, sewing, and similar operations. The U.S. components to be assembled abroad must be in such a condition that they are ready for assembly without further fabrication at the time they are exported from the United States. This means that nothing further needs to be done to the components in order to fit or to join them with other components. If this is true, then the components are merely assembled within the meaning of the law.

However, operations that are considered merely "incidental" to assembly will not cause otherwise eligible U.S. products to lose their eligibility. Such incidental operations may occur before, during, or after the assembly process. The cutting to length of materials in rolls such as wires, tapes, and ribbons is an operation incidental to the assembly of the wires, tapes, and ribbons. Other examples of incidental operations are the following:

1. Cleaning
2. Removal of rust, grease, paint, or preservative coatings

3. Application of preservative paint or coatings, including lubricants or protective encapsulation

4. Trimming, filing, or cutting off small amounts of excess materials

5. Separation by cutting of finished components, such as prestamped integrated circuit lead frames exported in multiple unit strips

6. Final calibration, testing, marking, sorting, pressing, and folding of assembled articles

These operations are considered to be incidental to assembly and not "manufacturing" operations.

Materials that are undefined in final dimensions and shapes and that must be cut or bent into specific patterns or shapes in the foreign country prior to assembly are insufficiently fabricated at the time of exportation to qualify as eligible fabricated components. Such materials undergo operations beyond those that are merely incidental to assembly. These types of operations are considered to be manufacturing or transforming operations.

The distinctions between incidental operations and manufacturing or transforming operations are very subtle and care should be taken in advance to secure Customs' opinion as to the legal status of any contemplated foreign operations. Examples of these distinctions are the following:

1. Cutting wire to length and winding it to form a coil does not disqualify the wire.

2. Bending metal components into a rectangle to form a bed frame does disqualify the metal components.

3. Painting an article with preservative paint does not disqualify the article.

4. Painting an article primarily to enhance its appearance does disqualify the article.

Other types of operations that will disqualify components are the following:

1. Melting materials and pouring them into molds or forms

2. Pattern cutting fabric into garment parts

3. Chemical treatment of components or assembled articles to impart new characteristics, such as showerproofing, permapressing, Sanforizing, dying, or bleaching of textiles

4. Machining, polishing, burnishing, peening, plating, embossing, pressing, stamping, extruding, drawing, annealing, tempering, case hardening, and similar operations, treatments, or processes that impart significant new characteristics or qualities to the articles

If a disqualifying process or operation occurs, the only articles disqualified are those subjected to the disqualifying process or operation. Any other qualifying U.S. components are not affected.

The special documentation that must be filed to obtain the duty exemption under tariff item 9802.00.80 is as follows:

1. *Assembler's Declaration.* A declaration, as set forth in the Customs Regulations, by the person performing the assembly operations abroad stating the nature of the assembly operations and the pertinent facts regarding the actual U.S. components contained in the assembled product.

2. *Endorsement by the Importer.* A declaration signed by the importer attesting to the correctness of the information set forth in the assembler's declaration and the correctness of the other facts contained in the entry papers regarding the 9802.00.80 exemption.

In addition to the above declarations, Customs frequently will request the importer to obtain a manufacturer's affidavit from each vendor of the U.S. components certifying that the components obtained from that vendor were actually manufactured in the United States. When a U.S. vendor is asked to supply such verification, it is often discovered that the components obtained from that vendor were imported and not made in the United States. Such imported components do not qualify for the exemption. Moreover, the importer is exposed to penalties for incorrectly certifying the U.S. origin of these components at the time of entry. To avoid this situation, the importer should verify the origin of components purchased in the United States prior to entry of the assembled goods.

Articles assembled abroad with U.S. components are considered to be products of the country of assembly for country of origin marking purposes. If an assembled article is made entirely of U.S. components and materials, it may be marked "assembled in [country] from material of U.S. origin."

SPECIAL DUTY RATE PROGRAMS

This section will discuss products that may be imported duty free or with reduced duties as a result of the special tariff treatment programs provided for in general note 3 of the Harmonized Tariff Schedule of the United States. The precautionary note given before regarding the generalized nature of this discussion bears repeating here. The five special programs discussed below could form the subject of an entire book if every ramification and exception to the general rules were spelled out. A complete explication of these subjects goes beyond the scope of this book. The reader is cautioned that, for many statements made in the materials below, there may be exceptions, which should be explored before utilizing the special provisions.

Products of Insular Possessions

Goods that are products of U.S. insular possessions other than Puerto Rico may be accorded duty free treatment if certain conditions are met. The possessions that are eligible for this special treatment are Guam, the Virgin Islands, Wake Island, Midway Islands, Kingman Reef, Johnston Island, and American Samoa. Although not a U.S. possession, the Commonwealth of Northern Mariana Islands is accorded the same tariff treatment as the listed possessions.

In order to qualify for duty free entry, all goods, except textile products, must meet the following requirements:

1. The goods must be shipped directly from the insular possession to the Customs territory of the United States.
2. The goods must be the growth or product of such possession, or they must be manufactured in such possession from materials that are the growth, product, or manufacture of such possession or the United States or both.
3. The goods must not contain foreign materials valued at more than 70% of the appraised value of the goods.

With regard to requirement 1, the goods may not enter the commerce of another country or territory before reaching the Customs territory of the United States. With regard to requirement 2, it has been held that the goods must undergo substantial manufacturing operations that go beyond mere finishing, sorting, or packing.

In determining the percentage by value of the foreign materials, as discussed in requirement 3, the value of foreign materials will be the actual purchase price of the foreign materials, plus the cost of transportation of those materials to the insular possession. Duties and taxes assessed by the insular possession and any charges that accrue after landing of the foreign materials are not considered part of the value of the foreign materials. In addition, no material shall be considered foreign if it could have been entered into the United States from its country of origin duty free, either at the time the finished goods from the insular possession enter the United States or at the time of importation of the foreign materials into the insular possession. Of course, materials manufactured in the United States are not considered foreign materials for the purpose of the percentage calculation.

Textile and apparel articles must meet all the above requirements, except that they may not contain foreign materials valued at more than 50% of the appraised value of the imported articles.

When goods from insular possessions are entered duty free under this provision, the importer must file at the time of entry or later a certificate of origin on Customs Form 3229, signed by the appropriate customs officer at the port of shipment from the insular possession.

Generalized System of Preferences (GSP)

There are approximately 136 countries, territories, and islands that are the beneficiaries of the Generalized System of Preferences (GSP) program. Referred to as the Beneficiary Developing Countries (BDCs), these political entities are found for the most part in Central and South America, Asia, and Africa. The current beneficiaries of the GSP program are set forth in appendix F.

The specific articles that may benefit from the GSP program are determined entirely by tariff classification. If the tariff number under which the goods are properly classified shows the word "Free" followed by an "A" in the "Special" rate of duty subcolumn, then those goods may be entered duty free if they meet the other qualifications. An example of this GSP designator is shown in the following modified excerpt from the Tariff Schedule (also see appendix A):

Heading/Subheading	Article Description	Rates of Duty General	Special
2838.00.00	Fulminates, cyanates and thiocyanates	3.1%	Free (A, E, IL) 1.2% (CA)

In the "Special" subcolumn at the far right above, the word "Free" followed by the "A" in parentheses indicates that this tariff item is eligible for GSP treatment, provided the other conditions discussed below are met. Note for future reference the designators "E" (Caribbean Basin Initiative), "IL" (United States-Israel Free Trade Area), and "CA" (United States-Canada Free-Trade Agreement) which will be discussed below.

The word "Free" followed by an "A*" indicates that some beneficiary countries are not eligible under GSP. Those BDCs that are not eligible for any given tariff number are listed in note 3 of the Tariff Schedule. In most instances, an "A*" indicates that one or two countries are not eligible. In rare cases, however, four or five countries may be ineligible.

In order to qualify for duty free treatment, eligible articles must be imported directly from the BDC into the Customs territory of the United States. In addition, an article must be wholly the growth, product, or manufacture of the beneficiary country or the article must be the result of a manufacturing or production process occurring in the beneficiary country that substantially transforms its constituent materials into a new and different article of commerce.

Duty free entry under GSP is allowed only if the sum of (1) the cost or value of the materials produced in the BDC, plus (2) the direct costs of processing operations performed in the BDC, is not less than 35% of the appraised value of the article at the time of its entry into the Customs territory of the United States. If the cost of materials and processing when added together are more than 35% of the appraised value of the article, then the article qualifies for duty free entry.

Only those materials that are manufactured in the BDC can be counted toward the 35% requirement. Materials imported into the BDC from the United States or other countries are not, except in very limited circumstances, considered to be part of the qualifying materials.

The words "direct costs of processing operations" refer to costs directly incurred in production or costs that can be reasonably allocated to the production of the goods under consideration. Such costs include the following:

1. All actual labor costs involved in the growth, production, manufacture, or assembly of the specific merchandise, including fringe benefits, on-the-job training, and the cost of engineering, supervisory, quality control, and similar personnel
2. Dies, molds, tooling, and depreciation on machinery and equipment that are allocable to the specific merchandise
3. Research, development, design, engineering, and blueprint costs insofar as they are allocable to the specific merchandise
4. Costs of inspecting and testing the specific merchandise

Costs that are not included in direct costs of processing operations are those that are not directly attributable to the merchandise or are not costs of manufacturing the product. These types of costs are the following:

1. Profit
2. General expenses of doing business that are either not allocable to the specific merchandise or are not related to the growth, production, manufacture, or assembly of the merchandise, such as administrative salaries, casualty and liability insurance, advertising, and salesmen's salaries, commissions, or expenses

The documentation required to obtain duty free treatment under GSP consists of the Certificate of Origin Form A, as evidence of the country of origin. Form A is normally prepared by the manufacturer of the merchandise, the exporter, or another party having knowledge of the necessary facts.

The manufacturer or other knowledgeable party who prepares Form A indicates what the qualifying percentage is. For example, if Form A indicates that the sum of qualifying materials, plus direct costs of processing operations, is 60% of the total value, then Customs will normally consider the 35% requirement to have been met. However, the qualifying percentage shown on Form A is subject to such verification as the district director may require.

At one time, Form A had to be certified by the government of the exporting country. Presently, such certification is required only if the exporting country has a verification agreement with the U.S. Customs Service. To date, no country has such an agreement with U.S. Customs. As matters now stand, a Form A made out and signed by the producer or other knowledgeable party is sufficient for U.S. Customs. However, some foreign governments still insist that goods exported from their countries under GSP documentation be accompanied by a Form A signed by governmental officials.

Caribbean Basin Economic Recovery Act (CBERA)

Approximately 25 countries and territories in the Caribbean Basin have been designated as beneficiary countries under the Caribbean Basin Economic Recovery Act (CBERA). These countries and territories are as follows:

Antigua and Barbuda	El Salvador	Netherlands Antilles
Aruba	Grenada	Panama
Bahamas, The	Guatemala	Saint Christopher and Nevis
Barbados	Guyana	Saint Lucia
Belize	Haiti	Saint Vincent and the Grenadines
Costa Rica	Honduras	Trinidad and Tobago
Dominica	Jamaica	Virgin Islands, British
Dominican Republic	Montserrat	

The articles eligible for duty free treatment under this program are identified in the Tariff Schedule. If the tariff number under which the goods are properly classified shows the word "Free" followed by an "E" or "E*" in the "Special" rate of duty subcolumn, then the goods may be entered duty free if they meet the other qualifications. For an example of how the "E" designator appears in the Tariff Schedule, see the illustration used in the discussion of GSP above.

Goods that are *not* eligible under CBERA are the following:

1. Certain textile and apparel items
2. Certain footwear, handbags, luggage, flat goods, work gloves, and leather apparel

3. Certain prepared or preserved tuna
4. Certain petroleum and petroleum products
5. Certain watches and watch parts
6. Certain sugars, syrups, and molasses
7. Certain articles of beef or veal

To qualify for duty free treatment under CBERA, an article must be imported directly from a beneficiary country into the Customs territory of the United States. In addition, an article must be wholly the growth, product, or manufacture of a beneficiary country or the article must be the result of a manufacturing or production process occurring in a beneficiary country that substantially transforms its constituent materials into a new and different article of commerce. In this regard, articles that are the result of simple combining or packaging operations, or the result of a dilution process that does not change the characteristics of the diluted substance, do not qualify for duty free treatment.

Duty free treatment is allowed only if the sum of (1) the cost or value of the materials produced in a beneficiary country or countries, plus (2) the direct costs of processing operations performed in a beneficiary country or countries, is not less than 35% of the appraised value of the article. In meeting the 35% requirement, the cost of materials and direct processing that are attributable to any beneficiary country may be counted. Therefore, materials that originate in any beneficiary country are qualifying.

For the purpose of CBERA, there are two additional rules that may be helpful in meeting the 35% requirement. They are as follows:

1. The cost or value of materials produced in the United States and in its Customs territory (other than Puerto Rico) may be counted toward the 35% requirement up to an amount not greater than 15% of the appraised value of the article.
2. For the purpose of the 35% requirement, the term "beneficiary country or countries" includes Puerto Rico and the U.S. Virgin Islands.

Rule 1 deals only with materials, while rule 2 deals with both materials and direct costs of processing operations. Therefore, Puerto Rican materials that are excluded under rule 1 may be counted under rule 2. Thus, Puerto Rican materials are not subject to the 15% limitation shown in rule 1.

The term "direct costs of processing operations" means the same thing under CBERA that it did under GSP. Specifically, this term refers to those costs either directly incurred in, or reasonably attributable to, the growth, production, manufacture, or assembly of the article under consideration. (Refer to the GSP discussion above which specifically lists those costs that are, and those costs that are not, part of the direct costs of processing operations.)

The documentation required to obtain duty free treatment under CBERA is the Certificate of Origin Form A. This is the same Form A as used for GSP but it is modified by deleting the words "Generalized System of Preferences" and inserting the words "Caribbean Basin Initiative." The form is filled out and signed by the manufacturer, exporter, or another party having knowledge of the necessary facts. Again, Form A need not be certified by any governmental authority.

The United States–Israel Free Trade Area (USIFTA)

The United States–Israel Free Trade Area (USIFTA) program applies only to products of Israel. The articles that are eligible for special treatment are indicated in the Tariff Schedule. Some articles may be completely duty free, while other articles receive only a lower duty rate than that shown as the general rate. If the tariff number under which an article is properly classified shows the word "Free" followed by the designation "IL" in the "Special" duty rate subcolumn, the article is eligible under the USIFTA and is duty free, provided it meets the other qualifications discussed below. For an example of how the "IL" designator appears in the Tariff Schedule, see the illustration used in the discussion of GSP above.

If an article is eligible under USIFTA but not completely duty free, a designation such as "2% (IL)" will appear in the "Special" duty rate subcolumn. This means the article is eligible and that the special duty rate under the USIFTA is 2% *ad valorem*. Where a 2% rate applies for the USIFTA, the general rate might be 5%. Thus, the duty rate under the USIFTA would be reduced by 60%.

To qualify for preferential treatment under the USIFTA, an article must be imported directly from Israel into the Customs territory of the United States. In addition, an article must be wholly the growth, product, or manufacture of Israel or the article must be the result of a manufacturing or production process occurring in Israel that substantially transforms its constituent materials into a new and different article of commerce. In this regard, articles that are the result of simple combining or packaging operations, or the result of a dilution process that does not change the characteristics of the diluted substance, do not qualify for preferential treatment.

Preferential treatment is allowed only if the sum of (1) the cost or value of the materials produced in Israel, plus (2) the direct costs of processing operations performed in Israel, is not less than 35% of the appraised value of the article. In order to count toward the 35% requirement, materials must originate in Israel. However, the cost or value of materials produced in the United States and in its Customs territory may be counted toward the 35% requirement up to an amount not greater than 15% of the appraised value of the article.

The term "direct costs of processing operations" means the same thing under the USIFTA that it did under GSP. Specifically, this term refers to those costs either directly incurred in, or reasonably attributable to, the growth, production, manufacture, or assembly of the article under consideration. (Refer to the GSP discussion above which specifically lists those costs that are, and those costs that are not, part of the direct costs of processing operations.)

The documentation required to obtain preferential treatment under the USIFTA is the Certificate of Origin Form A. This is the same Form A as used for GSP but it is modified by deleting the words "Generalized System of Preferences" and inserting the words "United States-Israel Free Trade Area." The form is filled out and signed by the manufacturer, exporter, or another party having knowledge of the necessary facts.

The United States–Canada Free-Trade Agreement (USCFTA)

The United States–Canada Free-Trade Agreement (USCFTA) program applies only to products that are shipped from Canada to the United States. Under the agreement, all qualifying goods will eventually be entitled to duty free entry into the United States. The period of time required for articles to reach duty free status varies, depending upon the class of goods. Some goods are given immediate duty free status, while other goods are to reach duty free status from the current level of general duty rates through a process of "staged reductions." Some staged goods will reach duty free status in five years by experiencing a 20% reduction in duty rates over a period of five years. Another group of staged goods will reach duty free status in 10 years, experiencing a 10% reduction in duty rates each year.

The articles that are eligible for special treatment are indicated in the Tariff Schedule. Some articles may be completely duty free, while other articles receive only a lower duty rate, as discussed above. If the tariff number under which an article is properly classified shows the word "Free" followed by the designation "CA" in the "Special" duty rate subcolumn, the article is eligible under the USCFTA and is duty free, provided it meets the other qualifications discussed below. For an example of how the "CA" designator appears in the Tariff Schedule, see the illustration used in the discussion of GSP above.

If an article is eligible under the USCFTA but not completely duty free, a designation such as "4.5% (CA)" will appear in the "Special" duty rate subcolumn. This means the article is eligible and the special duty rate under the USCFTA is 4.5% *ad valorem.*

Stated very generally, goods are eligible for this preference if both of the following occur:

1. The goods originate in Canada, the United States, or both.
2. The goods are directly shipped to the United States from Canada.

There are certain goods that are specifically excluded from eligibility for this preference and they include:

1. Goods that have merely undergone simple packaging or simple combining operations or have undergone mere dilution with water or with another substance that does not materially alter the characteristics of the goods.
2. Goods that have undergone any process or work, the sole purpose of which is to circumvent the rules of origin by making the goods appear eligible for the preference.

The Customs Regulations set forth specific classes of goods that are considered to originate in Canada, the United States, or both. For the purpose of the agreement, goods may be regarded as originating goods if they fall into one of the following classes:

1. Wholly of Canadian or U.S. origin
2. Transformed with a change in classification
3. Transformed without a change in classification

The largest group of eligible goods is, by far, those of class 2. Each class of goods will be discussed and explained separately.

Class 1—goods that are wholly of Canadian or U.S. origin—includes goods that are wholly obtained or produced in the territory of Canada, the United States, or both. Examples of goods that are wholly of Canadian or U.S. origin are the following:

1. Mineral goods extracted in the territory of Canada and/or the United States
2. Goods harvested in the territory of Canada and/or the United States
3. Live animals born and raised in the territory of Canada and/or the United States

Class 2—goods transformed with a change in classification—refers to goods that have been transformed by a processing operation that results in a change in classification, where the constituent materials are classified under one tariff heading and the finished product is classified under a different tariff heading.

Goods are eligible under the USCFTA primarily because of processing or manufacturing operations that change the original material from one classification in the Tariff Schedule to another classification, after processing. Eligibility is most frequently determined by such changes in classification, and by such changes in classification alone, without reference to the value of materials or direct costs of processing as a percentage of the appraised value. However, in a small number of instances, not only must there be a change in classification but there must also be a certain value content in terms of materials and labor expended in Canada. An example of a change in classification and an example of a change in classification plus the required value content are set forth below:

Section VI: Chapters 28 through 38.

(aa) A change to chapters 28 through 38 from any chapter outside that group.
(bb) A change to any subheading of chapters 28 through 38 from any other subheading within those chapters; provided, except for the other rules in this section, that the value of materials originating in the territory of Canada and/or the United States plus the direct cost of processing performed in the territory of Canada and/or the United States constitute not less than 50 percent of the value of the goods when exported to the territory of the United States.

The excerpt from the Tariff Schedule shown above deals with two of the classification change possibilities for goods in section VI of the Tariff Schedule, specifically for goods classifiable in chapters 28 through 38. The first example, designated "(aa)," states that goods are eligible if, as a result of processing in Canada, constituent materials classified in any chapter outside chapters 28 through 38 change to a classification in chapters 28 through 38. This is an example of a simple classification change which, by itself, makes the goods eligible for the preference. When an article meets the requirements stated in such a classification change, it is eligible for the preference without reference to the value of materials and labor originating in Canada.

The second example, designated "(bb)," is an illustration of a change in classification that is accompanied by a specific value-content requirement. In this case, not only must the classification change occur, but the value of materials originating in the territory of Canada and/or the United States, plus the direct cost of processing performed in the territory of Canada and/or the United States, must constitute not less than 50% of the value of the goods when exported to the territory of the United States.

Thus, the two examples show how goods of class 2 are eligible for the preference because they are transformed with a change in classification.

By far, the most frequent requirement is merely a change in classification. Tariff headnote 3(c) lists 146 specific rules for qualifying changes in classification, either with or without a value-content requirement. Of these 146 classification change rules, only 23 also have the value-content requirement as specified in example "(bb)" above.

Class 3 deals with goods that are eligible for the preference because they are transformed without a change in classification. This is a class of goods with apparently limited application, but it is included because there will be instances when certain goods ought to qualify even though there is no change in classification. An example is an assembly of goods that does not result in a change in classification (1) because the goods were imported unassembled or disassembled but classified as the finished goods by reference to General Rule of Interpretation 2(a) of the Tariff Schedule, or (2) because the tariff subheading for the goods provides for both the goods themselves and their parts. An example of (2) is a Canadian exporter who assembles barbers' chairs in Canada from parts imported into Canada from a third country. Both the imported parts and the finished barbers' chairs are classified under tariff subheading 9402.10. Goods of this nature may nevertheless be qualifying goods if:

1. The value of originating materials and the direct cost of assembling in Canada, the United States, or both constitute not less than 50% of the value of the goods when exported to the United States.
2. The assembled goods are not subsequently processed or further assembled in a third country.
3. The goods are shipped directly to the United States.

Goods meeting the above qualifications are considered eligible for the preference, even though there has been no change in classification.

In addition to the three classes of originating goods discussed above, there is a special rule regarding accessories, spare parts, and tools. This rule states that accessories, spare parts, or tools delivered with any piece of equipment, machinery, apparatus, or vehicle that form part of its standard equipment shall be treated as having the same origin as that equipment, machinery, apparatus, or vehicle if the quantities and values of such accessories, spare parts, or tools are customary for the equipment, machinery, apparatus, or vehicle.

Reference was made above to the value-content requirement which requires that the value of originating materials and the direct cost of assembling or processing in Canada, the United States, or both must constitute not less than 50% of the value of the goods when exported to the United States. The terms "value of originating materials," "direct cost of assembling or processing," and "value of goods when exported" all have very specialized meanings which are set forth in the Customs

Regulations and headnote 3 (c) of the Tariff Schedule. These sources define what costs are and what costs are not included within the meaning of these terms. These definitions are too lengthy to set forth here. Therefore, the importer who finds he or she must meet one of the few value-content requirements should refer specifically to the Customs Regulations or the headnote to determine the precise meaning of the terms.

The documentation required to obtain the preference under the USCFTA is the Exporter's Certificate of Origin. The Exporter's Certificate of Origin must be prepared on Customs Form 353, unless the exporter uses a computerized format or some other format approved by the Customs Service in Washington, D.C. The Exporter's Certificate of Origin is completed and signed by the manufacturer, the exporter, or another person with knowledge of the necessary facts.

The Exporter's Certificate of Origin does not have to be filed with the consumption entry for the goods. However, it must be in the importer's possession or available to him or her at the time the entry is filed and the preference is claimed. The Exporter's Certificate of Origin must be presented to the district director upon request.

In a somewhat unusual provision, the claim for preference under the USCFTA must be made at the time of filing the Customs entry. Failure to make a timely claim when the entry is presented to Customs will result in liquidation of the entry at the normal general rate of duty that applies to the goods. This claim requirement is certainly very different from the claim requirements for the other special duty rate programs discussed above. For all the other programs, a claim for preferential treatment could be made after the time of entry, as long as the claim was made prior to liquidation of the entry. This is not true under the USCFTA. Under this program, the claim for preference must be made at the time of filing the Customs entry.

Any evidence of the country of origin or of direct shipment to the United States submitted in support of a preference under the USCFTA is subject to such verification as the district director may require. If any further information requested by U.S. Customs to support the claim of preference is not properly tendered to Customs, the district director may refuse to grant the claim for preference.

The importer must retain the Exporter's Certificate of Origin for a period of five years from the date of entry, and it must be made available upon request to any Customs official during that time.

TEMPORARY IMPORTATIONS UNDER BOND (TIB)

Certain articles may be admitted into the United States, temporarily free of duty, under a Customs bond. Goods imported for sale or for sale on approval are not eligible for temporary importation under bond (TIB). The specific articles that may be admitted under TIB procedures are found in chapter 98 of the Tariff Schedule. The tariff numbers and descriptions are as follows:

9813.00.05   Articles to be repaired, altered or processed (including processes which result in articles manufactured or produced in the United States).
[Note: Merchandise will not be admitted under this provision if it is to be manufactured into a U.S. product which is:
1. Alcohol, distilled spirits, wine, or beer or any dilution or mixture of these.
2. A perfume or other commodity containing ethyl alcohol.
3. A product of wheat.]

9813.00.10   Models of women's wearing apparel imported by manufacturers for use solely as models in their own establishments.

9813.00.15   Articles imported by illustrators and photographers for use solely as models in their own establishments, in the illustrating of catalogues, pamphlets or advertising matters.

9813.00.20   Samples solely for use in taking orders for merchandise.

9813.00.25   Articles solely for examination with a view to reproduction, or for such examination and reproduction (except photoengraved printing plates for examination and reproduction); and motion-picture advertising films.

9813.00.30   Articles intended solely for testing, experimental or review purposes, including specifications, photographs and similar articles for use in connection with experiments or for study.

9813.00.35   Automobiles, motorcycles, bicycles, airplanes, airships, balloons, boats, racing shells and similar vehicles and craft, and the usual equipment of the foregoing; all the foregoing which are brought temporarily into the United States by nonresidents for the purpose of taking part in races or other specific contests.

9813.00.40   Locomotives and other railroad equipment brought temporarily into the United States for use in clearing obstructions, fighting fires or making emergency repairs on railroads within the United States, or for use in transportation otherwise than in international traffic when the Secretary of the Treasury finds that the temporary use of foreign railroad equipment is necessary to meet an emergency.

9813.00.45   Containers for compressed gases, filled or empty, and containers or other articles in use for covering or holding merchandise (including personal or household effects) during transportation and suitable for reuse for that purpose.

9813.00.50   Professional equipment, tools of trade, repair components for equipment or tools admitted under this heading and camping equipment; all the foregoing imported by or for nonresidents sojourning temporarily in the United States and for the use of such nonresidents.

9813.00.55   Articles of special design for temporary use exclusively in connection with the manufacture or production of articles for export.

9813.00.60   Animals and poultry brought into the United States for the purpose of breeding, exhibition or competition for prizes, and the usual equipment therefor.

9813.00.65   Theatrical scenery, properties and apparel brought into the United States by proprietors or managers of theatrical exhibitions arriving from abroad for temporary use by them in such exhibitions.

9813.00.70   Works of the free fine arts, engravings, photographic pictures and philosophical and scientific apparatus brought into the United States by professional artists, lecturers or scientists arriving from abroad for use by them for exhibition and in illustration, promotion and encouragement of art, science or industry in the United States.

9813.00.75   Automobiles, automobile chassis, automobile bodies, cutaway portions of any of the foregoing and parts for any of the foregoing, finished, unfinished or cutaway, when intended solely for show purposes.
              [Note: Articles under this heading will only be admitted under bond for a period of 6 months, and this period cannot be extended.]

Some of the above provisions require that special Customs forms be submitted at the time of entry. In addition, for some of the items there are restrictions on the way in which the items can be used in the United States.

The articles shown above are admitted duty free only because they must be exported from the United States. To ensure exportation, a Customs bond must be filed at the time of entry. To meet the terms of the bond, the articles must be exported within one year of their importation. The period for exportation may be extended for one or two additional one-year periods, but the total time the goods remain under bond in the United States may not exceed three years. Extensions of the original one-year period are granted only upon a written application to Customs for such an extension. A request for an extension must be submitted before the expiration of the original one-year period, otherwise it is untimely.

At the time of entry, the importer must show the chapter 98 tariff number and description he or she thinks applies to the goods to be temporarily imported. In addition, the importer must file a detailed statement indicating the intended use of the articles in the United States. This statement must be complete enough to permit Customs to determine that the goods are entitled to temporary entry under the tariff number chosen by the importer. The importer must also declare that the goods will not be used in any manner other than as stated by him or her and that the goods are not imported for sale or for sale on approval. The invoice filed with the entry must describe each article in detail and set forth the value of each item.

The bond required to be given at the time of entry is, in most cases, for an amount equal to twice the duties that would be paid if the goods were entered for consumption at their regular rates of duty.

Articles entered under the TIB provisions must be exported using special procedures that permit Customs to verify the fact of exportation of the articles. The articles may be exported from the port of entry or from another port. In either case, the importer must file Customs Form 3495 with the district director in sufficient time before exportation to permit Customs to examine and identify the articles prior to exportation. After Customs Form 3495 is filed, the importer will be notified where the goods are to be taken for examination and identification.

Under the procedures currently in use at some districts, the importer is notified at the time of filing the entry whether the goods will be examined by Customs prior to exportation. In many cases, Customs may not want to examine each shipment prior to exportation. This would probably hold true for a company that uses TIBs extensively and whose exportations are repetitive in nature.

After the goods entered under TIB have been properly exported, the bond given at the time of entry is canceled. If the articles are not properly exported within the original one-year period, or within any extensions of time granted by Customs, the importer becomes liable to pay liquidated damages in the amount of the bond. The demand for liquidated damages is made in writing, and the importer is permitted to file a petition for mitigation of the damages. Liquidated damages proceedings are described in chapter 11.

Chapter 13

Duty Drawback and Duty Relief for Damaged Goods

This chapter may be of particular interest to importers because it deals with (1) refunds of Customs duties that are available on imported materials or articles that are exported from the United States and (2) refunds of duties paid on imported goods that are damaged, defective, or irregular at the time of importation. A refund obtained when imported merchandise is exported is referred to as a "drawback" of duties; a refund of duties that results from the importation of inferior merchandise that is not exported is referred to as an "abatement" of duties.

DUTY DRAWBACK

"Drawback" refers to a refund or remission, in whole or in part, of a Customs duty, internal revenue tax, or other levied fee because of a particular use made of the merchandise on which the duty, tax, or fee was assessed or collected. This discussion will concentrate on refunds of duties, as opposed to taxes and fees.

The amount of duty that may be refunded as a result of drawback depends upon the particular type of drawback claim involved. Many types of drawback permit a refund of 99% of the duties paid on imported materials or articles. Thus, the savings available through the use of drawback procedures can be significant.

Every year millions of dollars in drawback entitlement go unclaimed. This occurs in part because the drawback procedure is considered too time-consuming in relation to the amount of refunds possible or, more likely, because many exporters are simply unaware of the duty drawback procedures that exist.

To determine whether he or she is eligible to receive duty refunds under drawback procedures, the **importer** need only ask himself or herself the two following questions:

1. Do I export goods from the United States?
2. Do the products I export contain any imported material?

If the answer to both questions is yes, the importer may be eligible to obtain duty drawback. The following chart illustrates various factual situations in which parties are qualified to receive duty refunds under drawback procedures:

Party	Step 1	Step 2	Step 3
A	Imports material	Manufactures goods from imported material	Exports manufactured goods
B	Buys material imported by another party	Manufactures goods from imported material	Exports manufactured goods
C	Buys an intermediate product manufactured in the United States with imported material	Further manufactures intermediate product into finished product	Exports finished product
D	Buys finished goods manufactured in the United States with imported material	Exports finished goods	
E	Imports finished goods	Exports finished goods in same condition as when imported	
F	Buys finished goods imported by another party (imported goods are not changed by importer)	Exports finished goods in same condition as when imported	
G	Imports goods that do not meet sample or specifications or goods shipped without the importer's consent	Exports these rejected goods	

All the parties designated as *A* through *G* would be eligible to receive refunds of the duties paid on the imported materials or articles, provided the proper procedures are followed and all necessary documents are presented to Customs. As can be seen, even parties who do not import the material or articles may be eligible to receive drawback on the imported items. It may be the case that many exporters do not apply for duty drawback because of the erroneous belief that drawback is available only to the person who imports the materials or articles. This is definitely not the case. Although there are other limited instances where drawback is available, the five most common types of drawback are the following:

1. Manufacturing drawback—direct identification
2. Manufacturing drawback—substitution
3. Same condition drawback—direct identification
4. Same condition drawback—substitution
5. Rejected merchandise drawback

Each type of drawback will be discussed individually. Initially, however, some general observations that apply to all types of drawback will be noted.

First, all records that are required to be kept by anyone with respect to a drawback claim must be retained for a period of at least three years after payment of the drawback claim.

Second, under the drawback law, it is the exporter of merchandise who is entitled to drawback, unless the manufacturer or producer who utilizes the imported material reserves the right to the drawback claim. A manufacturer or producer who reserves the right to the drawback claim may receive the drawback payment, provided satisfactory evidence is presented to show that the reservation was made with the knowledge and consent of the exporter.

Third, if the party who exports the merchandise and claims the drawback is not the importer of the materials or articles that form the basis of the claim, then the exporter-claimant must obtain a certificate of delivery or a certificate of manufacture and delivery to perfect the drawback claim. These documents establish the importation of the goods and the delivery of those goods to the claimant, with or without intervening manufacturing.

Manufacturing Drawback

All refunds of duty under manufacturing drawback are obtained as the result of a contract between the Customs Service and the drawback claimant. The contract referred to is not the normal type of contract document used when parties memorialize a commercial agreement. Rather, the drawback claimant submits to Customs a letter, referred to as a "drawback proposal," that contains an offer to operate under drawback law and regulations. Each proposal is required to:

1. Describe the manufacturing operation fully and method of compliance with all requirements of the drawback law and regulations.
2. State that the records of identification, manufacture or production, and storage as prescribed in the Customs Regulations will be maintained.
3. Contain an agreement to follow the methods and keep records concerning drawback procedures.

If the required proposal complies with all the laws and regulations, the Customs Service issues a "drawback acceptance," which is a letter from Customs to the manufacturer or producer accepting the proposal. The drawback proposal and the drawback acceptance by Customs, taken together, constitute a contract which is referred to as a specific drawback contract. This is the contract under which the drawback claimant operates and to which he or she is expected to adhere.

Under manufacturing drawback, the manufactured product must be exported within five years after the date of importation of the imported material that forms the basis of the drawback claim. In addition, the drawback entry and all the documents necessary to complete a drawback claim must be filed or applied for within three years after the date of exportation of the articles on which drawback is claimed.

Manufacturing Drawback—Direct Identification. Under this type of drawback, a claimant may file for drawback of duties that were paid on imported material that is utilized in the production of an article that is subsequently exported. As a general rule, the manufacture or production involved must change or transform an imported article into a new and different article having a distinctive character or use. Therefore, the manufacturing process involved must be sufficiently substantial and constitute more than a minor alteration.

It has been held that a change in form alone, where the merchandise before the process is the same as that after the process, is not sufficient in some circumstances to evidence a "manufacture or production" for drawback purposes. On the other hand, Customs has held that assembly is a manufacture for drawback purposes in some situations, depending upon the facts and circumstances. For example, a manufacture or production occurs where imported eyeglass frames are fitted with domestic lenses. In this case, it was held that a manufactured article having a different character or use resulted from the assembly process because an imported article that was not suited for commercial use was further manufactured into one that was suited for commercial use.

The above discussion represents the type of analysis that is involved in the determination of whether or not a sufficient manufacture occurs to permit drawback under manufacturing drawback. The term "direct identification" refers to the requirement that the drawback claimant be able to show precisely what imported material was utilized in the production of the specific shipments being exported. To meet this requirement, the claimant must maintain strict inventory control over the imported material during production and up to the time of exportation.

Manufacturing Drawback—Substitution. Under this type of drawback, the claimant may obtain refunds on imported material, even if the imported material is not physically used in the product to be exported. If imported duty paid merchandise is replaced during the manufacturing process with duty free or domestic merchandise of the same kind and quality, and the manufacture or production occurs within a period of three years from the receipt of the imported merchandise by the manufacturer or producer of the articles, drawback is allowed upon exportation of the articles, even though none of the imported merchandise may actually have been used in the manufacture or production of the exported articles. Even though the imported merchandise is not used in the exported articles, it must still be used in production and within the same three-year period as the substituted material. The amount of drawback is the same as that which would have been allowed had the merchandise been made with the imported material that was replaced.

Again, the manufactured product must be exported within five years after the date of importation of the imported material. The drawback claim must be filed within three years after the date of exportation of the articles on which drawback is claimed. Note that, under the substitution provision, the imported material or substituted material must be used in the manufacturing process within three years after the receipt of the imported material by the manufacturer. As with direct identification, the manufacturing process must be sufficiently substantial to qualify the exported article for drawback.

Same Condition Drawback

Under same condition drawback there is no requirement that a contract exist in order to obtain the benefits of the drawback procedure. However, an exporter-claimant who desires to export merchandise with benefit of drawback under this provision must file with the Customs Service a completed Customs Form 7539, along with a copy of the import entry or other documents identifying the import entry, the date of entry, and the port of entry where the merchandise was imported. The Customs form must certify that the merchandise is in the same condition as when imported and that the merchandise was not used within the United States before exportation. The completed Customs form 7539 must be filed with Customs at least five working days prior to the date of intended exportation of the merchandise, unless Customs has approved a shorter filing period or waived the filing of this prior notice of intent to export. Customs may or may not examine the merchandise prior to its exportation.

Same Condition Drawback—Direct Identification. Under this type of drawback, the claimant may file for a refund of duties on imported merchandise that is exported in the same condition as when imported, provided it did not undergo any manufacturing and was not used in the United States before exportation. To qualify, the goods must not have been processed, modified, or altered from their condition at the time of importation. However, the performing of incidental operations such as testing, cleaning, repacking, and inspecting of the imported merchandise will not be treated as a use of that merchandise for the purpose of disqualifying it from same condition drawback.

In one case, imported television sets had to be adjusted in the United States prior to exportation to a foreign country in order to make them completely operable in the foreign country. As a consequence of these adjustments, it was held that the exported television sets were not in the same condition as when imported, and therefore same condition drawback was denied.

In order to qualify for this type of drawback, the merchandise must be exported within three years of the date of its importation. Again, the drawback claim must be filed within three years after the date of exportation of the articles.

The term "direct identification" requires that the drawback claimant be able to prove exactly when and on what import documents the exported items were imported into the United States.

Same Condition Drawback—Substitution. Under this drawback provision, claimants may file for drawback on imported material or articles, even though the material or articles that are exported are not the exact material or articles that were imported. The substitution provision allows the replacement, prior to export, of the imported material with domestic material. In this case, however, the domestic material that stands as a replacement for the imported material must be "fungible merchandise." Fungible merchandise is merchandise that for commercial purposes is identical and interchangeable in all situations. In order for replacement merchandise to be fungible, it must be so close in characteristics to the merchandise it replaces that it is considered to be commercially interchangeable under all circumstances.

In addition, the imported and substituted merchandise both must be in the possession of the exporter during a certain legally defined time period which begins when the merchandise is received and ends three years after the importation of the merchandise. Again, the imported material must not have been used, manufactured, or altered while in the United States, except for those incidental operations discussed above. The substituted merchandise when exported must be in the same condition as was the imported merchandise when imported. The substituted merchandise must be exported within three years of the date of importation of the merchandise forming the basis of the claim. The drawback claim must be filed within three years after the date of exportation of the articles on which drawback is claimed.

Rejected Merchandise Drawback

Rejected merchandise drawback allows for drawback of duties upon the exportation of imported merchandise that does not conform to sample or specifications or that was shipped without the consent of the importer. The merchandise must be returned to Customs' custody for exportation within 90 days after the release of the goods from Customs' custody, unless Customs authorizes a longer time period. The exporter-claimant must file with Customs a drawback entry on Customs Form 7539, along with sufficient documentation to establish that the merchandise does not conform to sample or specifications or that the goods were shipped without the consent of the importer. If Customs is satisfied that the goods are rejected merchandise, it will designate a place for redelivery of the merchandise for examination.

The exporter-claimant must return the merchandise to Customs' custody within 90 days after its original release by Customs, unless the importer requests an extension of time. Customs normally will grant an extension of time for the redelivery of the goods beyond the 90 days if the importer has shown that the failure or inability to return the goods within the 90 days was for reasons beyond the control of the importer. If the merchandise is not returned to Customs within the original 90 days, or within any extension granted by Customs, the drawback claim will be denied.

Drawback under this provision is payable only to a claimant who is the importer of record of the merchandise or the actual owner named in the import entry.

It should be noted that rejected merchandise may also be exported under the provisions of the same condition drawback law and regulations discussed above. Therefore, in any case where the importer has failed to return the rejected merchandise to Customs within 90 days of release, an alternative claim for drawback may be filed under the same condition—direct identification provisions.

Filing of Drawback Claims

Some of the types of drawback discussed above are fairly straight-forward and the document preparation is not particularly difficult. This is especially true of rejected merchandise drawback and same condition—direct identification drawback. However, whenever manufacturing drawback or same condition—substitution drawback are involved, the documentation requirements and recordkeeping provisions can become quite complicated. For example, the records to be maintained for direct identification manufacturing drawback must show the following:

1. The date or inclusive dates of manufacture or production

2. The quantity and identity of the imported duty paid merchandise or drawback products used in the articles manufactured or produced, or, if claim for waste is waived and there are no multiple products, the quantity and identity of the imported merchandise or drawback products appearing in the articles manufac-tured or produced

3. The quantity and description of the articles manufactured or produced

4. The quantity of waste incurred; if claim for waste is waived and the appearing in basis is used, waste records need not be kept unless required to establish the quantity of imported duty paid merchandise or drawback products appearing in the articles

5. That the finished articles on which drawback is claimed were exported within five years after the importation of the duty paid merchandise.

In addition to these recordkeeping requirements, there are further recordkeeping requirements where substitution is involved, either for manufacturing or same condition drawback. Because of the complexity of the recordkeeping and the difficulty in preparing the drawback claims for manufacturing drawback and same condition—substitution drawback, claimants frequently utilize the services of "drawback specialists" in the presentation of their claims to Customs.

A small percentage of customs brokers perform services as drawback specialists. Independent companies also act as drawback specialists. In addition, the consulting groups of some of the large accounting firms offer services and consultations in connection with drawback procedures.

In any event, the importer who believes that he or she may be in a position to benefit from the drawback law and regulations should not hesitate to consult with a drawback specialist. Many drawback specialists provide their services on a contingency fee basis. That is, the specialist will perform all required services to obtain the drawback in return for a certain percentage of the refunds recovered. Some may also charge a one-time set-up fee for the drawback program. Since there is no charge under these circumstances for the privilege of consulting with a specialist regarding drawback possibilities, the advice of these specialists should at least be obtained.

DUTY RELIEF ON DAMAGED AND DEFECTIVE MERCHANDISE

When merchandise is discovered after importation to be damaged, defective, or irregular, refunds of duties may be made by the Customs Service to reflect the fact that the merchandise is either completely worthless or otherwise not first-quality merchandise. The amount of the allowances made in duties depends upon the nature of the merchandise and the extent of the deterioration, damage, defect, or irregularity.

Merchandise Completely Worthless at Importation

Perishable goods such as fruits, vegetables, fish, or meats that are condemned by health officers or other proper authorities are entitled to a full refund of duties if the condemnation occurs within 10 days after landing of the merchandise. Written notice of the condemnation must be given to Customs within five days of the date of condemnation.

Perishable merchandise that has not been condemned but that is nevertheless commercially worthless by reason of damage or deterioration is also entitled to a full refund of duties. Refunds will be permitted on an entire shipment or the deteriorated portion of a shipment. A written application for allowance in duties must be filed with Customs within 96 hours after unlading of the goods *and* before any portion of the shipment has been removed from the pier or other place of arrival.

Claims for allowances in duty on nonperishable merchandise are more diverse because the various types of problems permit different degrees of commercial inferiority in the goods. Goods may be rendered completely worthless by reason of damage or deterioration. Examples of these include broken glass items and rusted metal products.

When a shipment of nonperishable merchandise, or any portion of it, is found by Customs to be completely without commercial value in its imported condition by reason of damage or deterioration, those items with no commercial value are treated as nonimportations and a full refund of duties can be made. Although there is no set time limit for the importer's notification to Customs, the regulations do permit Customs to examine the merchandise to verify its condition. Therefore, notification to Customs of the inferior nature of the goods should occur within a reasonable time after importation. In addition, where only a portion of a shipment is without commercial value, the importer must segregate the good items from the bad items under Customs' supervision. Subsequent to segregation, Customs will examine all the items and determine by count, weight, or other means the percentage of the shipment that is without commercial value.

Merchandise Partially Damaged or Defective at Importation

Merchandise not completely worthless may be only partially inferior for various reasons, including damage, defects, or irregularities. Examples of these problems are the following:

1. A shipment of otherwise working clocks has all or most of the glass face covers broken (damage). Such clocks are not without commercial value and therefore the clocks are only partially damaged.
2. A shipment of otherwise working appliances has uniformly defective power switches that fail to turn the appliances on (defective). These switches must be replaced after importation.
3. Women's pantsuits with tops and bottoms were made from two different fabric lots. As a result, the color of the top does not quite match the color of the bottom, and this difference is noticeable (irregular).

Merchandise that is partially damaged, defective, or irregular may be appraised by Customs in its condition as imported, with an allowance made in value to the extent of the damage, defects, or irregularities. If the goods are subject to an *ad valorem* rate of duty (that is, percentage of the value), lowering the appraised value of the merchandise will result in a refund of duties on the shipment.

Since Customs may want to examine the merchandise and may request segregation under Customs' supervision, it is prudent for the importer to bring the problem to Customs' attention as soon as practicable after importation of the goods.

In the case of partially damaged or inferior goods, Customs often requests samples in lieu of a complete examination of the shipment. Copies of correspondence, telexes, or facsimiles between the importer and the seller may also be requested to verify the nature and extent of the damage, defects, or irregularities. The seller of the merchandise is usually the first person notified of the problem by the importer and the normal business communications from the buyer to the seller are usually accepted by Customs as supporting documents for the importer's claims regarding the inferior nature of the goods.

While establishing the nature of the damage or defect is relatively easy, establishing the amount of the allowance in value is a different matter. Granted the goods should not be appraised under transaction value at the price paid, what should the reduction in value be? The appraisement law and the Customs Regulations do not reveal any method for determining the lower appraised value. As a result, different Customs districts have developed different solutions to this problem.

One approach to the problem is to allow a reduction in value only to the extent that the importer receives a refund or rebate from the seller. If the importer originally paid $10,000 for the goods, but receives a $1,000 rebate from the seller, Customs would appraise the shipment at $9,000. The difficulty with this approach is that it does not take into consideration the commercial realities of the situation. Frequently it is the case that (1) the seller will make no rebate or (2) the seller's rebate is only a token acknowledgement of the extent of the problem and the amount rebated does not adequately compensate the importer for the full extent of the damage, defects, or irregularities.

A different approach, which attempts to deal with commercial realities, involves a reduction in the appraised value equal to the reduction in the importer's resale price. If (1) the purchase price of the goods is $10.00 each, (2) the importer can establish that he or she had presold, or could have sold, first-quality goods for $20.00 each, and (3) the importer establishes that he or she sold the inferior goods for only $15.00 each, then the goods can be appraised at $7.50 each ($15.00 divided by $20.00, times $10.00).

Since the Customs Regulations are silent regarding the method of appraisement to be used, any reasonable means of arriving at a lower appraised value ought to be acceptable.

Finally, the Customs Regulations state that where goods are partially damaged, defective, or irregular, no allowance may be made in the specific duties due or in the weight, quantity, or measure. Thus, goods subject only to a specific rate of duty (for example, 10 cents per piece) or to a compound rate of duty (for example, 10% plus 7 cents per linear foot) will receive no relief from duties on the specific rate that is applicable.

Chapter 14

Customs Bonded Warehouses and Foreign Trade Zones

This chapter will discuss Customs bonded warehouses and foreign trade zones and the uses to which these facilities may be put. Both permit the importation and storage of merchandise without the payment of duties. Many types of activities involving imported goods may be carried on in both facilities before entry for consumption or exportation of the goods. In general, foreign trade zones offer the importer greater latitude in manipulation of goods and in manufacturing merchandise from imported materials.

CUSTOMS BONDED WAREHOUSES

The types of Customs bonded warehouses and their uses are as follows:

1. *Class 1.* Premises owned or leased by the government and used for the storage of merchandise undergoing examination by the customs officer, under seizure, or pending final release from Customs' custody.

2. *Class 2.* Importers' private bonded warehouses used exclusively for the storage of merchandise belonging or consigned to the proprietor thereof.

3. *Class 3.* Public bonded warehouses used exclusively for the storage of imported merchandise.

4. *Class 4.* Bonded yards or sheds for the storage of heavy and bulky imported merchandise; stables, feeding pens, corrals, or other similar buildings or limited enclosures for the storage of imported animals; and tanks for the storage of imported liquid merchandise in bulk.

5. *Class 5.* Bonded bins or parts of buildings or elevators to be used for the storage of grain.

6. *Class 6.* Warehouses for the manufacture in bond, solely for exportation, of articles made in whole or in part of imported materials or of materials subject to internal revenue tax.

7. *Class 7.* Warehouses bonded for smelting and refining imported metal-bearing materials for exportation or domestic consumption.

8. *Class 8.* Bonded warehouses established for the purpose of cleaning, sorting, repacking, or otherwise changing in condition, but not manufacturing, imported merchandise.

Warehouses in classes 1 through 5 are all primarily for the storage of imported merchandise. The class 1 warehouse is owned or leased by the government, and it is this type of facility that may be used for the storage of "general order" merchandise when an entry for imported goods is not timely filed by the importer.

The class 2 warehouse is generally found on property owned or leased by the importer. Normally, such a warehouse is only a designated portion of a building used by the importer. By setting aside a portion of the importer's property, the importer may store imported goods without the payment of duties until such time as he or she desires to withdraw the goods and enter them for consumption. When only part of a building is used by the importer as a Customs bonded warehouse, the bonded and unbonded portions of the building must be effectively separated by partitions of substantial materials and construction, erected in such a manner as to render it impossible for unauthorized personnel to enter the bonded facility except by an easily detectable breaking and entering.

The class 3 warehouse, which is the one most used by importers, is a public facility whose only purpose is the storage of imported merchandise. Anyone who imports merchandise into the United States may store such goods in a public bonded warehouse without the payment of duties, until such time as the merchandise is withdrawn and entered for consumption. Warehouses of class 4 and 5 are also primarily storage facilities.

Warehouses of class 6 and class 7 are specialized warehouses that may be used for manufacturing and refining. Note, however, that general manufacturing of merchandise to be entered into the United States is not permitted under either class.

The class 8 warehouse is primarily intended for the manipulation of imported goods.

The Customs Service exercises supervision over all classes of warehouses. The district director may authorize a customs officer to supervise any particular transaction or procedure at any bonded warehouse facility. Supervision may be performed through periodic audits of the warehouse proprietor's records, quantity counts of goods in warehouse inventories, spot checks of selected warehouse transactions or procedures, and reviews of conditions of recordkeeping, security, or storage in a warehouse facility.

Merchandise that is deposited in any type of bonded warehouse becomes liable for the expenses of labor and storage attributable to those goods. Such charges become a lien upon the merchandise and withdrawal of the goods is normally not permitted without the payment of these charges.

Under proper circumstances, an importer may be granted permission by Customs to examine, sample, and repack merchandise in a bonded warehouse. The importer may be granted permission to have potential buyers examine the merchandise in the bonded warehouse.

The physical handling of merchandise in a bonded warehouse is referred to as manipulation. In the classes of warehouses intended primarily for the storage of goods, the type of manipulation that is permitted is of a limited nature. On the other hand, manipulation warehouses of the class 8 variety permit a wide range of activity, including cleaning, sorting, repacking, or otherwise changing the condition of the merchandise if such changes do not amount to a manufacture. A change in the condition of the merchandise is permissible even if such change results in a lower rate of duty or duty free status for the goods upon withdrawal for consumption.

Any type of merchandise may be entered into a bonded warehouse, except for perishable goods and explosive substances other than firecrackers. Dangerous and highly flammable merchandise may generally not be entered for warehouse without the written consent of the insurance company that insures the warehouse where the goods will be stored.

If merchandise has been entered under any other type of entry and has remained in the continuous custody of Customs, a warehouse entry may be substituted for the previous entry. If estimated duties were deposited on the previous entry, that entry will be liquidated for a refund of the estimated duties previously paid.

No abatement or reduction in duties can be made by Customs on account of any damage, loss, or deterioration of the merchandise that occurs while the goods are stored in the bonded warehouse. However, allowances in duties will be made for merchandise that is legally abandoned or intentionally destroyed in accordance with the procedures outlined in the Customs Regulations.

Merchandise is not permitted to remain in a bonded warehouse more than five years from the date of importation. Any merchandise that remains in a bonded warehouse after the five-year period may be sold by the government at auction, whether or not the duties have been paid.

When an importer desires to have merchandise stored in a bonded warehouse, he or she is required to file a warehouse entry. The warehouse entry is much like a consumption entry, and the documentation, bond, and other requirements must be met. No duties are required to be deposited at the time the warehouse entry is filed. Duties are paid when the merchandise is withdrawn from the warehouse for consumption. If the goods are exported, however, no duty is paid.

Goods entered on a warehouse entry are classified and appraised by the import specialist in the same manner as all other goods. Since the warehouse entry is accompanied by a bond, the goods may be withdrawn for consumption prior to completion of the classification and appraisement of the merchandise. If the goods are withdrawn before these procedures are completed, the duties required to be paid will be those that are estimated based upon the classification and value used at the time of entry filing. Goods that are withdrawn may therefore become subject to the payment of duties at a higher duty rate or at a higher value. If this occurs, a duty bill will be issued in the same manner as for the consumption entry.

The right to withdraw all or part of the merchandise stored in a bonded warehouse may be transferred to another party. Therefore, goods that are warehoused by one party may be sold to another party, along with the right to withdraw the merchandise from the warehouse. When this occurs, the purchaser who withdraws the goods would pay the required Customs duty.

Goods are removed from a bonded warehouse by filing a withdrawal document. Each withdrawal document filed must show the amount of goods in the warehouse before withdrawal, the quantity being withdrawn, and the quantity remaining in warehouse after the withdrawal. Merchandise cannot be withdrawn from a bonded warehouse in quantities less than an entire bale, cask, box, or other package.

Merchandise may be transferred from one warehouse to another warehouse, either at the same port or at another port. Merchandise may also be withdrawn for the purpose of transporting it elsewhere. After transportation, goods may be rewarehoused, partly rewarehoused and partly entered for consumption, exported, or admitted to a foreign trade zone in zone-restricted status. Goods may also be withdrawn from warehouse for direct or indirect exportation to another country.

Finally, goods may be withdrawn from warehouse and entered for consumption in the United States. This also is accomplished by the filing of a withdrawal document. Merchandise that is withdrawn from warehouse and entered for consumption must meet all legal requirements at the time of entry.

In summary, Customs bonded warehouses have many purposes. The most common of these are (1) storage and delay in the payment of duties owing on the goods and (2) the avoidance of duty payments entirely, where the shipment or a portion of the shipment is exported from the United States.

Temporarily storing goods in a bonded warehouse may also save an importer substantial amounts of duty when changes are about to occur in the tariff status of a given class of goods. For example, an importer may have merchandise that has been ordered and shipped to the United States but which has not yet arrived. These goods (currently dutiable) may be eligible for duty free entry under the Generalized System of Preferences or under some other provision that is to take effect within a short time after importation of the merchandise. In many circumstances, if a warehouse entry is filed and the goods are stored temporarily, the goods may later be withdrawn from warehouse and receive the benefit of the change in tariff status for those goods.

FOREIGN TRADE ZONES (FTZ)

Foreign trade zones are areas that, for legal purposes, are considered to be outside the Customs territory of the United States. These zones are established under the Foreign Trade Zones Act and the general regulations and rules of procedure of the Foreign Trade Zones Board. Merchandise in these zones may be stored, sold, broken up, repacked, assembled, distributed, sorted, graded, cleaned, and mixed with foreign or domestic merchandise. Other types of manipulation may be possible. Goods of any origin may be used for manufacturing in the foreign trade zone. After manufacture or manipulation in the zone, the merchandise may either be exported or transferred into the Customs territory of the United States. Many foreign trade zones today are used for the production of automobiles with imported and domestic auto parts. Since the duty rate on finished automobiles is substantially lower than the rate for automobile parts, significant duty savings are realized in this type of operation.

Duties are payable only on the actual quantity of foreign goods incorporated into the merchandise that is finally transferred from the zone into the Customs territory of the United States. Therefore, any manufacturing process that results in a significant amount of waste material may benefit from the duties saved on the waste, which need not be imported.

Goods may also be exhibited in a foreign trade zone. Importers may establish showrooms to display and demonstrate merchandise that they desire to sell at wholesale. These goods may be stored in the zone until the time of sale without the payment of duties. At the time such goods are sold, they may be entered into the commerce of the United States and duty paid. If not sold, the goods may be exported. Retail sales of merchandise, however, are not permitted in a foreign trade zone. Merchandise may be stored in a zone for an unlimited length of time, without the requirement that it be destroyed, exported, or entered for consumption.

Foreign trade zones are under the direct supervision of the District Director of Customs for the district in which they are located. The district director may require supervision of any transaction or procedure within a zone. Supervision is also performed through periodic audits of the operator's records, quantity counts of goods stored in the zone, spot checks of selected transactions or procedures, and review of record-keeping, security, or conditions of storage of goods in a zone. The district director may cause any merchandise to be examined before, or at the time of admission into a zone, or at any time thereafter, if such examination is considered necessary to carry out any laws or regulations.

Merchandise may be admitted directly into a zone from any place outside the Customs territory of the United States. Domestic merchandise may be admitted to a zone from U.S. Customs territory by any means of transportation. Merchandise may also be withdrawn from a bonded warehouse and transferred to a zone for admission in zone-restricted status. Merchandise of every kind may be admitted into a zone unless prohibited by law.

Any person desiring to have merchandise admitted into a foreign trade zone must complete an application on Customs Form 214. This form is sometimes referred to as a zone entry. Like other types of entries, the zone entry has a unique number that distinguishes it from all other zone entries. In addition, goods will not be admitted to a foreign trade zone unless the district director has issued a permit for such admission. Domestic merchandise may be admitted without a permit.

An application for admission to a zone must show the status for the goods that the applicant desires them to have. At the time Customs Form 214 is submitted, it must be accompanied by an invoice that meets all the invoicing requirements, as discussed previously. Notations as to classification and value need not be made on this invoice unless the applicant has requested that the goods be admitted in privileged status, as discussed below.

There are four different types of status that goods may have while in a foreign trade zone. They are as follows:

1. Privileged foreign status
2. Nonprivileged foreign status
3. Domestic status
4. Zone-restricted status

The status of merchandise in the zone will normally be that which has been applied for and granted by the district director at the time of filing the zone entry.

Foreign merchandise that has not been manipulated or manufactured so as to effect a change in tariff classification will be given status as privileged foreign merchandise upon proper application to the district director. Application for such status may be made at the time of filing the zone entry or at any time thereafter, before the merchandise has been manipulated or manufactured in the zone in a manner that has effected a change in tariff classification.

Privileged foreign merchandise is subject to tariff classification according to its character, condition, and quantity, and at the rate of duty and tax in force on the date of the filing of the application for privileged status. In effect, the rate of duty becomes fixed, regardless of any subsequent changes that take place in the goods before they are entered for consumption. Goods may enter the zone and secure a rate of duty based on the condition in which they enter the zone, regardless of the fact that they are processed in the zone and would have required a higher rate of duty, when later entered for consumption, had they not been accorded privileged foreign status.

The status of privileged foreign merchandise cannot be abandoned and remains applicable and binding on the merchandise even if it is changed in form by manipulation or manufacture. However, privileged foreign merchandise may be exported without the payment of taxes and duties.

Any foreign merchandise in a zone that does not have the status of privileged foreign merchandise or of zone-restricted merchandise is accorded the status of nonprivileged foreign merchandise. Domestic merchandise that in a zone has lost its identity as domestic merchandise will be treated as nonprivileged foreign merchandise.

Nonprivileged foreign merchandise is classified in accordance with its character, condition, and quantity at the time it is entered for consumption. Goods that would have taken a high rate of duty when imported may be put into the zone for manipulation or processing and entered at a lower resultant rate of duty. Components imported together as sets, which might be treated as an entirety for classification purposes, at a high rate of duty may be separated in the zone, with one portion entered at a lower rate of duty one day and the other portion entered separately at a higher rate on another day. These are considered legitimate uses of a foreign trade zone.

Domestic status may be granted to merchandise that is:

1. The growth, product, or manufacture of the United States on which all internal revenue taxes, if applicable, have been paid
2. Previously imported and on which duty and tax has been paid
3. Previously entered free of duty and tax

Any of the merchandise specified above may be returned to Customs territory from a zone free of quotas, duty, or tax.

Merchandise taken into a zone for the sole purpose of exportation, destruction, or storage may be given zone-restricted status. Zone-restricted status may be requested at any time for any merchandise located in a zone, but it cannot be abandoned once granted. Merchandise in zone-restricted status may not be removed to Customs territory for domestic consumption unless the Foreign Trade Zones Board determines that such return is in the public interest.

If an applicant desires zone-restricted status in order that merchandise may be considered exported for the purpose of any Customs law, such as for duty drawback purposes, all pertinent Customs requirements relating to an actual exportation must be complied with as though the admission of the merchandise into the zone constituted a lading on an exporting carrier at a point of final exit from the United States.

The dutiable value of merchandise withdrawn from a zone is the price actually paid or payable for the merchandise in the transaction that caused the merchandise to be admitted into the zone, less international shipment and insurance and U.S. inland freight costs. If there is no such price actually paid or payable, the dutiable value is the price actually paid or payable to the zone seller in the transaction that caused the merchandise to be transferred from the zone, less any included zone costs of processing or fabrication, general expenses and profit, and the international shipment and insurance and U.S. inland freight costs related to the merchandise transferred from the zone. If there is no price paid or payable to the zone seller, the dutiable value is the cost of all materials and zone processing costs, less any included zone costs of processing or fabrication, general expenses and profit, and the international shipment and insurance and U.S. inland freight costs related to the merchandise transferred from the zone. In determining the dutiable value, the appraising officer will use the valuation statute and all reasonable ways and means. An allowance in the dutiable value of zone merchandise may be made by the district director for damage, deterioration, or casualty while the merchandise is in the zone.

No merchandise in a zone, other than domestic status merchandise, may be manipulated in any manner or for any purpose, except under Customs permit. After proper application is made, the district director may grant permission to manipulate, manufacture, exhibit, or destroy merchandise in a zone. However, no application or permit is required for the manipulation, manufacture, exhibition, destruction, or transfer to Customs territory of domestic status merchandise, except when it is mixed or combined with merchandise in another zone status.

Merchandise may be transferred from one zone to another or may be exported. Merchandise in foreign status or composed in part of merchandise in foreign status may be entered for consumption from a zone. Merchandise that is entered for consumption from the foreign trade zone is classified and appraised in accordance with the rules previously discussed.

Chapter 15

Protection for Trademarks, Trade Names, and Copyrights

This chapter will examine the protection afforded by the U.S. Customs Service for trademarks, trade names, and copyrights. How this protection may be obtained by parties having rights in these properties and how Customs enforces these rights will be discussed. The procedures applicable to trademarks and trade names will be discussed together. Copyrights will be discussed separately.

TRADEMARKS AND TRADE NAMES

In order to obtain protection for a trademark or a trade name, a party must record the trademark or trade name with the Customs Service.

Recordation of Trademarks and Trade Names

Trademarks registered by the U.S. Patent Office may be recorded with the U.S. Customs Service if the registration is current. An application in letter form to record the trademark must be submitted to the Commissioner of Customs in Washington, D.C. The information and documents as set forth in the Customs Regulations must be provided, along with a fee of $190.00 for each class of goods for which the trademark protection is requested.

If the application to record the trademark is in proper form, Customs will record the trademark and issue a notice to all customs field officers showing a facsimile of the registered trademark and the other identifying information. Once this notice is received by customs field officers, special enforcement procedures are employed to detect the importation of goods that may impair the rights of the trademark holder.

The trade name or trade style used to identify a manufacturer or trader may be recorded with the U.S. Customs Service. Words or designs used as trademarks, even if registered with the U.S. Patent Office, will not be accepted for recordation as a trade name. Usually, the complete business name will be recorded unless convincing proof establishes that only a part of the complete business name is customarily used by the manufacturer or trader.

An application in letter form to record a trade name must be submitted to the Commissioner of Customs in Washington, D.C. Certain information and documents as set forth in the Customs Regulations must be supplied at the time of application, along with a fee of $190.00 for each trade name to be recorded.

After receipt of the application to record a trade name, Customs will publish a notice of tentative recordation of the trade name in the *Federal Register* and the *Customs Bulletin.* This notice will specify a procedure and a time period within which interested parties may oppose the recordation that has been requested. After consideration by Customs of any claims, rebuttals, and other relevant evidence submitted by interested parties who may wish to oppose the recordation, notice of final approval or disapproval of the application will also be published in the *Federal Register* and the *Customs Bulletin.* If approval of the application is given by Customs, the field offices are put on alert to detect merchandise imported in derogation of the recorded trade name.

Restrictions on Articles Bearing Recorded Marks and Names

Items of foreign or domestic manufacture bearing a trademark or trade name that copies or simulates a recorded trademark or trade name will be denied entry by Customs. Such articles are subject to seizure and forfeiture as prohibited importations. A "copying or simulating" trademark or trade name is one that so resembles the real trademark or trade name that it is likely to cause the public confusion, or to cause mistake, or to deceive. A copying or simulating trademark, however, is not the same thing as a "counterfeit" trademark, which is discussed separately below.

Foreign-made articles bearing a trademark identical with one owned and recorded by a citizen of the United States or a partnership, corporation, or association created or organized within the United States are subject to seizure and forfeiture as prohibited importations. Such items, which are referred to as genuine trademarked articles, will be denied entry by U.S. Customs.

The restrictions for copying and simulating marks and names and genuine trademarked articles do not apply, however, if any of the following conditions are met:

1. Both the foreign and the U.S. trademark or trade name are owned by the same person or business entity.
2. The foreign and domestic trademark or trade name owners are parent and subsidiary companies or are otherwise subject to common ownership or control.
3. The merchandise is imported by the party who recorded the trademark or trade name or by someone designated by that party to import the merchandise.
4. The party who recorded the trademark or trade name gives written consent to the importation in question, and such consent is furnished to the appropriate Customs officials.

In any case where any of the above conditions apply, the imported goods will not be subject to the restrictions mentioned. With regard to exceptions 1 and 2 above, Customs permits the unrestricted importation by any party of articles bearing simulating or copying marks or names or genuine trademarks if those marks or names are applied abroad by firms related to the U.S. trademark owner or by firms under common ownership or control with the U.S. trademark owner.

Genuine trademarked goods that are permitted entry into the United States because of exceptions 1 and 2 are known as grey market goods or parallel imports. The law, as interpreted by Customs, prohibits the importation of only genuine trademarked goods where an independent U.S. firm uses a U.S. trademark or has purchased the U.S. rights to a foreign trademark from an unrelated foreign firm.

Grey market goods are usually purchased abroad from authorized foreign distributors of the products and are imported into the United States by someone other than the U.S. trademark owner. Grey market goods are normally imported only if the purchaser can buy these goods at prices low enough to permit him or her to bring them to the United States and sell them at a discount to the prices charged by the U.S. trademark owner.

Considerable controversy surrounds the importation of grey market goods. However, Customs' interpretation of the law, as expressed in exceptions 1 and 2 above, has been upheld by the U.S. Supreme Court.

In any case where the exceptions set forth in 3 or 4 above apply, the goods will also not be seized. These exceptions both involve situations where the goods are imported with the authorization of the trademark or trade name owner.

Detention of Articles Bearing Recorded Marks and Names

When Customs discovers by physical examination or otherwise that a shipment contains articles subject to trademark or trade name restrictions, it will detain the shipment. A notice of detention of the articles is given to the importer in writing and the importer is given 30 days from the date of the notice to establish that any of the exceptions or conditions set forth above apply to the merchandise.

If the importer has not presented evidence to establish that any of the exceptions apply to the detained articles within the 30-day period, the merchandise will be seized and forfeiture proceedings instituted. The importer will be promptly notified of the seizure and the liability to forfeiture. In addition, he or she will be notified of his or her right to petition for relief in accordance with the Customs Regulations. If the importer is able to establish the existence of any of the exceptions during the 30-day period, the detained articles will be released to the importer.

Restrictions on Articles Bearing Counterfeit Trademarks

A counterfeit trademark is a spurious trademark that is identical with, or substantially indistinguishable from, a properly registered trademark. The term "spurious" refers to marks that are applied to goods without authorization of the trademark owner. Therefore, genuine trademarked articles cannot fall within the definition of the term "counterfeit." Any article imported into the United States bearing a counterfeit trademark will be seized by Customs and, in the absence of the written consent of the trademark owner, forfeited for violation of the Customs laws.

The owner of the trademark will be notified of the seizure and the quantity of the articles seized. Unless the trademark owner, within 30 days of notification, provides written consent for (1) importation of the articles, (2) exportation of the articles, (3) entry of the articles after obliteration of the trademark, or (4) other appropriate disposition, the articles will become subject to forfeiture. The importer must be advised of his or her right to petition for relief from the forfeiture in accordance with the procedures set forth in the Customs Regulations.

Redelivery of Merchandise Released from Customs Custody

When it is determined that merchandise that has been released from Customs' custody is subject to the trademark or trade name restrictions discussed above, the district director is authorized to issue a demand for redelivery of the merchandise under the terms of the Customs bond. If the merchandise is not redelivered to Customs' custody, a claim for liquidated damages will be issued in accordance with the Customs Regulations.

COPYRIGHTS

In order to obtain protection for works that have been registered for U.S. copyright, a party must record the copyright with the Customs Service.

Recordation of Copyrighted Works

Claims to copyright that have been registered with the U.S. Copyright Office may be recorded with U.S. Customs for import protection. The copyright owner, including any person who has acquired copyright ownership rights through an exclusive license, assignment, or otherwise, may file an application to record a copyright. An application in letter form to record a copyright to secure Customs protection against the importation of infringing copies must be made to the Commissioner of Customs in Washington, D.C. The information and documents as specified in the Customs Regulations must be submitted, along with a fee of $190.00 for each copyright to be recorded.

After the application has been accepted by Customs and the copyright recorded, a notice is sent to all customs field officers advising them of the details of the copyright.

Restrictions on Importations Violating Copyright Laws

Copies of protected works made without authorization of the copyright owner are made unlawfully. Such unlawful copies are infringing copies, which are referred to as piratical articles.

The importation of infringing copies of works copyrighted in the United States is prohibited by U.S. Customs. The importation of lawfully made copies is not a Customs violation. Articles determined to be noninfringing will not be detained by Customs, even though the copyright owner may object to a decision by a customs officer to release the goods to the importer. A prior Customs decision regarding the copyright at issue or a clearly controlling court opinion may provide an adequate basis upon which the district director may release the goods to the importer.

The district director will seize any imported article that he or she definitely determines is an infringing copy of a copyrighted work protected by Customs. The district director will also seize an imported article if the importer does not deny an allegation that the article is an infringing copy. Unless the articles may be returned to the country of export as provided in the Customs Regulations, the district director shall also implement forfeiture proceedings on the seized merchandise.

Suspicion of Infringement

If the district director is not certain but has reason to believe that an imported article may be an infringing copy of a recorded copyrighted work, he or she will withhold delivery, notify the importer of Customs' action, and advise the importer that he or she may file a statement denying that the article is an infringing copy. The district director will also advise the importer that the merchandise shall be considered an infringing copy, subject to seizure and forfeiture, unless a statement of denial of infringement is received from the importer within 30 days. If the importer of the suspected infringing copies files a denial of infringement as provided above, the district director will then furnish the copyright owner with a sample of the imported article, along with a notice stating that the imported items will be released to the importer if the copyright owner, within 30 days of the date of the notice, does not file the following with the district director:

1. A written demand for the exclusion from entry of the detained imported articles
2. A bond to insure the payment of damages to the importer or owner of the imported article for any loss or damage resulting from Customs' detention of the article in the event the Commissioner of Customs determines that the article is not an infringing copy

What occurs next in the administrative proceeding depends upon what response is received by the district director from the copyright owner. If the copyright owner asserts that the imported article is not an infringing copy or fails to present sufficient evidence or proof to substantiate a claim of infringement, the district director will release the detained shipment to the importer. In addition, all future importations of the same article, regardless of who imports it, shall be released without detention and notice to the copyright owner.

If the copyright owner fails to file a written demand for exclusion and to post the bond as requested by the district director, the district director will release the detained articles to the importer and notify the copyright owner of the release. In this case, all future importations of the same article, whether imported by the same or another party, become subject to detention by Customs. When such goods are detained in the future, the procedure discussed above is repeated, and the copyright owner is given the opportunity to file a written demand for exclusion of the imported articles, provided he or she is willing to post the necessary bond.

If the copyright owner files a written demand for exclusion of the detained imported articles and posts the required bond, the district director will promptly notify the importer and the copyright owner that each has 30 days within which to submit further evidence, legal briefs, or other pertinent material to substantiate the claim or denial of infringement. The burden of proof is on the party claiming that the article is in fact an infringing copy. At the close of the 30-day period specified for submission of evidence by each party, the district director forwards the entire file, together with a sample of the imported articles, to the Commissioner of Customs for a decision on the disputed claim of infringement.

The basic test for determining whether there has been an infringement of a copyright is whether substantial similarity exists between two works. The appropriate test for determining whether substantial similarity is present is whether an average person would recognize the alleged copy as having been appropriated from the copyrighted work. The substantial similarity test was developed in order to prevent a potential infringer from producing a supposedly new and different work by deliberately making trivial or insignificant variations in specific features of the copyrighted work. Two steps are involved in the test for infringement: access to the copyrighted work and substantial similarity not only of the general ideas but of the expression of those ideas.

After a review of the evidence, legal briefs, and other materials submitted by each party, the Commissioner of Customs will make a determination regarding the claim and denial of infringement. If the Commissioner of Customs determines that the detained article is an infringing copy, the district director will seize the imported article and either institute forfeiture proceedings or, under proper circumstances, permit the importer to return the article to the country of export. Articles seized or detained for violations or suspected violations of the copyright law may be returned to the country of export whenever it is shown to the satisfaction of the district director that the importer had no reasonable grounds for believing that his or her actions constituted a violation of the law. If the articles are not permitted to be exported, forfeiture proceedings will be commenced. In any event, the bond posted by the copyright owner is returned to him or her.

If the Commissioner of Customs determines that the detained article is not an infringing copy, the district director will release all detained merchandise to the importer and transmit the copyright owner's bond to the importer. The determination of the proper amount of monetary damages due the importer under the bond is an issue that must be resolved by the importer, the copyright owner, and the surety who issued the bond.

Redelivery of Articles Subject to Copyright Restrictions

Whenever it is determined by Customs that articles released from Customs' custody are subject to the prohibitions or restrictions that apply to infringing copies, a demand for redelivery of the articles to Customs' custody will be made under the terms of the Customs bond. If the articles are not redelivered to Customs' custody, a claim for liquidated damages will be made in accordance with the Customs Regulations.

Chapter 16

Administrative Rulings Issued by Customs

There are many situations in which an importer would like to know exactly how a specific import transaction will be legally treated by the Customs Service. Since oral opinions and oral advice of customs officers regarding any particular transaction are not binding on the Customs Service, the agency has devised certain procedures by which importers may request written rulings that are legally binding upon the Customs Service.

This chapter deals with the issuance of such rulings to importers and other interested persons by the Customs Service. It discusses the situations in which rulings may be requested, the procedures to be followed in requesting these rulings, the conditions under which rulings will be issued, the legal effect of those rulings when issued, and the publication of rulings in the *Customs Bulletin*.

Questions regarding Customs' ruling procedures can be answered by any district office of the Customs Service at various locations throughout the United States.

GENERAL INFORMATION ABOUT CUSTOMS RULINGS

A Customs ruling may be requested by any individual, corporation, partnership, association, or other legal entity that has a direct interest in the question or questions presented in the ruling request, either as an importer, exporter, or otherwise.

A "ruling" is a written statement issued by the Customs Service that interprets and applies the provisions of the Customs and related laws to a specific set of facts. A "ruling letter" is a ruling issued to a specific person, company, or other legal entity in response to a written request for a ruling. A "published ruling" is a ruling that has been published in the *Customs Bulletin*.

The Customs Service will not issue rulings in response to oral requests. However, oral inquiries may be made to customs officers regarding existing rulings, the scope of such rulings, the types of transactions with respect to which the Customs Service will issue rulings, and the procedures to be followed in submitting ruling requests.

No ruling letters will be issued with regard to transactions or questions that are only hypothetical in nature or in any instance in which it appears that a ruling would be detrimental to the sound administration of the Customs laws and regulations. Also, no ruling letter will be issued in regard to a completed transaction.

Customs will not issue ruling letters with respect to any issue that is pending before the U.S. Court of International Trade, the U.S. Court of Appeals for the Federal Circuit, or any other court of appeal from these courts. However, litigation before any court not previously mentioned will not preclude the issuance of a ruling letter by Customs, provided neither the Customs Service nor any of its officers is named as a defendant.

A "Customs transaction" is an act or activity to which the Customs and related laws apply. A "prospective" Customs transaction is one that is contemplated or is currently being undertaken but has not resulted in the arrival of any merchandise, in the filing of any entry or other document, or in any other act that would bring the transaction under the jurisdiction of any Customs Service field office. According to U.S. Customs, the proper administration of the Customs laws requires that persons engaging in any transaction affected by those laws fully understand the consequences of the transaction prior to its occurrence. For this reason, the Customs Service will usually give full and careful consideration to written requests from importers or other interested parties for rulings setting forth a definitive interpretation of applicable laws, regarding a specifically described Customs transaction that is being contemplated.

A "current" Customs transaction is one that is presently under consideration by a Customs field office. These transactions involve the actual importation of merchandise, whose classification, appraisement, or other legal status is still being determined by district customs officers. A question arising in connection with such a current Customs transaction will normally be resolved by the district office in accordance with the principles and precedents previously announced by the Headquarters of the Customs Service or the courts. If questions cannot be resolved on the basis of clearly established rules set forth in the Customs laws; in the Customs Regulations; or in applicable Treasury decisions, rulings, opinions, or court decisions published in the *Customs Bulletin*, the district field office may, on its own initiative or at the request of the importer, forward the unresolved questions to Headquarters of the Customs Service for consideration. The procedures to be used in the resolution of disputes involving current transactions is described more fully below.

A "completed" Customs transaction is one that has been acted upon by a Customs Service field office, where that office has issued a determination that is final in nature, except for appeal rights by way of protest or petition. Any questions arising in connection with liquidated Customs entries or any other completed Customs transaction may not be the subject of a ruling request.

HOW RULING REQUESTS ARE SUBMITTED

Ruling requests must be in the proper form, be addressed to the proper office, and contain certain general and specific information in order that Customs can answer them.

Form and General Content

A request for a ruling from Customs should be in the form of a letter. Requests for valuation and other rulings should be addressed to the Commissioner of Customs, Attention: Office of Regulations and Rulings, Washington, D.C. 20229. Requests for tariff classification rulings should be addressed to the Regional Commissioner of Customs, New York Region, Attention: Classification Ruling Requests, New York, N.Y. 10048, or to any area or district office of the Customs Service.

Each request for a ruling must contain a complete statement of all pertinent facts related to the transaction. Such facts include the names, addresses, and other identifying information of all interested parties; the name of the port or place at which any article involved in the transaction will arrive or be entered, or the Customs office that will otherwise have jurisdiction over the activities described in the transaction; and a description of the specific transaction itself, with details appropriate to the type of ruling requested.

Specific Information Included in Ruling Request

The Customs transaction involved in the ruling request must be described in sufficient detail to permit the proper application of the relevant Customs and other laws. In addition, the information shown below should be included in the ruling request.

Type of Customs Transaction. The specific information required to be submitted to Customs in a ruling request depends upon whether the ruling involves tariff classification or valuation. The following guidelines should be observed if a classification or valuation ruling is requested. If classification or appraisement is not involved, then the following requirements may be disregarded.

If the proper classification under the Tariff Schedule of the United States is requested, the request should include a full and complete description of the article to be imported and, where appropriate, information as to the article's chief use in the United States; its commercial, common, or technical designation; and, where the article is composed of two or more materials, the relative quantity of each (by weight and by volume) and the value of each material. Each request for a ruling submitted to area or district offices will be limited to five merchandise items, all of which must be of the same class or kind.

Rulings issued by the New York region or by other area or district offices are limited to prospective transactions, that is, transactions that will occur in the future. The requesting party may, however, send any classification ruling request, at his or her option, directly to the Director, Commercial Rulings Division, U.S. Customs Service, Washington, D.C. 20229. The Headquarters of the Customs Service retains authority to review independently all tariff classification ruling letters issued by the New York region and other area and district offices. If the importer or other person to whom a ruling letter is issued disagrees with the tariff classification set forth in a ruling issued by the New York region or other area or district offices, he or she may petition the Director, Commercial Rulings Division, U.S. Customs Service, Washington, D.C. 20229, for a review of the ruling.

If the transaction involves the valuation of an article for Customs purposes, the request for a ruling should include all information that would be considered pertinent under the terms of the appraisement law. Information of the type that would normally be required on the invoice should also be set forth in the request. The request should also describe the terms of the transaction (whether FOB, CIF, X-Factory, or some other terms), the relationship of the parties, whether the transaction is arm's-length, whether there have been other sales of the same or similar merchandise from the country of exportation, and the nature of any agency relationships that exist.

Samples and Descriptive Literature. Each request for a ruling regarding the status of an article to be imported under the Customs laws should be accompanied by descriptive literature, photographs, drawings, or other pictorial representations of the article and, whenever possible, by a sample of the article, unless a precise description of the article is not essential to the ruling requested. Any laboratory analysis that may have been done regarding the article should be included. Any samples submitted in connection with the request become a part of the Customs Service file and will be retained until the ruling is issued. If the requester desires the return of the sample, the ruling request should so state and should specify the desired means of return. Samples should only be submitted with the understanding that all or part of them may be damaged or consumed in the course of examination, testing, analysis, or other actions undertaken in connection with the ruling request.

Related Documents. If the questions presented in the ruling request directly relate to matters set forth in any invoice, contract, agreement, or other document pertinent to the transaction, a copy of the document must be submitted wih the request. The original document should not be submitted inasmuch as any documents or exhibits furnished with the request become a part of the Customs Service file and cannot be returned. The relevant facts contained in any documents submitted, and an explanation of their bearing on the question or questions presented, must be expressly set forth in the ruling request.

Prior or Current Transactions. Each request for a ruling must state, to the best knowledge of the requester, whether the same transaction, or one identical to it, has ever been considered, or is currently being considered, by any Customs Service office, or whether, to the requester's knowledge, the issues involved have ever been considered, or are currently being considered, by the U.S. Court of International Trade, the U.S. Court of Appeals for the Federal Circuit, or any court of appeal from these courts. If the transaction described in the ruling request is only one in a series of similar and related transactions, that fact must also be stated.

Statement of Legal Position. If the request for a ruling seeks to establish a specific legal determination or conclusion with regard to a matter at issue, the ruling request must include a statement setting forth the legal arguments and basis for that particular determination or conclusion, along with a citation of all relevant supporting authority, whether in the form of Customs rulings or court decisions. It is not necessary, however, that the request state a legal position on any matter.

Statement Regarding Confidential Information. Information that is claimed to constitute trade secrets or privileged or confidential commercial or financial information regarding the business transactions of private parties, the disclosure of which would cause substantial harm to the competitive position of the person making the request, or any other interested party, must be identified clearly and the reasons set forth why such information should not be disclosed. Where applicable, this statement should contain the reasons why the disclosure of the information would prejudice the competitive position of the person making the request or of another interested party. Requests for confidential treatment of information are usually honored by Customs. The important thing is to let Customs know what particular items of information should not be revealed in the event the ruling is published. Every ruling issued by Customs has the potential to be published in one form or another.

ISSUANCE OF RULINGS BY CUSTOMS

The Customs Service will endeavor to issue a ruling letter setting forth its determination with respect to a specifically described Customs transaction whenever a request for such a ruling is submitted in accordance with proper procedures and whenever it is in the sound administration of the Customs laws to do so. Otherwise, a request for a ruling will be answered by an information letter or, in those situations in which general information is likely to be of little or no value, by a letter stating that no ruling can be issued.

Any person or company engaging in a Customs transaction for which a binding tariff classification ruling letter has been issued by Customs must insure that a copy of the ruling letter is attached to all documents filed with the Customs Service office having responsibility for the transaction or must otherwise indicate with the information filed for that transaction that a ruling has been received. Any person receiving a ruling setting forth the tariff classification of merchandise must set forth such classification in the documents or information filed in connection with any subsequent entry of that merchandise; the failure to do so may result in a rejection of the entry and the assessment of such penalties as may be appropriate. A ruling received after the filing of such documents or information with Customs must immediately be brought to the attention of the appropriate Customs Service field office.

A ruling letter must be based on the information set forth in the ruling request. No part of the ruling letter, including names, addresses, or information relating to the business transactions of private parties, is deemed to constitute privileged or confidential commercial or financial information or trade secrets exempt from disclosure under the Freedom of Information Act, unless the information claimed to be exempt from disclosure is clearly identified and the reasons for the exemption are stated. Before the ruling letter is issued, the person submitting the ruling request will be notified of any decision adverse to his or her claim for exemption from disclosure and will, upon written request to Customs within 10 working days of notification, be permitted to withdraw the ruling request. All ruling letters issued by the Customs Service will be available, upon written request, for inspection and copying by any person, except that any portions determined to be exempt from disclosure will be deleted.

LEGAL STATUS AND EFFECT OF RULING LETTERS

A ruling letter issued by the Customs Service represents the official position of the Customs Service with respect to the particular transaction or issue described in the letter and is binding on all Customs Service personnel until modified or revoked. In the absence of a change of practice or other modification or revocation that affects the principle of the ruling set forth in the ruling letter, that principle may be cited by anyone as authority in the disposition of transactions involving the same circumstances. A ruling letter is generally effective on the date it is issued and may be applied to all entries that are unliquidated or to other transactions on which Customs has not taken final action on that date.

Each ruling letter is issued on the assumption that all information furnished in the ruling request and set forth in the ruling letter, either directly, by reference, or by implication, is accurate and complete in every material respect. The application of a ruling letter by Customs field offices to the transaction involved is subject to (1) a verification of the facts incorporated in the ruling letter, (2) a comparison of the transaction described in the ruling letter to the actual transaction, and (3) the satisfaction of any conditions on which the ruling was based. If a customs officer reviews the specific transaction and the ruling letter associated with it and believes the ruling letter should be modified or revoked, he or she will forward his or her findings and recommendations to the Headquarters of the Customs Service for reconsideration of the ruling, prior to any final disposition with respect to the transaction currently under consideration. If the transaction described in the ruling letter and the actual transaction are the same, and any and all conditions set forth in the ruling letter have been satisfied, the ruling will be applied to the transaction.

Each ruling letter setting forth the proper classification of an article under the Tariff Schedule of the United States will be applied only with respect to transactions involving articles identical to the samples submitted with the ruling request or to articles whose description is identical to the description set forth in the ruling letter. Each ruling letter setting forth the proper valuation of an article under the valuation law will be applied only with respect to transactions involving the same merchandise and like facts.

A ruling letter is subject to modification or revocation without notice to any person, except the person to whom the letter was addressed. Accordingly, no other person should rely on a ruling letter or assume that the principles of that ruling will be applied to any transaction other than the one described in the letter.

MODIFICATION OR REVOCATION OF RULING LETTERS

Any ruling letter that is found to be in error or not in accordance with the current views of the Customs Service may be modified or revoked. Modification or revocation of a ruling letter is accomplished by Customs by giving notice to the person to whom the ruling letter was addressed and, where appropriate, by the publication of a notice or other statement in the *Customs Bulletin*.

The modification or revocation of a ruling letter will not be applied retroactively with respect to the person to whom the ruling was issued, or to any person directly involved in the transaction to which that ruling related, provided the following conditions are met:

1. The request for a ruling contained no misstatement or omission of material facts.
2. The facts subsequently developed are not materially different from the facts on which the ruling was based.
3. There has been no change in the applicable law.
4. The ruling was originally issued with respect to a prospective transaction.
5. All the parties involved in the transaction acted in good faith in reliance upon the ruling, and retroactive modification or revocation would be to their detriment.

None of these conditions, however, will preclude the retroactive modification or revocation of a ruling if the transaction involved was not prospective at the time the ruling was issued, since such a transaction was not entered into in reliance upon a ruling from the Customs Service.

A ruling letter modifying or revoking an earlier ruling letter will be effective on the date it is issued. The Customs Service may, under proper circumstances, delay the effective date of such a ruling for a period of up to 90 days from the date of issuance. Such a delay may be granted with respect to the party to whom the ruling letter was issued or to any other party, provided such party can demonstrate to the satisfaction of Customs that it reasonably relied upon the earlier ruling to its detriment. All parties applying for a delay will be issued a separate ruling letter setting forth the period of any delay to be provided. Where appropriate, Customs may decide to delay its decision for all affected parties, regardless of demonstrated reliance. When this occurs, a notice announcing the delay will be published in the *Customs Bulletin* and individual ruling letters will not be issued.

PUBLICATION OF CUSTOMS DECISIONS

Within 120 days after issuing any important decision relating to any Customs transaction, whether prospective, current, or completed, the Customs Service will publish the decision in the *Customs Bulletin* or otherwise make it available for public inspection. Customs decisions that are important enough to publish include any letter ruling, internal advice memorandum, or protest review decision.

Rulings Regarding a Rate of Duty or Charge

Any ruling regarding a rate of duty or charge that is published in the *Customs Bulletin* will establish a uniform practice. A published ruling may (1) result in a change of practice, (2) limit the application of a court decision, (3) otherwise modify an earlier ruling with respect to the classification or valuation of an article or any other action found to be in error or no longer in accordance with the current views of the Customs Service, or (4) revoke a previously published ruling or a previously issued ruling letter.

Changes of Customs Practice or Position

Before the publication of a ruling that has the effect of changing a practice and that results in the assessment of a higher rate of duty, a notice will be published in the *Federal Register* indicating that the prior practice is under review. Interested parties will be given an opportunity to make written submissions with respect to the correctness of any contemplated change. No advance notice will be provided with respect to rulings that result in a change of practice but no change in the rate of duty.

Before the publication of a ruling that has the effect of changing a position of the Customs Service and that results in a restriction or prohibition, a notice will be published in the *Federal Register* indicating that the prior position is under review. Interested parties will be given an opportunity to make written submissions with respect to the correctness of any contemplated change.

Effective Dates

Unless otherwise provided in the ruling itself, all rulings published will be applied immediately. If the ruling involves merchandise, it will apply to all unliquidated entries, except that a change of practice resulting in the assessment of a higher rate of duty or increased duties shall be effective only as to merchandise entered for consumption or withdrawn from warehouse for consumption on or after the 90th day after publication of the change in the *Federal Register*.

INTERNAL ADVICE REQUEST PROCEDURES

Advice or guidance as to the interpretation or application of the Customs and related laws with respect to a specific Customs transaction may be requested by Customs Service field offices from the Headquarters of the Customs Service at any time, whether the transaction is prospective, current, or completed. Advice as to the proper application of the Customs and related laws to a current transaction may be sought by a Customs Service field office whenever that office is requested to do so by an importer or other person having an interest in the transaction. Advice or guidance is furnished by headquarters to assist Customs personnel in the orderly processing of Customs transactions under consideration by them and to insure the consistent application of the Customs and related laws in the various districts throughout the United States.

With respect to current Customs transactions, the procedures discussed below for seeking internal advice will be followed.

Requests by Field Offices

If any Customs Service office has issued a ruling letter regarding a particular Customs transaction and the Customs Service field office having jurisdiction over that transaction believes that the ruling should be modified or revoked, the field office will forward its views to the Headquarters of the Customs Service, with a request that the ruling be reconsidered. The field office must notify the importer to whom the ruling letter was issued, in writing, that it has requested headquarters to reconsider the ruling.

Requests by Importers and Others

If the importer or other person to whom a ruling letter is issued disagrees with the Customs Service field office having jurisdiction over the transaction as to the proper application of the ruling to the transaction, the field office will, upon written application by the importer, request advice from the Headquarters of the Customs Service as to the proper application of the ruling to the transaction. The importer may not use this internal advice procedure to request reconsideration of a Customs ruling with which he or she disagrees.

When No Ruling Has Been Issued

When no ruling has been issued and a difference of opinion exists between the field office and the importer as to the interpretation or application of the Customs and related laws to a particular current transaction, the Customs field office should seek internal advice when requested to do so by the importer, provided the importer could have done so while the transaction was still prospective. The importer must make a request in writing when asking the field office to seek internal advice.

The importer's request must be made to the field office having jurisdiction over the transaction in question. The request must contain a complete statement setting forth a description of the transaction, the specific questions presented, the applicable law, and any arguments for the conclusions advocated. The importer's request must also specify whether, to the knowledge of the importer, the same transaction, or one identical to it, has ever been considered, or is currently being considered, by any Customs Service office. In addition, the request must indicate at which port or ports of entry identical or substantially identical merchandise has been entered.

All requests submitted by importers for internal advice will be reviewed by the field office to which they are submitted. In the event that a difference of opinion exists as to the description of the transaction or as to the point or points at issue, the person submitting the request will be so advised in writing. If agreement cannot be reached between the importer and the field office, the statements of both the importer and the field office will be forwarded to Headquarters of the Customs Service for consideration.

Advice furnished by headquarters in response to a request for internal advice represents the official position of the Customs Service as to the application of the Customs laws to the facts of a specific transaction. If the field office believes that the advice furnished by headquarters should be reconsidered, the field office shall promptly request such reconsideration. Otherwise, the advice furnished by headquarters will be applied by the field office in its disposition of the Customs transaction in question. Within 120 days after issuing an internal advice memorandum, the Customs Service will publish the decision in the *Customs Bulletin* or otherwise make it available for public inspection.

Harmonized Tariff Schedule of the United States (1991), Annotated

Heading/ Subheading	Stat. Suf. & cd	Article Description	Units of Quantity	Rates of Duty		
				1		2
				General	Special	
9013		Liquid crystal devices not constituting articles provided for more specifically in other headings; lasers, other than laser diodes; other optical appliances and instruments, not specified or included elsewhere in this chapter; parts and accessories thereof:				
9013.10		Telescopic sights for fitting to arms; periscopes; telescopes designed to form parts of machines, appliances, instruments or apparatus of this chapter or section XVI:				
		Telescopic sights for rifles:				
9013.10.10	00 2	Not designed for use with infrared light..............	No......	20%	Free (A,E,IL) 14% (CA)	45%
9013.10.30	00 8	Other................	No......	2.2%	Free (A,E,IL) 1.5% (CA)	35%
9013.10.40	00 6	Other................	No......	8%	Free (A,E,IL) 5.6% (CA)	45%
9013.20.00	00 2	Lasers, other than laser diodes.............	No......	3.9%	Free (A,E,IL) 2.7% (CA)	35%
9013.80		Other devices, appliances and instruments:				
9013.80.20	00 5	Hand magnifiers, magnifying glasses, loupes, thread counters and similar apparatus.............	No......	6.6%	Free (A,E,IL) 4.6% (CA)	45%
9013.80.40	00 1	Door viewers (door eyes).............	No......	5.8%	Free (A,E,IL) 4% (CA)	60%
9013.80.60	00 6	Other.............	X.......	9%	Free (A,E,IL) 6.3% (CA)	45%
9013.90		Parts and accessories:				
9013.90.20	00 3	Of telescopic sights for rifles.............	X.......	20%	Free (A,E,IL) 14% (CA)	45%
9013.90.40	00 9	Other.............	X.......	9%	Free (A,E,IL) 6.3% (CA)	45%

Title 19, United States Code, Section 1401a

Section 1401a. Value

(a) Generally

    (1) Except as otherwise specifically provided for in this chapter, imported merchandise shall be appraised, for the purposes of this chapter, on the basis of the following:

        (A) The transaction value provided for under subsection (b) of this section.

        (B) The transaction value of identical merchandise provided for under subsection (c) of this section, if the value referred to in subparagraph (A) cannot be determined, or can be determined but cannot be used by reason of subsection (b) (2) of this section.

        (C) The transaction value of similar merchandise provided for under subsection (c) of this section, if the value referred to in subparagraph (B) cannot be determined.

        (D) The deductive value provided for under subsection (d) of this section, if the value referred to in subparagraph (C) cannot be determined and if the importer does not request alternative valuation under paragraph (2).

        (E) The computed value provided for under subsection (e) of this section, if the value referred to in subparagraph (D) cannot be determined.

        (F) The value provided for under subsection (f) of this section, if the value referred to in subparagraph (E) cannot be determined.

    (2) If the value referred to in paragraph (1) (C) cannot be determined with respect to imported merchandise, the merchandise shall be appraised on the basis of the computed value provided for under paragraph (1) (E), rather than the deductive value provided for under paragraph (1) (D), if the importer makes a request to that effect to the customs officer concerned within such time as the Secretary shall prescribe. If the computed value of the merchandise cannot subsequently be determined, the merchandise may not be appraised on the basis of the value referred to in paragraph (1) (F) unless the deductive value of the merchandise cannot be determined under paragraph (1) (D).

    (3) Upon written request therefor by the importer of merchandise, and subject to provisions of law regarding the disclosure of information, the customs officer

concerned shall provide the importer with a written explanation of how the value of that merchandise was determined under this section.

(b) Transaction value of imported merchandise

(1) The transaction value of imported merchandise is the price actually paid or payable for the merchandise when sold for exportation to the United States, plus amounts equal to—

(A) the packing costs incurred by the buyer with respect to the imported merchandise;

(B) any selling commission incurred by the buyer with respect to the imported merchandise;

(C) the value, apportioned as appropriate, of any assist;

(D) any royalty or license fee related to the imported merchandise that the buyer is required to pay, directly or indirectly, as a condition of the sale of the imported merchandise for exportation to the United States; and

(E) the proceeds of any subsequent resale, disposal, or use of the imported merchandise that accrue, directly or indirectly, to the seller.

The price actually paid or payable for imported merchandise shall be increased by the amounts attributable to the items (and no others) described in subparagraphs (A) through (E) only to the extent that each such amount (i) is not otherwise included within the price actually paid or payable; and (ii) is based on sufficient information. If sufficient information is not available, for any reason, with respect to any amount referred to in the preceding sentence, the transaction value of the imported merchandise concerned shall be treated, for purposes of this section, as one that cannot be determined.

(2) (A) The transaction value of imported merchandise determined under paragraph (1) shall be the appraised value of that merchandise for the purposes of this chapter only if—

(i) there are no restrictions on the disposition or use of the imported merchandise by the buyer other than restrictions that—

(I) are imposed or required by law,

(II) limit the geographical area in which the merchandise may be resold, or

(III) do not substantially affect the value of the merchandise;

(ii) the sale of, or the price actually paid or payable for, the imported merchandise is not subject to any condition or consideration for which a value cannot be determined with respect to the imported merchandise;

(iii) no part of the proceeds of any subsequent resale, disposal, or use of the imported merchandise by the buyer will accrue directly or indirectly to the seller, unless an appropriate adjustment therefor can be made under paragraph (1) (E); and

(iv) the buyer and seller are not related, or the buyer and seller are related but the transaction value is acceptable, for purposes of this subsection, under paragraph (B).

(B) The transaction value between a related buyer and seller is acceptable for the purposes of this subsection if an examination of the circumstances of the sale of the imported merchandise indicates that the relationship between such buyer and seller did not influence the price actually paid or payable; or if the transaction value of the imported merchandise closely approximates—

    (i) the transaction value of identical merchandise, or of similar merchandise, in sales to unrelated buyers in the United States; or

    (ii) the deductive value or computed value for identical merchandise or similar merchandise;

but only if each value referred to in clause (i) or (ii) that is used for comparison relates to merchandise that was exported to the United States at or about the same time as the imported merchandise.

(C) In applying the values used for comparison purposes under subparagraph (B), there shall be taken into account differences with respect to the sales involved (if such differences are based on sufficient information whether supplied by the buyer or otherwise available to the customs officer concerned) in—

    (i) commercial levels;

    (ii) quantity levels;

    (iii) the costs, commissions, values, fees, and proceeds described in paragraph (1); and

    (iv) the costs incurred by the seller in sales in which he and the buyer are not related that are not incurred by the seller in sales in which he and the buyer are related.

(3) The transaction value of imported merchandise does not include any of the following, if identified separately from the price actually paid or payable and from any cost or other item referred to in paragraph (1):

(A) Any reasonable cost or charge that is incurred for—

    (i) the construction, erection, assembly, or maintenance of, or the technical assistance provided with respect to, the merchandise after its importation into the United States; or

    (ii) the transportation of the merchandise after such importation.

(B) The customs duties and other Federal taxes currently payable on the imported merchandise by reason of its importation, and any Federal excise tax on, or measured by the value of, such merchandise for which vendors in the United States are ordinarily liable.

(4) For purposes of this subsection—

(A) The term "price actually paid or payable" means the total payment (whether direct or indirect, and exclusive of any costs, charges, or expenses incurred for transportation, insurance, and related services incident to the international shipment of the merchandise from the country of exportation to the place of importation in the United States) made, or to be made, for imported merchandise by the buyer to, or for the benefit of, the seller.

(B) Any rebate of, or other decrease in, the price actually paid or payable that is made or otherwise effected between the buyer and seller after the date of the importation of the merchandise into the United States shall be disregarded in determining the transaction value under paragraph (1).

(c) Transaction value of identical merchandise and similar merchandise

(1) The transaction value of identical merchandise, or of similar merchandise, is the transaction value (acceptable as the appraised value for purposes of this chapter under subsection (b) of this section but adjusted under paragraph (2) of this subsection) of imported merchandise that is—

(A) with respect to the merchandise being appraised, either identical merchandise or similar merchandise, as the case may be; and

(B) exported to the United States at or about the time that the merchandise being appraised is exported to the United States.

(2) Transaction values determined under this subsection shall be based on sales of identical merchandise or similar merchandise, as the case may be, at the same commercial level and in substantially the same quantity as the sales of the merchandise being appraised. If no such sale is found, sales of identical merchandise or similar merchandise at either a different commercial level or in different quantities, or both, shall be used, but adjusted to take account of any such difference. Any adjustment made under this paragraph shall be based on sufficient information. If in applying this paragraph with respect to any imported merchandise, two or more transaction values for identical merchandise, or for similar merchandise, are determined, such imported merchandise shall be appraised on the basis of the lower or lowest of such values.

(d) Deductive value

(1) For purposes of this subsection, the term "merchandise concerned" means the merchandise being appraised, identical merchandise, or similar merchandise.

(2) (A) The deductive value of the merchandise being appraised is whichever of the following prices (as adjusted under paragraph (3)) is appropriate depending upon when and in what condition the merchandise concerned is sold in the United States:

(i) If the merchandise concerned is sold in the condition as imported at or about the date of importation of the merchandise being appraised, the price is the unit price at which the merchandise concerned is sold in the greatest aggregate quantity at or about such date.

(ii) If the merchandise concerned is sold in the condition as imported but not sold at or about the date of importation of the merchandise being appraised, the price is the unit price at which the merchandise concerned is sold in the greatest aggregate quantity after the date of importation of the merchandise being appraised but before the close of the 90th day after the date of such importation.

(iii) If the merchandise concerned was not sold in the condition as imported and not sold before the close of the 90th day after the date of importation of the merchandise being appraised, the price is the unit price at which the merchandise being appraised, after further processing, is sold in the greatest aggregate quantity before the 180th day after the date of such importation. This clause shall apply to appraisement of merchandise only if the importer so elects and notifies the customs officer concerned of that election within such time as shall be prescribed by the Secretary.

(B) For purposes of subparagraph (A), the unit price at which merchandise is sold in the greatest aggregate quantity is the unit price at which such merchandise is sold to unrelated persons, at the first commercial level after importation (in cases to which subparagraph (A) (i) or (ii) applies) or after further processing (in cases to which subparagraph (A) (iii) applies) at which such sales take place, in a total volume that is (i) greater than the total volume sold at any other unit price, and (ii) sufficient to establish the unit price.

(3) (A) The price determined under paragraph (2) shall be reduced by an amount equal to—

   (i) any commission usually paid or agreed to be paid, or the addition usually made for profit and general expenses, in connection with sales in the United States of imported merchandise that is of the same class or kind, regardless of the country of exportation, as the merchandise concerned;

   (ii) the actual costs and associated costs of transportation and insurance incurred with respect to international shipments of the merchandise concerned from the country of exportation to the United States;

   (iii) the usual costs and associated costs of transportation and insurance incurred with respect to shipments of such merchandise from the place of importation to the place of delivery in the United States, if such costs are not included as a general expense under clause (i);

   (iv) the customs duties and other Federal taxes currently payable on the merchandise concerned by reason of its importation, and any Federal excise tax on, or measured by the value of, such merchandise for which vendors in the United States are ordinarily liable; and

   (v) (but only in the case of a price determined under paragraph (2) (A) (iii)) the value added by the processing of the merchandise after importation to the extent that the value is based on sufficient information relating to cost of such processing.

(B) For purposes of applying paragraph (A)—

   (i) the deduction made for profits and general expenses shall be based upon the importer's profits and general expenses, unless such profits and general expenses are inconsistent with those reflected in sales in the United States of imported merchandise of the same class or kind, in which case the deduction shall be based on the usual profit and general expenses reflected in such sales, as determined from sufficient information; and

   (ii) any State or local tax imposed on the importer with respect to the sale of imported merchandise shall be treated as a general expense.

(C) The price determined under paragraph (2) shall be increased (but only to the extent that such costs are not otherwise included) by an amount equal to the packing costs incurred by the importer or the buyer, as the case may be, with respect to the merchandise concerned.

(D) For purposes of determining the deductive value of imported merchandise, any sale to a person who supplies any assist for use in connection with the production or sale for export of the merchandise concerned shall be disregarded.

(e) Computed value

   (1) The computed value of imported merchandise is the sum of—

   (A) the cost or value of the materials and the fabrication and other processing of any kind employed in the production of the imported merchandise;

   (B) an amount for profit and general expenses equal to that usually reflected in sales of merchandise of the same class or kind as the imported merchandise that are made by the producers in the country of exportation for export to the United States;

(C) any assist, if its value is not included under subparagraph (A) or (B); and

(D) the packing costs.

(2) For purposes of paragraph (1)—

(A) the cost or value of materials under paragraph (1) (A) shall not include the amount of any internal tax imposed by the country of exportation that is directly applicable to the materials or their disposition if the tax is remitted or refunded upon the exportation of the merchandise in the production of which the materials were used; and

(B) the amount for profit and general expenses under paragraph (1) (B) shall be based upon the producer's profits and expenses, unless the producer's profits and expenses are inconsistent with those usually reflected in sales of merchandise of the same class or kind as the imported merchandise that are made by producers in the country of exportation for export to the United States, in which case the amount under paragraph (1) (B) shall be based on the usual profit and general expenses of such producers in such sales, as determined from sufficient information.

(f) Value if other values cannot be determined or used

(1) If the value of imported merchandise cannot be determined, or otherwise used for the purposes of this chapter, under subsections (b) through (e) of this section, the merchandise shall be appraised for the purposes of this chapter on the basis of a value that is derived from the methods set forth in such subsections, with such methods being reasonably adjusted to the extent necessary to arrive at a value.

(2) Imported merchandise may not be appraised, for the purposes of this chapter, on the basis of—

(A) the selling price in the United States of merchandise produced in the United States;

(B) a system that provides for the appraisement of imported merchandise at the higher of two alternative values;

(C) the price of merchandise in the domestic market of the country of exportation;

(D) a cost of production, other than a value determined under subsection (e) of this section for merchandise that is identical merchandise or similar merchandise to the merchandise being appraised;

(E) the price of merchandise for export to a country other than the United States;

(F) minimum values for appraisement; or

(G) arbitrary or fictitious values.

This paragraph shall not apply with respect to the ascertainment, determination, or estimation of foreign market value or United States price under subtitle IV of this chapter.

(g) Special rules

(1) For purposes of this section, the persons specified in any of the following subparagraphs shall be treated as persons who are related:

(A) Members of the same family, including brothers and sisters (whether by whole or half blood), spouse, ancestors, and lineal descendants.

(B) Any officer or director of an organization and such organization.

(C) An officer or director of an organization and an officer or director of another organization, if each such individual is also an officer or director in the other organization.

(D) Partners.

(E) Employer and employee.

(F) Any person directly or indirectly owning, controlling, or holding with power to vote, 5 percent or more of the outstanding voting stock or shares of any organization and such organization.

(G) Two or more persons directly or indirectly controlling, controlled by, or under common control with, any person.

(2) For purposes of this section, merchandise (including, but not limited to, identical merchandise and similar merchandise) shall be treated as being of the same class or kind as other merchandise if it is within a group or range of merchandise produced by a particular industry or industry sector.

(3) For purposes of this section, information that is submitted by an importer, buyer, or producer in regard to the appraisement of merchandise may not be rejected by the customs officer concerned on the basis of the accounting method by which that information was prepared, if the preparation was in accordance with generally accepted accounting principles. The term "generally accepted accounting principles" refers to any generally recognized consensus or substantial authoritative support regarding—

(A) which economic resources and obligations should be recorded as assets and liabilities;

(B) which changes in assets and liabilities should be recorded;

(C) how the assets and liabilities and changes in them should be measured;

(D) what information should be disclosed and how it should be disclosed; and

(E) which financial statements should be prepared.

The applicability of a particular set of generally accepted accounting principles will depend upon the basis on which the value of the merchandise is sought to be established.

(h) Definitions

As used in this section—

(1) (A) The term "assist" means any of the following if supplied directly or indirectly, and free of charge or at reduced cost, by the buyer of imported merchandise for use in connection with the production or the sale for export to the United States of the merchandise:

(i) Materials, components, parts, and similar items incorporated in the imported merchandise.

(ii) Tools, dies, molds, and similar items used in the production of the imported merchandise.

(iii) Merchandise consumed in the production of the imported merchandise.

(iv) Engineering, development, artwork, design work, and plans and sketches that are undertaken elsewhere than in the United States and are necessary for the production of the imported merchandise.

(B) No service or work to which subparagraph (A) (iv) applies shall be treated as an assist for purposes of this section if such service or work—

(i) is performed by an individual who is domiciled within the United States;

(ii) is performed by that individual while he is acting as an employee or agent of the buyer of the imported merchandise; and

(iii) is incidental to other engineering, development, artwork, design work, or plans or sketches that are undertaken within the United States.

(C) For purposes of this section, the following apply in determining the value of assists described in subparagraph (A) (iv):

(i) The value of an assist that is available in the public domain is the cost of obtaining copies of the assist.

(ii) If the production of an assist occurred in the United States and one or more foreign countries, the value of the assist is the value thereof that is added outside the United States.

(2) The term "identical merchandise" means—

(A) merchandise that is identical in all respects to, and was produced in the same country and by the same person as, the merchandise being appraised; or

(B) if merchandise meeting the requirements under subparagraph (A) cannot be found (or for purposes of applying subsection (b) (2) (B) (i) of this section, regardless of whether merchandise meeting such requirements can be found), merchandise that is identical in all respects to, and was produced in the same country as, but not produced by the same person as, the merchandise being appraised.

Such term does not include merchandise that incorporates or reflects any engineering, development, artwork, design work, or plan or sketch that—

(I) was supplied free or at reduced cost by the buyer of the merchandise for use in connection with the production or the sale for export to the United States of the merchandise; and

(II) is not an assist because undertaken within the United States.

(3) The term "packing costs" means the cost of all containers and coverings of whatever nature and of packing, whether for labor or materials, used in placing merchandise in condition, packed ready for shipment to the United States.

(4) The term "similar merchandise" means—

(A) merchandise that—

(i) was produced in the same country and by the same person as the merchandise being appraised,

(ii) is like the merchandise being appraised in characteristics and component material, and

(iii) is commercially interchangeable with the merchandise being appraised; or

(B) if merchandise meeting the requirements under subparagraph (A) cannot be found (or for purposes of applying subsection (b) (2) (B) (i) of this section, regardless of whether merchandise meeting such requirements can be found), merchandise that—

(i) was produced in the same country as, but not produced by the same person as, the merchandise being appraised, and

(ii) meets the requirements set forth in subparagraph (A) (ii) and (iii).

Such term does not include merchandise that incorporates or reflects any engineering, development, artwork, design work, or plan or sketch that—

        (I) was supplied free or at reduced cost by the buyer of the merchandise for use in connection with the production or the sale for export to the United States of the merchandise; and

        (II) is not an assist because undertaken within the United States.

(5) The term "sufficient information," when required under this section for determining—

  (A) any amount—

    (i) added under subsection (b) (1) of this section to the price actually paid or payable,

    (ii) deducted under subsection (d) (3) of this section as profit or general expense or value from further processing, or

    (iii) added under subsection (e) (2) of this section as profit or general expense;

  (B) any difference taken into account for purposes of subsection (b) (2) (C) of this section; or

  (C) any adjustment made under subsection (c) (2) of this section;

means information that establishes the accuracy of such amount, difference, or adjustment.

Notice of Redelivery (Customs Form 4647)

DEPARTMENT OF THE TREASURY
U.S. CUSTOMS SERVICE
134.51,134.52,141.113,C.R.

NOTICE OF REDELIVERY—MARKINGS, ETC.

PORT	ENTRY NO.	DATE OF ENTRY	No. of Cases Released
			No. of Cases Retained

MARKETING STATUTE, ETC.

☐ Section 304, T.A.

☐ Wool Products Labeling Act

☐ Schedule 7, Part 2E Headnote 4 TSUSA

☐ Fur Products Labeling Act

☐ Foreign Assets Control Regulations

☐ Textile Fiber Products Identification Act

☐ Other

FROM (Include Phone No.)

TO IMPORTER—Redelivery is hereby ordered of the following shipment for the reason stated above. Deliver to Customs all merchandise which has been released to you under the terms of the entry bond. This shipment can not be released unless brought into conformity with the statute indicated. Articles not returned or properly marked within 30 days of this notice become liable for liquidated damage.

DESCRIPTION OF MERCHANDISE	QUANTITY	MARKS—NUMBERS

☐ You are authorized to mark the merchandise at a place other than public stores. When marking is accomplished complete certification below and return both copies of this form ☐ with ☐ without a sample of the marked merchandise of this office. Merchandise must be held until marking is verified or notification received that marking is acceptable.

☐ Merchandise to be marked under customs supervision.

REMARKS:

SIGNATURE OF CUSTOM OFFICER	DATE

IMPORTER—COMPLETE APPROPRIATE ITEMS	Place	Date	Time
☐ Merchandise is to be marked at place other than Public Stores.			
☐ Merchandise to be ☐ exported ☐ destroyed under customs supervision in lieu of marking.	Place	Date	Time

I (we) guarantee the payment of all expenses incident to above action.

☐ I certify that the merchandise has been marked to indicate the country of origin as required by Section 304, Tariff Act 1930. Sample ☐ is ☐ is not submitted herewith.

SIGNATURE OF IMPORTER	DATE

☐ _____: Supervise the required action as set forth in this notice.

☐ Marking waived pursuant to your request dated _____

☐ The merchandise has been ☐ legally marked ☐ exported ☐ destroyed or, ☐ the certified marking accepted, except as noted on reverse.

SIGNATURE OF CUSTOMS OFFICER	DATE

Previous editions may be used)

Customs Form 4647 (092083)

Request for Information
(Customs Form 28)

DEPARTMENT OF THE TREASURY
UNITED STATES CUSTOMS SERVICE

REQUEST FOR INFORMATION

Approved Through 4/30/
OMB No. 1515-00

19 U.S.C. 1481, 1499,
1500, 1508, and 1509

(General Information/Instructions on reverse)

1. DATE OF REQUEST

2. DATE OF ENTRY & IMPORTATIO

3. MANUFACTURER/SELLER/SHIPPER

4. CARRIER

5. ENTRY NO.

6A. INVOICE DESCRIPTION OF MERCHANDISE

6B. INVOICE NO.

7. TSUS ITEM NO.

8. COUNTRY OF ORIGIN/EXPORTATION

9. CUSTOMHOUSE BROKER AND REFERENCE OR FILE NO.

10. TO:

11. FROM:

PRODUCTION OF DOCUMENTS AND/OR INFORMATION REQUIRED BY LAW:
If you have provided the information requested on this form to U.S. Customs at other ports, please indicate the port of entry to which it was supplied, and furnish a copy of your reply to this office, if possible.

A. PORT

B. DATE INFORMATION FURNISHE

12. PLEASE ANSWER INDICATED QUESTION(S)

A. Are you related (see reverse) in any way to the seller of this merchandise? If you are related, please describe the relationship, and explain how this relationship affects the price paid or payable for the merchandise.

B. Identify and give details of any additional costs/expenses incurred in this transaction, such as:

  (1) packing

  (2) commissions

  (3) proceeds that accrue to the seller (see reverse)

  (4) assists (see reverse)

  (5) royalties and/or license fees (see reverse)

13. PLEASE FURNISH INDICATED ITEM(S)

A. Copy of contract (or purchase order and seller's confirmation thereof) covering this transaction, and any revisions thereto.

B. Descriptive or illustrative literature or information explaining what the merchandise is, where and how it is used, and exactly how it operates.

C. Breakdown of component materials or ingredients by weight and the actual cost of the components at the time of assembly into the finished article.

D. Submit samples:
  Article no. and description _____

  from container no. _____

  mark(s) and no. _____

Samples consumed in analysis, and other samples whose return is not specifically requested, will not normally be returned.

E. See item 14. below.

14. CUSTOMS OFFICER MESSAGE

15. REPLY MESSAGE (Please print or type. Use additional sheets if more space is needed.)

16. CERTIFICATION It is required that an appropriate corporate/company official execute this certificate and/or endorse all correspondence in response to the information requested (NOTE: NOT REQUIRED IF FOREIGN FIRM COMPLETES THIS FORM).

I hereby certify that the information furnished herewith or upon this form in response to this inquiry is true and correct, and that any samples provided were taken from the shipment covered by this entry.

A. NAME AND TITLE/POSITION OF SIGNER (Owner, Importer, or Corporate/Company Official - Print or Type)

B. SIGNATURE

C. TELEPHONE NO.

D. DATE

17. CUSTOMS OFFICER (Print or Type)

18. TEAM DESIGNATION

19. TELEPHONE NO.

(Paperwork Reduction Act Notice on reverse)

Customs Form 28 (122386

Notice of Action
(Customs Form 29)

NOTICE OF ACTION *This is NOT a Notice of Liquidation*			1. DATE OF THIS NOTICE
2. CARRIER	3. DATE OF IMPORTATION	4. DATE OF ENTRY	5. ENTRY NO.
6. MFR/SELLER/SHIPPER	7. COUNTRY	8. CUSTOMHOUSE BROKER AND FILE NO.	

9. DESCRIPTION OF MERCHANDISE

10. TO	11. FROM

12. THE FOLLOWING ACTION, WHICH WILL RESULT IN AN INCREASE IN DUTIES,—

☐ IS **PROPOSED.** IF YOU DISAGREE WITH THIS PROPOSED ACTION, PLEASE FURNISH YOUR REASONS IN WRITING TO THIS OFFICE WITHIN 20 DAYS FROM THE DATE OF THIS NOTICE. AFTER 20 DAYS THE ENTRY WILL BE LIQUIDATED AS PROPOSED.

☐ HAS BEEN **TAKEN.** THE ENTRY IS IN THE LIQUIDATION PROCESS AND IS NOT AVAILABLE FOR REVIEW IN THIS OFFICE.

TYPE OF ACTION

A. ☐ RATE ADVANCE

B. ☐ VALUE ADVANCE

C. ☐ EXCESS ☐ WEIGHT ☐ QUANTITY

D. ☐ OTHER *(See below)*

13. EXPLANATION *(Refer to Action letter designations above)*

14. CUSTOMS OFFICER *(Print or Type)*	15. TEAM DESIGNATION	16. TELEPHONE

DEPARTMENT OF THE TREASURY
U. S. CUSTOMS SERVICE
152.2 C. R.

CUSTOMS FORM 29
(2-1-79)

261

Beneficiary Developing Countries under the Generalized System of Preferences

Independent Countries

Angola
Antigua and Barbuda
Argentina
Bahamas, The
Bahrain
Bangladesh
Barbados
Belize
Benin
Bhutan
Bolivia
Botswana
Brazil
Burkina Faso
Burundi
Cameroon
Cape Verde
Chad
Colombia
Comoros
Congo
Costa Rica
Côte d'Ivoire
Cyprus
Djibouti
Dominica
Dominican Republic
Ecuador
Egypt

El Salvador
Equatorial Guinea
Fiji
Gambia, The
Ghana
Grenada
Guatemala
Guinea
Guinea Bissau
Guyana
Haiti
Honduras
Hungary
India
Indonesia
Israel
Jamaica
Jordan
Kenya
Kiribati
Lebanon
Lesotho
Madagascar
Malawi
Malaysia
Maldives
Mali
Malta
Mauritania
Mauritius
Mexico
Morocco
Mozambique
Nepal
Niger
Oman
Pakistan
Panama

Papua New Guinea

Peru

Philippines

Poland

Rwanda

St. Kitts and Nevis

Saint Lucia

Saint Vincent and the
   Grenadines

Sao Tome and Principe

Senegal

Seychelles

Sierra Leone

Solomon Islands

Somalia

Sri Lanka

Sudan

Suriname

Swaziland

Syria

Tanzania

Thailand

Togo

Tonga

Trinidad and Tobago

Tunisia

Turkey

Tuvalu

Uganda

Uruguay

Vanuatu

Venezuela

Western Samoa

Yemen Arab Republic
   (San'a)

Yugoslavia

Zaire

Zambia

Zimbabwe

Nonindependent Countries and Territories

Anguilla

Aruba

British Indian Ocean
 Territory

Cayman Islands

Christmas Island
 (Australia)

Cocos (Keeling) Islands

Cook Islands

Falkland Islands
 (Islas Malvinas)

French Polynesia

Gibraltar

Greenland

Heard Island and
 McDonald Islands

Macau

Montserrat

Netherlands Antilles

New Caledonia

Niue

Norfolk Island

Pitcairn Islands

Saint Helena

Tokelau

Trust Territory of the
 Pacific Islands (Palau)

Turks and Caicos
 Islands

Virgin Islands, British

Wallis and Futuna

Western Sahara

Bibliography

Code of Federal Regulations, Title 19, Customs Duties. 2 vols. Washington, D.C.:
  U.S. Government Printing Office, 1990.
  Updated annually in April. Volume 1 is considered indispensable to every
  company's Customs department. Available at government bookstores.
Customs Cooperation Council (CCC). *Alphabetical Index to the Harmonized
  Commodity Description and Coding System and Its Explanatory Notes.* 2
  vols. Brussels: CCC, 1987.
  Periodic supplements. Helpful aid in beginning classification analysis.
  Recommended for companies with large product lines.
_____. *Compendium of Classification Opinions: Harmonized Commodity
  Description and Coding System.* Brussels: CCC, 1987.
_____. *Explanatory Notes: Harmonized Commodity Description and Coding
  System.* 4 vols. Brussels: CCC, 1986.
  Periodic supplements. Indispensable to anyone engaged in classification
  analysis under the Harmonized Tariff Schedule of the United States.
International Trade Alert. New York: American Association of Exporters and
  Importers.
  Published weekly and available through membership or subscription.
  Contains briefs on recent changes implemented by U.S. Customs and other
  federal agencies in import/export procedures. Also contains transportation-
  related information affecting international shipment of commercial cargo.
  Recommended for companies whose import operations are sensitive to
  procedural changes.
Sherman, Saul L., and Hinrich Glashoff. *Customs Valuation: Commentary on the
  GATT Customs Valuation Code.* ICC Publication 429. Paris: ICC
  Publishing, 1988; distributed in United States and Canada by Kluwer Law
  and Taxation Publishers, Norwell, Mass.
  Scholarly treatment of appraisement principles involved in the valuation
  law currently adopted by the United States. Recommended for serious stu-
  dents of customs valuation, attorneys, and customs brokers.
Sturm, Ruth F. *Customs Law & Administration.* 3d ed. 2 vols. Dobbs Ferry,
  N.Y.: Oceana Publications, 1990.
  Periodic supplements. Organized by Customs subject matter. Contains for

each subject references to precedential Treasury decisions, Customs decisions, and court cases. Recommended for attorneys.

United States Code, Volume 7, Title 19, Customs Duties. 13th ed. Washington, D.C.: U.S. Government Printing Office, 1989.

Periodic supplements. Contains all laws relating to Customs matters but is not widely available in public reference rooms. Available through government bookstores.

United States Code Annotated, Title 19, Customs Duties. 3 vols. 1978. Reprint. St. Paul, Minn.: West Publishing, 1984.

Periodic supplements. Contains all Customs laws with annotations showing legislative history and interpretations by courts. Widely available in large public reference rooms. Recommended for attorneys and customs brokers.

U.S. International Trade Commission. *Harmonized Tariff Schedule of the United States.* USITC 2333. Washington, D.C.: U.S. Government Printing Office, 1991.

Periodic supplements. Recommended for every company's Customs department.

U.S. Treasury Department. Customs Service. *Customs Bulletin.* Washington, D.C.: U.S. Government Printing Office.

Periodic publication, approximately twice monthly. Available by subscription. Contains proposed and final rule changes, Treasury decisions, Customs decisions, reported Customs cases of the U.S. Court of International Trade and the U.S. Court of Appeals for the Federal Circuit. Also contains currency exchange rates used by U.S. Customs for conversion of Customs transactions invoiced in foreign currencies. Recommended for large importing companies, attorneys, and customs brokers.

_____. *Importing into the United States.* Washington, D.C.: U.S. Government Printing Office, 1986.

Reprinted every several years. Contains helpful information about import requirements of U.S. Customs and other federal agencies. Available at government bookstores.

Index

About the Author

MICHAEL J. HORTON is an attorney based in Oakland, California. A former officer of the United States Customs Service, he has practiced Customs law exclusively since 1977. He appears frequently as a guest speaker on import procedures before international trade associations and business schools in the San Francisco Bay area, and has received professional recognition in other areas as well.